Pirates Through the Ages

Biographies

Pirates Through the Ages

Biographies

Elizabeth Shostak
Sonia G. Benson, Contributing Writer
Jennifer Stock, Project Editor

GALE
CENGAGE Learning™

Detroit • New York • San Francisco • New Haven, Conn • Waterville, Maine • London

GALE
CENGAGE Learning

Pirates Through the Ages: Biographies
Elizabeth Shostak

Project Editor: Jennifer Stock

Rights Acquisition and Management:
  Robyn Young

Composition: Evi Abou-El-Seoud

Manufacturing: Wendy Blurton

Imaging: John Watkins

Product Design: Kristine Julien

For product information and technology assistance, contact us at
Gale Customer Support, 1-800-877-4253.
For permission to use material from this text or product,
submit all requests online at **www.cengage.com/permissions.**
Further permissions questions can be emailed to
permissionrequest@cengage.com

Cover photographs reproduced by permission of Private Collection/Peter Newark Historical Pictures/The Bridgeman Art Library International (William Kidd), INTERFOTO/Alamy (Blackeard), and Stock Montage/Archive Photos/Getty Images (John Paul Jones).

While every effort has been made to ensure the reliability of the information presented in this publication, Gale, a part of Cengage Learning, does not guarantee the accuracy of the data contained herein. Gale accepts no payment for listing; and inclusion in the publication of any organization, agency, institution, publication, service, or individual does not imply endorsement of the editors or publisher. Errors brought to the attention of the publisher and verified to the satisfaction of the publisher will be corrected in future editions.

Library of Congress Cataloging-in-Publication Data

Benson, Sonia.
   Pirates through the ages reference library / Sonia G. Benson, Elizabeth Shostak, Laurie Edwards.
      3 v. cm.
   Includes bibliographical references and index.
      ISBN 978-1-4144-8662-8 (set) -- ISBN 978-1-4144-8663-5 (almanac) --
   ISBN 978-1-4144-8664-2 (biographies) -- ISBN 978-1-4144-8665-9
   (primary sources)
      1. Pirates--History--Handbooks, manuals, etc. I. Shostak, Elizabeth, 1951-
   II. Edwards, Laurie, 1954- III. Title.
   G535.B38 2011
   910.4'5--dc22   2010051978

Gale
27500 Drake Rd.
Farmington Hills, MI, 48331-3535

ISBN-13: 978-1-4144-8662-8 (set)   ISBN-10: 1-4144-8662-6 (set)
ISBN-13: 978-1-4144-8663-5   ISBN-10: 1-4144-8663-4
(Almanac)   (Almanac)
ISBN-13: 978-1-4144-8664-2   ISBN-10: 1-4144-8664-2
(Biographies)   (Biographies)
ISBN-13: 978-1-4144-8665-9   ISBN-10: 1-4144-8665-0
(Primary Sources)   (Primary Sources)
ISBN-13: 978-1-4144-8666-6   ISBN-10: 1-4144-8666-9
(Cumulative Index)   (Cumulative Index)

This title is also available as an e-book.
ISBN-13: 978-1-4144-8667-3 ISBN-10: 1-4144-8667-7
Contact your Gale, a part of Cengage Learning sales representative for ordering information.

Printed in Singapore
1 2 3 4 5 6 7 15 14 13 12 11

Table of Contents

Pirates Through the Ages: Biographies

Reader's Guide

On April 8, 2009, in waters about 350 miles (563 kilometers) off the coast of Somalia, four pirates boarded the *Maersk Alabama* in a botched attempt to seize the cargo ship. After a stand-off with the ship's crew, the Somali pirates took the captain, Richard Phillips (1963–), hostage and sped off in a life boat. They were soon surrounded by military warships and helicopters from several nations, and for five days the pirates held the captain at gunpoint on the small boat. Footage of the hostage situation was broadcast to millions of television viewers throughout the world. In the end, U.S. Navy snipers killed the pirates and rescued Phillips. But piracy experts noted that the rescue of Phillips was the exception; at the time of his rescue, pirates held hundreds of other hostages in Somalia. The *Maersk Alabama* incident, only one among hundreds of pirate attacks in the waters off Somalia over the period of a few years, brought international attention to the rise in piracy in the twenty-first century, after many twentieth-century history books had pronounced piracy a thing of the past.

For most of us, it is difficult to connect the Somali pirates—young men and boys in t-shirts and jeans using modern technology and carrying automatic weapons—with the familiar image of pirates we have known since childhood: the swarthy seafarers with peg-legs or eye patches wearing tri-cornered hats and bearing parrots on their shoulders, who are known for phrases like "avast, me hearties," "shiver me timbers," and "aarr." The familiar image, a product of both fact and fantasy, is based on the historical era known as the golden age of piracy, a brief period during the late eighteenth and early nineteenth century when famous pirates like Blackbeard (Edward Teach; c. 1680–1718), William Kidd (c. 1645–1701), and Bartholomew Roberts (1682–1722) ruled large areas of the Caribbean

Sea. But Somali piracy and golden age piracy both take their place in a long, global history of similar pirate eras, periods when seas in certain regions became infested with pirates who managed to resist law enforcement agents for extended periods of time.

Who were these pirates? Pirates through the ages have been as diverse as the rest of the human population. Pirate leaders have ranged from poor English sailors to highly successful Chinese businessmen and ferocious Scandinavian warriors. Like most criminal paths, piracy has drawn courageous adventurers, sadistic psychopaths, and many who fall somewhere in between. Most were drawn to piracy as a rare means to lift themselves out of poverty, but not all pirates chose their trade. Many sailors were forced into it by pirates who raided their ships. Others, on the other hand, traveled long distances and some even converted to new religions for the opportunity to get rich by raiding ships at sea. Pirates have come from all nationalities and races. The Chinese pirates included women among their ranks, and there were also several notorious European women pirates, but overall, the overwhelming majority of pirates have been men.

On land and at sea, pirates have always sought places where they could carry out their plundering (robbing of goods by force) while living outside the law. They spent much of their lives on the high seas, the open waters of the ocean that are outside the limits of any country's territorial authority. At sea, most pirates have established their own codes of conduct and social structures. Pirates also need land to carry out large-scale operations. In pirate havens, usually remote sea ports or islands without any strong governmental presence, pirates have been able to establish rough societies of their own where they live and carry out their business under their own rules. In pirate havens, as at sea, pirates defied law enforcement authorities—but only for a time. After every major pirate era, law and order has been restored, pirate havens have been destroyed, and many notorious pirates have faced prison or the hangman's noose.

Pirates have fascinated people from ancient times to the present day. Studying them provides insight into history and human nature in all its complexity. Historians study pirates in a surprisingly wide variety of contexts, such as the wars they fought in, their contribution to the settlement of new lands, the social institutions they have established at sea, and the social classes from which they arose. Lawmakers and international diplomats ponder the unique challenges of trying to stop piracy by establishing law and order on the high seas. Fiction writers, poets, playwrights, and filmmakers have all been drawn to the romantic aspects of piracy, such as the courage and ingenuity of the raiders, their thrilling adventures, the freedom of the seas, and the brotherhood of pirates.

The abundance of legends and writings about pirates has led to a strangely comfortable image of piracy in modern times. Children dress as pirates for Halloween, watch pirate cartoons on TV, and play pirate video games. In studying real piracy, though, it quickly becomes apparent that pirates are dangerous, and often violent, criminals. Pirates have murdered, raped, tortured, and enslaved their victims. They have disrupted trade and made sea travel a terrifying experience. Though they may fascinate us with their adventures at sea, they are predators who do a great deal of harm in the world.

Pirates v. privateers

Many of history's major pirate eras began with governmental policies that encouraged the licensing of privateers, private ships or ship owners commissioned by their government to raid enemy ships during war-time. The actual work that pirates and privateers do is the same. They attack ships, usually merchant vessels, or coastal communities, and they use violence or the threat of violence to rob their victims of valuables, sometimes taking the ship itself as a prize. The main difference between pirates and privateers is that pirates work solely for their own profit, while privateers, at least in theory, work for their country. While piracy is illegal, privateering is considered legal, at least by the nation that licenses the privateers.

The history of pirates cannot be separated from the history of privateers. Since ancient times, warring nations have frequently enlisted privateers to destroy their enemies' trade and harass military shipping. Ancient Greece, the Ottoman Empire, late eighteenth-century Vietnam, and the European nations of Spain, England, the Netherlands, and France, to name a few, all relied heavily on privateers in war-time. Privateers often greatly aided their countries. Some privateers, such as Englishman Francis Drake (1540–1596), were considered heroes and went on to prestigious careers in their countries. Other privateers, however, took a very different path. When wars ended, they found themselves armed, equipped with sea vessels, and highly skilled at raiding enemy ships, but suddenly unemployed. Many simply continued to raid ships as pirates. The nations that had originally enlisted the privateers' services soon found they had no control over their activities, and often had to muster new naval forces to pursue them.

The many names for sea raiders—corsairs, buccaneers, filibusters, freebooters, picaroons, sea rovers, sea dogs—all signify people who raid at or from the sea, but whether they mean "pirate," "privateer," or a little of both may differ in context.

Coverage and features

Pirates Through the Ages: Biographies profiles twenty-six pirates and privateers. Included are some of the most famous pirates of the golden age, such as Blackbeard, William Kidd, and Bartholomew Roberts; fierce corsairs of the Barbary Coast, including Barbarossa and Dragut Reis; and English and American privateers such as Francis Drake, John Paul Jones, and Jean Lafitte. Also featured are buccaneers such as Henry Morgan and William Dampier; female pirates Cheng I Sao, Anne Bonny and Mary Read, and Grace O'Malley; and pirate hunter Woodes Rogers. The volume includes more than fifty photographs and illustrations, a timeline, sources for further reading, and an index.

U·X·L Pirates Through the Ages Reference Library

Pirates Through the Ages: Almanac presents a comprehensive history of the major pirate eras throughout history and around the globe. The volume's twelve chapters cover ancient and medieval pirates, the Barbary corsairs, the privateers of Spanish Main and the United States, the buccaneers of the Caribbean, the golden age of piracy, piracy in Asia, modern piracy, and pirates in popular culture. Each chapter features informative sidebar boxes highlighting glossary terms and issues discussed in the text. Also included are nearly sixty photographs and illustrations, a timeline, a glossary, a list of research and activity ideas, sources for further reading, and an index providing easy access to subjects discussed throughout the volume.

Pirates Through the Ages: Primary Sources presents eighteen full or excerpted written works, poems, interviews, or other documents that were influential throughout the history of piracy. Included are the tale of the kidnapping of Julius Caesar by pirates, a letter from a captive of the

Barbary corsairs, a pirate trial transcript, and an example of ship's articles. Also featured are literary works such as *Treasure Island* and *The Corsair*, and interviews with Somali and Strait of Malacca pirates. More than fifty photographs and illustrations, a timeline, sources for further reading, and an index supplement the volume

A cumulative index of all three volumes in the U•X•L Pirates Through the Ages Reference Library is also available.

Comments and suggestions

We welcome your comments on *Pirates Through the Ages: Biographies* and suggestions for other topics to consider. Please write: Editors, *Pirates Through the Ages: Biographies*, Gale Cengage Learning, 27500 Drake Road, Farmington Hills, Michigan 48331-3535; call toll free: 1-800-877-4253; fax to 248-699-8097; or send e-mail via http://www.gale.cengage.com.

Timeline of Events

2000 BCE: The Phoenicians begin maritime trading in regions of the Mediterranean; as trade expands, piracy emerges.

1220–1186 BCE: The Sea People, a band of sea raiders, dominate the Mediterranean Sea, attacking merchant ships and coastal towns.

c. 750 BCE: Greek poet Homer writes the *Odyssey*; the epic poem is the first known written description of piracy.

421–339 BCE: Greek city-states engage pirates to attack their enemies in the Peloponnesian Wars in a system similar to what will later become known as privateering.

74 or 75 BCE: Roman statesman Julius Caesar is captured by Cilician pirates and held for ransom.

June 8, 793: Vikings attack the religious center at Lindisfarne, England.

1100s: A group of Germanic towns form the Hanseatic League to secure trade routes in the Baltic Sea and fight piracy.

1200s: The Wokou, a group of pirates that originated in Japan, attack the coasts of Korea and China.

1217: French pirate **Eustace the Monk** is killed by English forces at Sandwich.

1243: England's Cinque Ports, a league of sea towns, begins to license private merchant ships to raid enemy ships and ports. This is considered the origin of the privateer system that Europe would use for centuries to come.

1392: A powerful band of pirates known as the Victual Brothers attacks Norway's major city, Bergen, and sets up headquarters in Visby, Sweden.

1492: Spain captures Granada from the Moors and begins to expel the Moors from Spain. Tens of thousands of Spanish Muslims migrate to the Barbary Coast in northern Africa.

1492: Explorer Christopher Columbus, serving Spain, arrives on a Caribbean island, beginning an era of Spanish exploration and colonization in the Americas.

1494: The Catholic pope issues the Treaty of Tordesillas. Under the treaty, Portugal receives authority to control the non-Christian lands in the designated eastern half of the world, and Spain is awarded the lands in the west.

1516: Barbary corsair Aruj leads a large force of corsairs in an attack on the city-state of Algiers. The corsairs gain control of the city and the surrounding region.

1523: French privateer Jean Fleury captures two Spanish ships returning to Spain from Mexico. They are loaded with Aztec treasure that conquistador Hernán Cortéz was sending to the Spanish king.

1530: The Spanish king leases the island of Malta to the Knights of Malta under the condition that they fight "enemies of the Holy Faith." The Knights begin raiding Muslim ships and enslaving Muslim captives.

1533: Barbary corsair **Barbarossa** is named admiral-in-chief of the Ottoman navy. He launches a series of raids in Italy.

1550s: Wealthy Chinese businessman Wang Zhi commands a large force of Wokou pirate fleets, comprised of hundreds of junks and, by some estimates, about twenty thousand pirates.

1551: Corsair **Dragut Reis** captures Tripoli from the Knights of Malta. He is made ruler of Tunis as reward for this service to the Ottoman Empire.

1562: To protect its ships from piracy, Spain requires all ships carrying goods from the Spanish Main to Spain to join one of the two treasure fleets formed annually.

1567: In the Battle of San Juan de Ulúa, **John Hawkins** and his fleet of illegal traders are badly defeated by Spanish naval forces in Mexico.

1577–60: English privateer **Francis Drake** circumnavigates (sails around) the globe, raiding Spanish ships in the Pacific and bringing home an enormous booty.

1593: Irish pirate **Grace O'Malley** writes to Queen Elizabeth I requesting permission to continue sea raiding.

1628: Dutch privateer Pieter Pieterszoon Heyn, commanding an enormous fleet, captures a Spanish treasure fleet.

1600–40: A group of French hunters, called buccaneers, establish a rough lifestyle in the Caribbean, living part-time on the island of Tortuga and hunting feral animals on the northwest coast of Hispaniola.

1606–8: English pirate **John Ward** and Dutch pirate Simon de Danser join the Barbary corsairs. They are among the first in a long line of "renegades," or Europeans who converted from Christianity to Islam and raided Christian ships and ports with the Barbary corsairs.

Late 1620s: Hoping to expel the buccaneers, Spanish colonial officials exterminate feral animals in the northwestern region of Hispaniola. The buccaneers, no longer able to hunt, become full-time sea raiders.

1631: Corsair **Murat Reis** raids Baltimore, Ireland, capturing 103 prisoners to be sold into slavery.

1655: English ruler Oliver Cromwell sends naval forces to attack Santo Domingo, Hispaniola. The English forces fail to take over Santo Domingo, but take control of Jamaica. Under the English, Port Royal, Jamaica, becomes a pirate haven.

1656: English naval officer **Christopher Myngs** is sent to Jamaica to help defend the island against the Spanish. Myngs enlists the help of buccaneers.

1660s: **François L'Olonnais** joins the buccaneers on Tortuga. The pirate will become known as "The Flail of the Spaniards."

1661: Chinese pirate commander **Kho Hsing Yeh** attacks the Dutch colony at Formosa (present-day Taiwan) with a fleet of nine hundred junks and twenty-five thousand troops, pushing the Dutch military off the island. Under Kho Hsing Yeh and his sons, Formosa will remain a pirate kingdom for twenty years.

1668: Privateer **Henry Morgan**, chief of the buccaneers in Port Royal, leads a raid on the well-defended port city of Portobelo, Panama, where treasure from Peru is held for shipping to Spain on the annual treasure fleets.

1678: Alexander O. Exquemelin's *The Buccaneers of America* is first published in Dutch.

1690: The golden age of piracy begins.

1690s: The African island of Madagascar in the Indian Ocean becomes a pirate base in the Pirate Round, a course in which pirates raid African slave traders and merchant ships transporting valuable Asian goods from the shores of India and the Middle East back to Europe.

June 7, 1692: A major earthquake strikes Port Royal, Jamaica, killing thousands, toppling part of the city into the sea, and forcing pirates to look for another base of operations.

August 1695: Pirate captain **Henry Every** raids the well-armed *Ganj-i-sawii*, the Indian emperor's richly laden treasure ship, making every man in his crew wealthy. The raid inspires many heroic legends in England.

1697: English buccaneer **William Dampier** publishes *A New Voyage Round the World*, describing the species, habitats, climates, and native peoples he encountered during his travels.

1701: After a lengthy trial in England, **William Kidd** is hung for piracy, though he claims to have been fulfilling his obligations as a privateer. His body is hung over the Thames River as a warning to all pirates.

1710: In India, Maratha navy commander **Kanhoji Angria** captures the British East India Company's island headquarters off Bombay and sets up a well-fortified pirate base there.

1714: Pirates of the Caribbean, led by Benjamin Hornigold, **Blackbeard**, and Charles Vane, establish a base in Nassau, a port in the Bahamas; other pirates soon join them there.

February 1717: **Samuel Bellamy** and his crew seize an English slave ship, the *Whydah*, near Cuba, and refit it for piracy.

May 1718: With a fleet of heavily armed pirate vessels, Blackbeard blockades the harbor of Charleston, North Carolina.

September 5, 1718: By this date, Bahamas governor **Woodes Rogers** has granted pardons to more than six hundred pirates on the condition that they stop raiding.

November 1718: English troops commanded by Lieutenant Robert Maynard battle with Blackbeard's fleet; Blackbeard is killed in hand-to-hand combat.

December 1718: The gentleman-turned-pirate **Stede Bonnet** is executed in Charleston, North Carolina.

1720: **Anne Bonny and Mary Read** are among a group of pirates brought to trial in Jamaica. The story of these two female pirates causes a sensation in Europe and the Americas.

1721: England passes the Piracy Act, which punishes people who trade with or aid pirates.

March 1722: In the largest pirate trial of the golden age, 268 pirates who had sailed under the command of **Bartholomew Roberts** are tried at Cape Coast Castle, a slave-trading center in West Africa.

1724: *A General History of the Robberies and Murders of the Most Notorious Pirates* is published by Captain Charles Johnson.

1730: The golden age of piracy ends.

April 19, 1775: The Battles of Concord and Lexington begin the American Revolution.

March 1776: The Continental Congress passes legislation allowing American privateers to raid British warships and merchant ships.

September 23, 1779: Continental Navy commander **John Paul Jones** defeats a Royal Navy warship and utters his famous line, "I have not yet begun to fight."

1788: With the aid of Chinese pirates, the Vietnamese Tay Son rebels defeat Vietnam's military and take control of the country.

1804: The United States sends its recently established naval forces to Tripoli in an attempt to force the Barbary corsairs to stop demanding tribute payments from U.S. merchant ships in the Mediterranean.

1807: Chinese pirate chief Cheng I dies, having organized and led the largest pirate confederation ever known to history, comprised of an estimated 40,000 to 70,000 pirates. His wife **Cheng I Sao** takes command of the pirate empire.

1810: Cheng I Sao accepts a general pardon for the pirates in her confederation, ending the huge and powerful Chinese pirate empire.

1812: As the United States prepares for war with Britain in the War of 1812, it once again enlists the aid of American privateers.

1814: Lord Byron publishes *The Corsair*, a long poem in which the pirate captain Conrad is portrayed as a brooding, romantic hero. The poem is an instant success.

January 1815: In the Battle of New Orleans, the last battle of the War of 1812, privateer **Jean Lafitte** aids U.S. forces in defeating the British invasion of the city.

1826: Persian Gulf pirate **Rahmah ibn Jarbir al-Jalahimah** blows up his own ship, rather than allowing himself to be captured by his enemies.

1830s: A combined force of British Royal Navy and English East India Company ships set up an antipiracy base in Singapore. After a long series of fierce battles with the pirates of the Strait of Malacca and surrounding areas over the next thirty years, the antipiracy forces destroy the pirates.

1856: The leading powers of Europe sign the Declaration of Paris, which prohibits privateering. The United States does not sign.

1861: In the first year of the American Civil War, Southern privateers raid scores of Union ships.

1883: Robert Louis Stevenson publishes his children's adventure story *Treasure Island.* His pirate character, Long John Silver, becomes the best-known pirate in popular culture.

1982: The United Nations Convention on the Law of the Sea, which authorizes official ships of all states to seize known pirate ships on the high seas, is signed by 158 nations.

1984: Underwater explorer Barry Clifford discovers the pirate ship *Whydah* off Cape Cod. Relics recovered from the sunken ship and can be viewed today at the Whydah Museum in Provincetown, Massachusetts.

1992: The International Maritime Bureau (IMB), a division of the International Chamber of Commerce (ICC), establishes the IMB Piracy Reporting Centre, based in Kuala Lumpur, Malaysia, to track pirate attacks around the world.

1998: Political unrest in Indonesia leads to a surge in pirate activity in the Strait of Malacca.

1998: Chinese pirates posing as customs officials hijack a Hong Kong cargo ship, the *Cheung Son,* killing the entire twenty-three-member crew. China captures and prosecutes the pirates, executing thirteen of them.

2000: Piracy peaks worldwide, with a reported 469 attacks during the year; 65 percent of the attacks occur in Southeast Asia.

2003: *Pirates of the Caribbean: The Curse of the Black Pearl*, the first in a series of Disney pirate movies featuring Captain Jack Sparrow, is a huge box-office success.

2004: Under the Regional Cooperation Agreement on Combating Piracy and Armed Robbery against Ships in Asia (ReCAAP), Malaysian, Indonesian, and Singapore naval forces begin to work together to combat piracy.

June 2, 2008: The UN Security Council passes Resolution 1816, which authorizes foreign warships to enter Somali waters to stop piracy by any means necessary.

April 8, 2009: The world watches the aftermath of the botched hijacking of the U.S. cargo ship *Maersk Alabama*, after four Somali pirates take the ship's captain, Richard Phillips, hostage.

2009: Two hundred seventy-one pirate attacks were attributed to Somali pirates—more than half of the worldwide total.

July 2010: A new court near Mombasa, Kenya, built with international donations through the United Nations, is established as a place to try pirates from the region for their crimes.

Words to Know

A

act of reprisal: A document granting permission to individuals to raid the vessels of an enemy in response to some harm that enemy had done.

admiralty court: A court that administers laws and regulations pertaining to the sea.

antihero: A leading character or notable figure who does not have the typical hero traits.

artillery: Large weapons, such as cannons, that discharge missiles.

asylum: Refuge or protection in a foreign country, granted to someone who might be in danger if returned to his or her own country.

B

barbarians: People who are not considered civilized.

barge: A large, flat-bottomed boat used to transport cargo, usually over inland waterways.

barnacle: A shell-like marine animal that attaches itself to the underwater portion of a ship's hull.

barque: A simple vessel with one mast and triangular sails.

bey: The word for a local ruler in Tripoli and Tunis.

bireme: A swift galley ship with two banks of oars, and sometimes a square sail.

blunderbuss: A short musket with a flared muzzle.

bond: A type of insurance in which one party gives money to another party as a guarantee that certain requirements will be followed. If these requirements are not followed, the party that issued the bond keeps the money permanently.

booty: Goods stolen from ships or coastal villages during pirate raids or attacks on enemies in time of war.

buccaneer: A seventeenth-century sea raider based in the Caribbean Sea.

caravel: A small, highly maneuverable sailing ship.

careening: A regular process of cleaning the bottom of a ship.

cat-o'-nine-tails: A whip with nine knotted cords.

cleric: A member of the clergy, or church order.

clinker-built: Construction for boats using overlapping wooden planks.

city-state: An independent, self-governing city and its surrounding territory.

coast guard: A government agency responsible for enforcing laws on the seas and navigable waters.

commerce raiding: Also *guerre de course*, a naval strategy in which a weaker naval power attacks its stronger opponent's commercial shipping.

convoy: A collection of merchant ships traveling together for protection, often escorted by warships.

copyright laws: Laws that grant the creator the exclusive right to distribute, copy, use, or sell his or her product.

corsair: A pirate of the Barbary Coast.

cutlass: A short, heavy, single-edged sword.

dey: The word for a local ruler in Algiers.

digital technology: A data technology system that converts sound or signals into numbers, in the form of a binary format of ones and zeros.

duel: A prearranged fight with deadly weapons to settle a quarrel under specific rules.

dynasty: A succession of rulers from the same family line.

Execution Dock: The place in London where pirates were hanged; their bodies were often displayed to discourage others from turning to piracy.

extortion: The use of authority to unlawfully take money.

failed state: A state without a functioning government above the local level.

flintlock pistol: A small and comparatively lightweight gun that loads through the front of the barrel.

flota: A Spanish treasure fleet that transported goods and riches from the New World to Spain every year.

frigate: A three-masted, medium-sized warship.

galiot: A small, fast galley using both sails and oars.

galleon: A large, square-rigged sailing ship with three or more masts that was used for commerce and war.

galley: A long, low ship used for war and trading that was mainly powered by oarsmen, but might also use a sail.

grapeshot: A cluster of small iron balls usually shot from a cannon.

grenado: An early form of hand grenade comprised of hollow balls made of iron, glass, or wood and filled with gunpowder.

guild: An association for people or towns with a similar trade or interest.

harem: The area of a Muslim household historically reserved for wives, concubines, and female relatives.

high seas: The open waters of the ocean that are outside the limits of any country's territorial authority.

hijack: To take over by force.

hypocrisy: Pretending to have qualities or beliefs one does not really have.

I

impalement: A process of torture and execution by inserting a long stake through the length of the body and then leaving the person to die a slow and painful death.

impressment: The practice of forcibly recruiting sailors to serve in the navy.

indentured servant: A person working under a contract that commits him or her to an employer for a fixed period of time, typically three to seven years.

intellectual property: A product of someone's intellect and creativity that has commercial value.

J

junk: A Chinese form of sailboat.

jurisdiction: The sole right and power to interpret and apply the law in a certain area.

K

keel: A strong beam that extends along the entire length of the bottom of a ship and supports its frame.

knight: A man granted a rank of honor by the monarch for his personal merit or service to the country.

L

letter of marque: A document licensing a private ship owner to the seize ships or goods of an enemy nation.

M

mangrove: A tropical tree or shrub characterized by an extensive, impenetrable system of roots.

maritime: Relating to the sea.

maritime law: The set of regulations that govern navigation and trade on the seas.

maroon: To strand an individual on a deserted island or shore with few provisions.

matchlock: A musket in which gun powder is ignited by lighting it with a match.

melodrama: A drama, such as a play, film, or television program, characterized by exaggerated emotions, stereotypical characters, and an extravagant plot.

mercenary: A seaman or soldier hired by a government to fight its battles.

militia: A volunteer military force made up of ordinary citizens.

monopoly: Exclusive control or possession of something.

musket: A muzzle-loading shoulder gun with a long barrel.

mutiny: An open rebellion by seamen against their ship's officers.

myth: A traditional story that is partly based on a historical event and serves to explain something about a culture.

nautical mile: A unit of distance used for sea navigation. One nautical mile equals 6,080 feet (1.9 kilometers). One mile across land equals 5,280 feet (1.6 kilometers).

navigator: A person who charts the routes of ships at sea.

nostalgia: A bittersweet longing for something from the past.

organized crime syndicate: A group of enterprises run by criminals to carry out illegal activities.

pagan: A person who does not accept the Christian religion.

parody: A spoof, or a work that mocks something else.

patent: A government grant that gives the creator of an invention the sole right to make, use, and sell that invention for a set period of time.

piragua: A dugout canoe.

pirate base: A place where pirates lived under their own rule and maintained their own defense system.

pirate haven: A safe place for pirates to harbor and repair their ships, resupply, and organize raiding parties.

plunder: To rob of goods by force, in a raid or in wartime.

prahu: A swift, light, seagoing vessel propelled by oars and used by the pirates of Southeast Asia.

privateer: A private ship or ship owner commissioned by a state or government to attack the merchant ships of an enemy nation.

prize: The goods, human captives, and ships captured in pirate raids.

R

rack: A piece of equipment used for torture; a person tied on a rack is slowly stretched by the wrists and ankles, causing extreme pain.

ransom: A sum of money demanded for the release of someone being held captive.

reprisal: An act of revenge against an enemy in wartime.

rigging: The system of ropes, chains, and other gear used to support and control the masts and sails of a sailing vessel.

rudder: A vertical, flat piece of wood or metal attached with hinges to a ship's stern (rear) that is used to steer the ship.

S

sack: To plunder a captured city.

scurvy: A disease caused by a lack of vitamin C, characterized by spongy and bleeding gums, bruising, and extreme weakness.

sea shanty: A sailor's work song.

ship's articles: The written sets of rules and conditions under which pirates operated on any given expedition.

ship of the line: A large, heavy warship designed for line of battle combat.

siege: A military blockade that isolates a city while an attack is underway.

sloop: A fast vessel with a single fore-and-aft rigged mast, meaning that the mast was positioned for sails set lengthwise along the ship.

smuggling: Illegally importing and exporting goods.

swashbuckler: A daring adventurer; also a drama about a swashbuckler.

T

tanker: A ship constructed to carry a large load of liquids, such as oil.

territorial waters: Waters surrounding a nation over which that nation exercises sole authority.

terrorism: The systematic use of violence against civilians in order to attain goals that are political, religious, or ideological.

timbers: The frames or ribs of a ship that are connected to the keel and give the hull its shape and strength.

trawler: A fishing boat that uses open-mouthed fishing nets drawn along the sea bottom.

tribute: Payment from one ruler of a state to another, usually for protection or to acknowledge submission.

Tower of London: A fortress in London, England, that was famously used as a prison.

V

vigilante: Someone who takes the law into his or her own hands without the authority to do so.

W

walk the plank: A form of punishment in which a person is forced to walk off the end of a wooden board extended over the side of a ship and into the sea.

war of attrition: A conflict in which a nation tries to wear down its opponent in small ways, hoping to gradually weaken the enemy's forces.

Kanhoji Angria

BORN: c. 1669 • Harne, Maharashtra, India

DIED: July 4, 1729 • India

Indian pirate, admiral

"Angria and his successors continued to be a menace to the existence of Bombay, while the Angrian territory became the [criminal sanctuary] of the Indian seas, where desperadoes of all nationalities were made welcome."

– John Biddulph, English administrator in India
THE PIRATES OF MALABAR, AND AN ENGLISHWOMAN IN INDIA TWO HUNDRED YEARS AGO.

Denounced by the English as a pirate, Kanhoji Angria (also spelled Conajee Angria or Kanhoji Angre) was hailed in his native India as a fighter who defended local ports from foreign dominance in the early 1700s. He was an important admiral of the Maratha Empire's navy, and he devoted his entire life to attacking European traders. Angria led several successful attacks against English interests in western India and remained undefeated upon his death.

Early life

Kanhoji Angria was born around 1669 in Harne, a village in the Konkan region of Maharashtra state in western India. Few details about his childhood are known, except that his father was a naval officer in service of the Maratha Empire. The Maratha Empire established Hindu rule in 1674 after a successful revolt against the Muslim Mughal Empire, which ruled all of South Asia (present-day Bangladesh, Bhutan, India, Nepal, and Pakistan).

It is likely that, from an early age, Angria gained seafaring knowledge from his father. As a young man, he joined the Maratha navy. In 1690

1

Twenty-first Century Piracy in the Arabian Sea

Pirates have operated in the Arabian Sea since ancient times. Beginning in at least 3000 BCE, merchant ships from Arabia and India sailed in the Arabian Sea, trading cargoes of metal ores, teak (a type of wood), grains, spices, and other goods. The wealth from such trade attracted pirates, who either robbed these vessels or demanded payment in return for safe passage through their territory.

In Angria's time, merchants trading in the Arabian Sea made fortunes stealing the gold, silver, jewels, spices, and similar goods for which Europeans were willing to pay high prices. While stronger government controls in the countries bordering these waters eventually stamped out piracy in much of the Arabian Sea, it continued to flourish into the twenty-first century in a few areas, particularly along the coast of Somalia. Modern-day pirates often prey on the large and slow-moving tankers that carry petroleum from the Persian Gulf, which lies to the east of the Arabian Peninsula, to ports throughout the

world. But twenty-first-century pirates off the coast of Somalia have also seized other cargo ships, as well as passenger vessels. In the early 2000s the Gulf of Aden, situated along Somalia's northern coast between the Red Sea and the Arabian Sea, was the most vulnerable seaway in the world to acts of piracy.

Piracy off the coast of Somalia increased dramatically after the 1991 collapse of Somalia's government. In the vacuum of power that followed, commercial fishing interests began illegal operations in Somali waters, and without any law enforcement or military capacity, Somalia was unable to stop them. Worried about this threat to their livelihood, Somali fishermen confronted these commercial vessels and demanded a "tax," or payment for the right to use these waters. Before long, what began as a small-scale effort to protect local fishing rights escalated into full-blown, highly organized piracy. Somali pirates, using small, motorized boats and armed with automatic weapons, overtake larger and

Angria was named deputy commander of the Maratha fleet, and eight years later he rose to the position of admiral. In this role, he served several successive Maratha emperors. He patrolled the west coast of India, ensuring that any foreign ships had permission to be in the region. Angria also considered it his right to attack and seize any merchant ships that had not paid him for a pass known as a *dastak* to trade in these waters. The Marathas supported these actions, because they prevented foreigners from gaining too much economic power in the region. But the English condemned Angria's activities as piracy.

Piracy in the Arabian Sea

Piracy had been a way of life in the Indian Ocean for centuries. (The Indian Ocean is the body of water located between Africa, southern Asia, slower ships that have small (and usually unarmed) crews. The pirates easily board these vessels, either anchoring them at sea while they await ransom payment or forcing them to dock at Somali ports where they unload the cargo.

Piracy is a highly profitable business in Somalia, where successful pirates live in luxurious homes while most of the country's impoverished residents barely survive. Pirates often ask as much as two million dollars as ransom for a ship's crew. In 2008 Somalis captured the largest vessel ever seized by pirates, the Saudi supertanker *Sirius Star*, which was loaded with 2.2 million barrels of oil valued at one hundred million dollars and carrying twenty-five crew members. First demanding twenty-five million dollars for the release of the ship and crew, the pirates later reduced this amount to fifteen million. The ship was released in January 2009 after the payment of an unspecified amount. In 2008 Somali pirates made an estimated fifty million dollars from piracy.

To help protect shipping in the Arabian Sea, one of the world's busiest seaways, a coalition of countries created the Maritime Security Patrol Area in the Gulf of Aden in 2008. Countries participating in the task force's mission have included the United States, Canada, Australia, Great Britain, France, Germany, the Netherlands, Portugal, Spain, Italy, Denmark, Pakistan, Republic of Korea, Singapore, and Turkey.

One of the difficulties in dealing with Somali pirates is that there is no clear agreement about which country should have jurisdiction to prosecute them. Authorities fear that if pirates are tried in Europe, judges might be required to grant them asylum on grounds that the pirates would face the death penalty if they were handed over to Somali authorities. On the other hand, authorities point out that prosecution in Africa is not a good option either, because government corruption in many African countries could prevent pirates from having to stand trial at all. In 2009 judges from leading industrial countries pledged to work toward the creation of a fair and effective system for trying accused pirates and sentencing those who are convicted.

Australia, and Antarctica.) Frequent trade in the Arabian Sea, the part of the Indian Ocean that lies between India's western coast and the Horn of Africa (the easternmost projection of Africa), had attracted pirates to these waters long before Europeans began trading there. When Italian explorer Marco Polo (1254–1324) traveled through the Indian Ocean on his way to China in the late thirteenth century, he saw the hundreds of pirate ships that came out from the district of Gujarat, on India's northwestern coast, every summer. These pirates sailed in fleets of twenty to thirty ships, patrolling the area with only a few miles between each ship. This created a net that few merchant vessels could escape.

European sea trade did not begin in the Arabian Sea until the sixteenth century, after a sea route was found around the continent of Africa. Before then, Europeans who traded in Asia had to make the long and difficult journey across land, a trek of several thousand miles. But in 1498 Portuguese explorer Vasco da Gama (1469–1524) became the first European to sail around the continent of Africa and across the Arabian Sea to India's western coast, often referred to at that time as the Malabar Coast. This sea route was much faster than the overland route, and by the early 1500s, European merchant vessels were frequently present in this seaway. Among the first European traders in India were the Portuguese, who established a trade colony at Goa on the Malabar Coast. The Dutch and the English soon became Portugal's chief trade rivals in the region.

In 1600 a group of English merchants received a government charter to form the East India Company. This organization was created for the purpose of trade with Asia. It soon became a major economic force in India and increasingly challenged the Portuguese and Dutch interests there. After defeating the Portuguese in a sea battle in 1612, the East India Company established several trading posts along the Malabar Coast. Its northern base was located at Surat, in Gujarat, and its southern base was about 163 miles (263 kilometers) down the coast at Bombay (present-day Mumbai). Soon England became a major economic force in India and southeast Asia. England authorized the East India Company to govern the parts of the country in which it operated. Though Asian leaders generally welcomed the opportunity to trade with England, some were concerned that England had too much power in the region.

The increase in trade led to an increase in piracy against merchant vessels. In addition to Asian pirates, numerous European pirates operated in the Arabian Sea. Among them were **Henry Every** (c. 1653–1699; see entry) and **William Kidd** (1645–1701; see entry).

Angria's success as a pirate

By the end of the 1600s, Angria was the most formidable of the pirates on the Malabar Coast, controlling the seas from Surat to Bombay—the same area where the East India Company had concentrated its trade—and building a series of strong forts along the coast. He claimed this territory as his and acted as its governor.

As of about 1703, Angria commanded a fleet of about ten ghurabs and some fifty smaller vessels known as gallivats. Each ghurab, a warship with sails, could carry between sixteen and thirty cannons. Although the much larger European ships carried many more heavy guns and therefore had the capacity to overcome a group of ghurabs, Angria took advantage

The East India Company (EIC) port at Bombay (present-day Mumbai), India. When an EIC agent demanded that Kanhoji Angria stop harassing English ships in Bombay waters, the pirate refused. © WORLD HISTORY ARCHIVE/ALAMY.

of the fact that the merchant vessels had to reduce speed as they entered the shallower waters near the coast. He would hide his gallivats, which were propelled with oars as well as a sail and carried only a few cannons, as a merchant ship drew near. Once the ship slowed down, the quick-moving gallivats would attack from behind. This kept them out of the ship's line of fire while they tried to disable the ship. Then the ghurabs moved in with heavier fire. After the targeted ship suffered sufficient damage, the pirates were able to board the craft and capture it.

Once the pirates came aboard, the Europeans lost any advantage that their heavier firepower might have given them. Angria's men outnumbered the crews on European ships and were also more skilled in hand-to-hand combat. The pirates seized goods and took prisoners, demanding high ransoms for their return. (A ransom is a sum of money demanded for the release of someone being held captive.)

Beginning around 1702, Angria made it a particular point to attack English ships, which were the richest and most plentiful foreign vessels in the Indian Ocean. He captured a small ship and held its six English crewmen for ransom that year, sending word to the East India Company at Bombay that he would give them reason to remember and fear his name. When an agent of the East India Company was sent to Angria two years later to demand that the pirate admiral stop harassing English ships in Bombay waters, Angria replied that he had done the English many favors, but that they had broken their promises to him; therefore, he would seize their ships wherever they sailed along the Malabar Coast. The pirate did not explain exactly what these promises may have been, but Angria reportedly wanted the English to supply him with guns and ammunition if he cooperated with them, and they did not agree to this demand.

In 1707 Angria's forces dealt the East India Company a major blow when they attacked and blew up the frigate *Bombay*. Three years later, Angria captured the East India Company's island headquarters off the coast of Bombay and established a pirate base there. (A pirate base is a place where pirates lived under their own rule and maintained their own defense system.) Next he launched a two-day battle against the *Godolphin*. But the pirates were not able to win this battle, and opted to withdraw rather than face defeat.

Agrees to a treaty

In November 1712 Angria seized an armed yacht belonging to the East India Company's governor of Bombay, as well as a smaller vessel, the *Anne*. During the battle, an English employee of the East India Company, Mr. Chown, was killed, and his teenage widow was held for ransom. Earlier that year, Angria had angered Portugal by seizing a large fleet of Portuguese merchant vessels. The Portuguese now approached the English with an idea—to join forces against the pirate admiral. The English chose not to participate in this plan, but the possibility of an allied attack against him rattled Angria to the point that he decided to make peace with the English. During the ransom negotiations, Angria agreed to stop attacking English ships, or ships of any nation arriving in Bombay harbor, and English merchant ships would be allowed to trade in all ports in Angria's territory, if they paid the usual taxes. In return England paid a ransom of thirty thousand rupees for the English hostages.

For a time Angria spared English ships from attack but continued to prey on vessels from other countries. But by 1716 the pirate had begun to harass English ships again. Early that year, he captured an East India Company ship near Bombay harbor, as well as several others belonging to private merchants. In addition, ships under his command that entered

Bombay refused to pay regular harbor dues, or fees paid to local authorities for the right to use a harbor. When the governor of Bombay sent formal complains to Angria, the pirate responded with defiance.

During the next several years, the English made many efforts to stop Angria. But none of these were successful. They made several raids on Angria's forts, but these, according to Tim Travers in *Pirates: A History*, were "incredibly incompetent" and resulted in high casualties for the English and a further erosion of their profits. In one such attack at Khanderi, a fortified island of the coast of Bombay, in November 1718, an English captain marched up to the gates of the fort, took out his pistol, and tried to shoot off the lock on the gates. But the bullet bounced off the metal and hit the captain in the face, prompting the English to make a hasty retreat.

Defends Colaba

In 1721 the English government sent a squadron under Commodore Thomas Matthews (1676–1751) to control the piracy along the Malabar Coast. The English, with the assistance of Portugal, planned a major assault against Angria at his fortress at Colaba, an island in Bombay harbor. Some sixty-five hundred men prepared to invade the fortress by land, while Matthews and ten ships were to fire on the fort from the water. But Angria's spy network informed him of these plans, and he requested help from the Maratha leaders. They quickly sent twenty-five thousand soldiers to help defend Colaba.

The assault began on December 24. A small number of the land forces succeeded in breaching the fortress's walls, but most were fought off, only to be surprised by Angria's counterattack. His troops, which included a mounted force on elephants, overwhelmed the Europeans. The Portuguese began to retreat, as did the English. Furious at the outcome of the battle, Matthews accused the Portuguese of treachery, and in a confrontation with the Portuguese commander, Matthews struck the officer in the face with his cane. Matthews's behavior seriously offended the Portuguese, who accused the English forces of constant drunkenness and bickering. Soon after the defeat at Colaba, the Portuguese signed a peace agreement with Angria.

The situation continued to worsen for the East India Company. Angria increased his attacks on its ships, seizing the *Eagle* and the *Hunter* in 1723. After the appointment of a new colonial governor in Bombay that

Kanhoji Angria's pirate empire came to an end in 1756 when English forces attacked Geriah, the stronghold of his son, Tolaji, who then surrendered. MARY EVANS PICTURE LIBRARY/EVERETT COLLECTION.

year, however, Angria's activities against the English decreased. The pirate died in 1723, having evaded all efforts by the English to defeat him. He was buried in a tomb in the Alibag, a city in the Maharashtra region of India.

Angria's legacy

Because he acted in service to the Maratha Empire, Angria considered his actions legal. Like Western privateers, who were commissioned by a state or government to attack the merchant ships of enemy nations, Angria believed that his attacks furthered the interests of the Maratha Empire. In his view, his actions prevented European merchants from gaining an unacceptable level of economic influence on the Malabar Coast.

Angria was respected as a powerful and fair leader. His contemporaries described him as a strong man who was confident fighting at sea or on land but who did not love fighting merely for its own sake. He admired diplomacy and used it to advance the interests of those he governed. He also admired learning and was deeply religious.

Angria was an intelligent naval commander. He organized his forces effectively and was willing to make alliances that would contribute to his aims. For example, he sometimes sought the cooperation of the many European pirates who were attracted to the Arabian Sea in the early 1700s. In fact, one of Angria's best ships was captained by a Dutch pirate.

Angria had three wives, as well as many mistresses. His marriages produced seven children, including two sons, Sekhoji and Sambhaji, who vied for control of Angria's naval empire after his death. Sekhoji continued to harass English and European ships, but died in 1733, and the strength and organization of the Angrian forces began to decline. They were finally defeated in 1756, when another son, Tolaji (also spelled Tulagee), surrendered to the English after his stronghold at Geriah was attacked.

For More Information

BOOKS

Biddulph, John. *The Pirates of Malabar, and an Englishwoman in India Two Hundred Years Ago.* William Clowes and Sons, Limited, 1907. Available online at www.columbia.edu/itc/mealac/pritchett/00generallinks/biddulph/index.html (accessed on January 3, 2011).

Travers, Tim. *Pirates: A History.* Brimscombe Port Stroud, England: The History Press, 2009, p. 249.

PERIODICALS

Risso, Patricia. "Cross-Cultural Perceptions of Piracy: Maritime Violence in the Western Indian Ocean and Persian Gulf Region during a Long Eighteenth Century." *Journal of World History* (Fall 2001): p. 293.

WEB SITES

"Prosecution of Piracy." *Security Law Brief: Georgetown Law Center on National Security and the Law.* www.securitylawbrief.com (accessed on January 3, 2011).

Barbarossa

BORN: c. 1478 • Lesbos, Greece

DIED: 1546 • Istanbul, Turkey

Turkish pirate, admiral

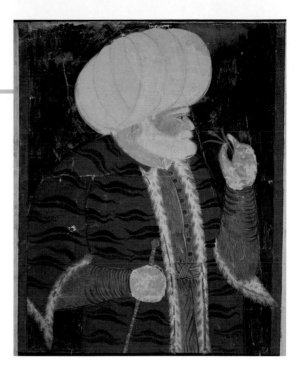

"Whence on the sea's horizon comes that roar? / Can it be Barbarossa now returning / From Tunis or Algiers or from the Isles? / Two hundred vessels ride upon the waves, / Coming from lands the rising Crescent lights: / O blessed ships, from what seas are ye come?"

– Yahya Kemal Beyath, twentieth-century Turkish poet
ENGRAVED ON BARBAROSSA'S STATUE AT HIS TOMB IN ISTANBUL, TURKEY.

Barbarossa. © THE ART GALLERY COLLECTION/ALAMY.

Barbarossa, whose birth name is Hizir, was one of the most famous Barbary corsairs. The corsairs were sea raiders based in Mediterranean port cities along the Barbary Coast, an area roughly encompassing the present-day countries of Morocco, Algeria, Tunisia, and northwest Libya. In the early 1500s Barbarossa made the Ottoman Empire the dominant naval power in the Mediterranean. With his older brother Aruj, he successfully defended the northern coast of Africa from invasion by the Spanish. (Both brothers would become known as Barbarossa, though Hizir would become more famous under this name.) Later he took command of the Ottoman navy. His pirate fleets controlled the entire Mediterranean, raiding Christian ships for treasure and for slaves, demanding protection money from traders, and plundering (robbing of goods by force) coastal cities from Spain to Italy.

Early life

Hizir was born around 1478 on the Greek Island of Lesbos. He was the youngest of four sons born to Yakup Aga, a Turkish Muslim, and his Christian wife. (Muslims are followers of the Islamic religion.) Some evidence suggests that Aga's wife may have been the daughter of a Greek priest. Aga had reportedly served in the Turkish cavalry and had been granted land on Lesbos, then under Turkish administration.

Little is known about Hizir's childhood. Since people in the Aegean, the part of the Mediterranean that lies between the coasts of Turkey and mainland Greece, relied heavily on trade to make a living, it is likely that Hizir learned seafaring skills at an early age. He reportedly spoke at least six languages fluently and was also a skilled engineer. As a young man, he joined his oldest brother, Aruj, in piracy.

There are various accounts about how the brothers first became pirates. One report says that Aruj and another brother, Ilyas, were on a trading voyage when their boat was attacked by a Christian galley. (A galley is a long, low ship used for war and trading that was mainly powered by oarsmen, but might also use a sail.) Ilyas was killed, and Aruj was captured and forced to work as a galley slave. It was a year before the family was able to pay his ransom and free him. (A ransom is a sum of money demanded for the release of someone being held captive.) After this, according to one story, Aruj returned to Lesbos and, with Hizir, joined a crew of pirates in the Aegean. Other historians say that Aruj went to the Egyptian city of Alexandria, where the local ruler gave him a small galley with which to attack Christian ships in revenge for his treatment. In yet another story, Aruj went to the coast of Turkey and obtained a privateering license from the government. This license gave sailors legal permission to attack the merchant ships of an enemy nation. Although these details vary, it is known that Aruj was operating as a pirate in the northern Aegean by the late 1400s, and that Hizir soon joined him.

Pirate brothers gain fame

With Aruj as leader, the pirate brothers made several successful attacks in the northern Aegean, capturing Christian merchant galleys and taking their crews as slaves. But a peace agreement between the Ottoman Turks and the Christian Knights Hospitallers of St. John, a religious military order based on the eastern Aegean island of Rhodes, forced the brothers to move their operations westward. In 1505 they sailed to Djerba, a small island off the coast of Tunisia, in North Africa, and established a pirate base there. (A pirate base is a place where pirates lived under their own rule and maintained their own defense system.) With a privateering license from the Tunisian government, they set out toward the waters along Italy's western coast.

The brothers raided towns as far north as the port of Genoa before turning south again. Near the island of Elba they captured two galleys owned by the pope, the head of the Catholic Church. This was a nearly impossible feat, considering that the brothers were working from two small galleys and they were attacking heavily armed warships. The attack stunned all of Europe. Soon afterward, they seized the *Cavalleria*, a Sicilian warship on its way to the port of Naples. Their success made the brothers wealthy and famous. Because of his bright red hair and beard, Aruj was nicknamed Barbarossa, which means "Red Beard" in Italian.

Hundreds of sailors joined them. They continued making raids on Sicily and the southern tip of Italy until 1511, when they shifted operations westward to Algiers, the capital of Algeria.

The dominant political conflict in the Mediterranean at this time was the ongoing struggle between Muslim and Christian powers. In the seventh century Muslim armies had conquered North Africa, spreading Islam across this entire region and into parts of southern Europe, including Spain, the Balkans, and parts of Italy. Christian kings had struggled since then to win back these territories and in 1492 succeeded in expelling the remaining Muslims from Spain. Many displaced Muslims migrated to the Barbary Coast and became pirates. From here, they launched pirate attacks on Spain's Mediterranean coast. This led Spain to begin military engagements against North Africa. By this time, Muslim lands in the Mediterranean had come under the administrative control of the Ottoman Turks. The Ottoman governor of Algeria, having received word of a planned Spanish assault, asked the Barbarossa brothers for help in defending the country from invaders.

After a few successful raids, the brothers lost a major battle against the Spanish in which Aruj was almost killed. After this, the Barbarossas decided they would stop at nothing to keep the Spanish from entering Barbary territory. In 1516 Aruj led a military uprising against the dey (a local ruler in Algiers), killing him and becoming ruler in his place. But tensions continued to escalate between Aruj and the Spanish. In 1518 he led a major assault on Spanish forces at Oran, to the west of Algiers, but he was outnumbered. After a twenty-day siege, the Spanish captured the city, executing Aruj and defeating the pirate's forces.

The terror of the Mediterranean

Hizir was immediately named the new Algerian leader, and he set out to avenge his brother's death. In honor of his brother, Hizir dyed his hair and beard red, and he, too, took the name Barbarossa. He soon became even more successful and famous than his brother. Barbarossa forced the Spanish out of several territories they had seized on the Algerian coast and in 1519 defeated an army sent to invade the city of Algiers. With the Spanish expelled, Algiers became the major base for the Barbary pirates. The slaves and goods traded in its marketplace brought immense riches to the city.

In 1522 the Ottoman sultan Suleiman I (1494–1566) sent Barbarossa to the Aegean to join his forces in an attack against the Knights Hospitallers. In gratitude for Barbarossa's help in this successful battle, which expelled the order from Rhodes, Suleiman gave the pirate the title Khayr ad-Din, which means "goodness of the faith" or "gift of God."

Returning to the Barbary coast, Barbarossa launched numerous raids along the western shores of Italy and against the islands of Corsica and Sardinia. In 1529 he captured Peñón, a Spanish fortress on the Algerian coast that was the last serious threat to his operations. Two years later he attacked the North African city of Tripoli (in present-day Libya), which Spain had given to the displaced Knights Hospitallers. Although this assault did not succeed, it conveyed the message that Spain could no longer feel secure in the region.

Barbarossa became the terror of the Mediterranean. In one raid alone, on the Spanish island of Majorca, he took some six thousand slaves. He flew his own battle flag, decorated with a six-pointed star known as the Seal of Solomon. Above this star was an image of the Zulfiqar sword, one of the oldest symbols of Islam. This sword, believed to have been owned by the Muslim prophet Muhammad (c. 570–632) and passed down to his descendants, has a V-shaped blade that represents its alleged mystical powers and speed. The Arabic writing at the top of the flag said, "Mohammed! Reveal good news to the believers that the conquest is soon."

Galley Slaves

Life as a galley slave, the fate of many men captured by the Barbary corsairs, was brutal. Galleys were designed to hold two or more rows of oars, which propelled the ships when the wind was not strong enough to fill their sails. Two, four, or even six galley slaves were chained to each oar and were forced to row on command, sometimes for many hours at a time. Men who grew tired were severely beaten. Exhaustion and hunger took the lives of many within just months or even weeks after capture. The need for new galley slaves was one motivation for the raids that the Barbary corsairs made against their enemies.

The use of galley slaves gave the corsairs the advantage in speed. Waiting at their positions during battle, slaves were ready to move the ship quickly if circumstances required. However, there was also a disadvantage to relying on slave labor. Because slaves were not part of the fighting forces on corsair galleys, these vessels had to carry many extra men to conduct the actual attacks. Lacking the capacity to carry weeks' worth of food and water for this many men,

Barbary slave galleys were not able to remain at sea for extended periods. They kept close to shore, where they could resupply frequently and obtain replacement slaves, if necessary.

Barbary corsairs were not the only seafarers who used galley slaves. Starting in the late Middle Ages (c. 500–c. 1500), France began sentencing convicted criminals to galleys, rather than to prison. France also forced prisoners of war to work as galley slaves. The prospect of this fate struck fear in the hearts of the English, who were often at war with the French.

Ottoman pirates themselves were sometimes captured and made to serve as galley slaves. At the Knights Hospitallers's castle in Bodrum, Turkey, the remains of thirteen galley slaves were discovered during an archaeological dig in 1993. The skeletons, still shackled, appear to have been discarded in a rubbish dump. Evidence found among the bones reveals that the victims were most likely Ottoman Turkish sailors enslaved by the Knights and then slaughtered.

Serving the sultan

From the early 1530s, Barbarossa was increasingly called upon to serve the sultan. The Christian city-state of Venice had sent a fleet to challenge Ottoman seizure of Christian islands in the Ionian Sea, which lies between mainland Greece and Italy, and the sultan asked Barbarossa to lead the Ottoman defense. The pirate succeeded in recapturing several of the islands, and the sultan named him admiral-in-chief of the Ottoman navy in 1533. With a fleet of about forty powerful new galleys, Barbarossa sailed back to the western shores of Italy and sacked (captured and plundered) the city of Fondi, perhaps hoping to capture the beautiful young widow of the town's deceased lord. Barbarossa sent some twenty thousand of the sultan's elite fighting corps, known as *janissaries*, to raid the city. After destroying Fondi's defenses, the janissaries carried off many women and children to be ransomed or sold as slaves. So alarming were Barbarossa's raids in Italy that, when he sailed near the mouth of the Tiber River, which flows through Rome, residents rang the city's church bells to sound an alarm.

Meanwhile trouble was brewing in Tunis. The exiled local leader, Mulei Hassan, wanted to regain the city and asked support from King Charles V (1500–1558). Charles had immense power; he was king of both Spain and Italy and the ruler of the Holy Roman Empire, an alliance of Christian kingdoms across central and western Europe. Charles dispatched a huge Spanish force to recapture Tunis for Hassan. Barbarossa did not succeed in stopping Spain at Tunis, but he was able to defend Oran from a second wave of attack. He then sailed for the Italian port of Naples, then held by the Spanish, and captured the city in 1537.

The defeat of Naples caused Pope Paul III (1468–1549) to organize the Holy League, an alliance between Spain, the pope, Venice, Genoa, and the Knights of Malta (formerly known as the Knights Hospitallers) that aimed to end Ottoman control of the Mediterranean. A fleet was assembled in 1538. In command was Admiral Andrea Doria (1466–1560). This force met Barbarossa's fleet at Preveza, Greece, in September. But despite its superior numbers, this Christian force was no match for Barbarossa. He sank or destroyed thirteen enemy galleys, capturing another thirty-eight. It was a stunning victory and a triumph for the Ottomans, whose control of the Mediterranean was now secure. For the next thirty years, Ottoman power in the region remained absolute.

Later career

In 1540 King Charles launched another invasion of Algiers but failed to capture the city. With no Christian force able to defeat him, Barbarossa continued raiding European targets. In 1543 he captured the French city of Nice. France decided to support Barbarossa against their mutual enemy, Spain, and from the French port of Toulon, the corsair planned additional raids on Spanish targets. After several months, however, the French became anxious for the pirate to leave. Eventually the French king, Francis I (1494–1547), paid Barbarossa a huge bribe to get the corsair to leave France. Thirty-two French treasury officials spent three whole days loading sacks with money to give the corsair before he finally set sail. He left the

The tomb of Barbarossa in Istanbul, Turkey. © CHRIS HELLER/ALAMY.

coast of France in May 1544 with his Ottoman galleys as well as a fleet of French vessels.

Next Barbarossa sacked Reggio, at the southern tip of Italy, taking men, women, and children to be sold as slaves. Farther up the coast at

Porto Ercole, the terrified residents gave the pirate thirty men as a bribe to ensure the town's safety. Barbarossa took the men but then burned the city. After capturing the island of Giglio, the pirates beheaded its leaders. The island of Lipari also offered a bribe, but Barbarossa refused. When the town surrendered, the pirate had the residents beaten. When his janissaries found a group who had hidden in the cathedral, they stripped them of their clothing and possessions and then killed them.

In 1544 Barbarossa was called to Genoa, in northern Italy, to negotiate for the release of Ottoman pirate **Dragut Reis** (also known as Turgut Reis; 1514–1565; see entry), who had been captured in 1541 by the Genoese and sentenced to work as a galley slave. Barbarossa's diplomacy consisted of a simple threat: He would lay siege to Genoa if the city did not accept a ransom payment to free Dragut. The Genoans were persuaded, accepting an amount worth the modern equivalent of about $1.25 million.

The following year, the sultan called Barbarossa back to the Ottoman capital of Istanbul. Leaving the government of Algiers to his son, Hasan Pasha, Barbarossa retired from his political position and lived quietly in Istanbul. He built a large palace, where he spent the last year of his life dictating his memoirs. He died in 1546. His tomb is located in Istanbul on the northern shore of the Bosphorus, the narrow body of water joining the Mediterranean with the inland Black Sea.

The Barbary corsairs after Barbarossa

Barbarossa is remembered as the commander who strengthened the Ottoman navy and made it the leading force in the Mediterranean. After his death, the Ottomans continued to dominate these waters and expand their power. The Ottomans suffered a major defeat at Lepanto in 1571, but rebuilt their navy and ventured farther east, entering the Atlantic Ocean and attacking various European targets. In the early 1600s the Ottomans raided southwestern England; within a few years, they reached the coasts of Ireland, Norway, and Sweden. At the height of their expansion, they sailed as far as Iceland.

The Barbary corsairs remained a significant presence in the Mediterranean for more than two centuries after Barbarossa's death. Their piracy, which was a major risk to international trade, provoked the United States to fight two wars against the Barbary states, resulting in the corsairs' final defeat in 1815.

For More Information

BOOKS

Konstam, Angus. *Piracy: The Complete History.* Oxford, England: Osprey, 2008.

Travers, Tim. *Pirates: A History.* Brimscombe Port Stroud, England: The History Press, 2009.

WEB SITES

"Galley Slave Exhibit." *The Bodrum Museum of Underwater Archaeology.* http://bodrum-museum.com/museum/depts/galley_slaves.htm (accessed on January 3, 2011).

"Ottoman Empire: Flags with the Zulfikar Sword." *Flags of the World.* http://flagspot.net/flags/tr-zulf.html (accessed on January 3, 2011).

Samuel Bellamy

BORN: c. 1689 • Devon, England
DIED: April 26, 1717 • Massachusetts, United States

English pirate

> "I am a free Prince, and I have as much Authority to make War
> on the whole World as he who has a hundred Sail of Ships at Sea, and
> an Army of 100,000 Men in the Field; and this my Conscience tells me."

Samuel Bellamy's career as a pirate was brief but spectacular. Operating in the Caribbean in the early 1700s, he seized many merchant vessels and enriched himself and his crew with plunder, or goods stolen by force. Bellamy, however, did not consider himself an outlaw. Like many other pirates in the region at the time, he saw his actions as a rebellion against government authority.

Bellamy's most audacious feat was the capture of the slave vessel *Whydah*, which he renovated and took as his own flagship. Just months later as he sailed the *Whydah* north to New England, the ship was wrecked in a huge storm, and Bellamy and most of his crew were killed.

Early life

Samuel Bellamy, sometimes called "Black Sam," was born around 1689 in Devon, a county in southwest England. He left England for the Americas during his youth and by the 1710s he was well-known in the Caribbean as an experienced seafarer. According to some accounts, Bellamy left England to seek his fortune as a privateer. (Privateers are private ships or ship owners commissioned by a state or government to attack the merchant ships of an enemy nation.) The Caribbean was an attractive area for privateers, because of the numerous Spanish treasure ships in the area. Since the 1490s, Spain had taken vast quantities of gold, silver, pearls, gems, and other valuable materials from its colonies in Central and South America. The goods were taken to ports in the Caribbean, where they were loaded onto treasure ships to be transported back to Spain. Spain was England's most powerful rival in the Caribbean, and the English often encouraged privateering against Spanish vessels. Bellamy's primary motive in going to the Americas, some historians believe, was to seek treasure.

Other stories, however, suggest that Bellamy first arrived in the Americas as a crewman on a ship that traded along the New England coast. He met and fell in love with Maria Hallett, who lived in Eastham, Massachusetts, a town on the coast of Cape Cod. Because Maria's parents would not allow her to marry Bellamy, who was penniless, the sailor decided to go south to search for treasure. In 1714 a devastating hurricane sank twelve Spanish ships that were carrying a fortune in gold, off the coast of Florida. Adventurers from all parts of the Atlantic Ocean were eager to find the wrecks and salvage what treasure they could for themselves, and this hope may have been what first drew Bellamy to the Caribbean.

Joins pirates in the Bahamas

By 1716 Bellamy was serving on the pirate ship of Benjamin Hornigold (d. 1719), who had established a base at the English settlement of New Providence, an island in the Bahamas, which lie north of Cuba and to the southeast of Florida. New Providence was an ideal pirate haven. (A pirate haven is a safe place for pirates to harbor and repair their ships, resupply, and organize raiding parties.) The island is located close to major trade routes, providing pirates easy access to merchant vessels passing by. A small fort protected the island, and its large harbor in the town of Nassau could hold more than one hundred ships. Moreover, the islanders welcomed the pirates, eager for their business. By about 1717, New Providence had attracted more than five hundred pirates, who served on a dozen or more small sailing ships.

As a member of Hornigold's crew, Bellamy served alongside Edward Teach, the notorious pirate known as **Blackbeard** (c. 1680–1718; see entry). But their relationship did not last long. In the summer of 1716, Bellamy decided to leave Hornigold. Historians believe that Bellamy may have disagreed with Hornigold's policy not to attack English merchant ships. Although Hornigold adhered to the conventions of privateering, which held that English ships were off-limits, Bellamy and many of the other young sailors serving with Hornigold saw no reason to obey this rule.

Captains his own ship

Bellamy became captain of the *Mary Anne*, a sailing vessel that Hornigold's crew had stolen. Hornigold's dissatisfied crew joined Bellamy's ship, and Bellamy parted ways with Hornigold. For a time Bellamy joined forces with French pirate Olivier Le Vasseur (c. 1688–1730), preying on ships in the Virgin Islands. Bellamy seized a large merchant ship, the *Sultana*, which he converted for his own use as a well-armed pirate ship. Soon he had a crew of about two hundred men, among them French, Dutch, and Spanish sailors, as well seamen from the North American colonies. The crew also included at least fifty Africans as well as three Native Americans. Most of these pirates had been merchant sailors who, frustrated by hard work and low pay, wanted a chance for more independence and adventure. Others had gone to sea to avoid political or religious persecution. And many of the Africans were escaped slaves who worked as equals to the other sailors aboard pirate vessels.

The youngest of Bellamy's pirates was eleven-year-old John King. The boy had been on a voyage with his mother when Bellamy captured their ship. John was so fascinated by the pirates that he begged to join them and eventually persuaded Bellamy to take him on. When the boy's mother objected, John allegedly screamed and threatened until she finally agreed. He is the youngest pirate in historical record.

Bellamy was known as a captain who treated his men fairly. Like many other pirates, he ruled his ship according to laws known as ship's articles. (Ship's articles are written sets of rules and conditions under which pirates operated on any given expedition.) Each crewman had to sign the ship's articles, which explained their rights and responsibilities. For example, ship's articles provided details about how plunder should be divided among the men, what punishments should be given for offenses, and how men should be compensated for injuries. Bellamy's articles specified that sailors' individual disagreements should be settled onshore in a duel. They also stated that any man who lost a limb or became disabled should receive eight hundred dollars, with lesser amounts for less serious injuries. Historians note that pirate ship's articles were much more democratic than contracts on merchant or naval ships at the time and gave sailors many more rights than they would have been given on other vessels.

Seizes the *Whydah*

Bellamy enjoyed a successful pirate career in the Caribbean. In less than one year, he captured dozens of ships and much valuable treasure. In February 1717 he set his sights on a particularly attractive target, the English slave ship *Whydah*. This vessel was a galley, a long, low ship used for war and trading that was mainly powered by oarsmen, but might also use a sail. The *Whydah* had three sails and carried eighteen cannons to protect it from pirate attacks. Having picked up a cargo of several hundred African slaves on the coast of West Africa, the *Whydah* arrived in the Caribbean to sell its cargo.

Slaves were a valuable commodity in the Americas. They provided necessary labor on the sugar, coffee, cotton, and tobacco plantations that had been established by European colonists. The Spanish and Portuguese had been the first Europeans to bring African slaves to the Americas. By the early 1700s, however, England dominated this trade. English ships sailed from England to West Africa with goods, such as cloth, tools, and other objects, that they traded for men, women, and children who had been captured and sold into slavery. Crossing the Atlantic, the slave traders sold the slaves in the Caribbean. With their profits, they bought sugar, rum, cotton, and other products to sell back in England. This transatlantic slave trade, which became known as the Triangular Trade, brought enormous wealth to the colonies and to England.

When Bellamy spied the *Whydah*, the ship was en route back to England after having sold its cargo, and it was loaded with a fortune in rum, gold dust, and coins worth many thousands of dollars. Although the *Whydah* was a fast ship, two of Bellamy's pirate vessels caught up with it. After a brief fight, the *Whydah*'s commander, Captain Lawrence Prince, surrendered to the pirates. The slave ship, a fine vessel that had been built in 1715, had sustained very little damage. Bellamy ordered his men to transfer their loot and cannons onto the *Whydah* and gave Prince one of the pirate vessels.

Final voyage

After refitting the *Whydah*, Bellamy headed north. Historians have debated why the pirate chose to leave the Caribbean, where there were more ships to plunder. Many believe that the pirate captain was headed back to New England to see his beloved, Maria Hallett, and perhaps win her parents'

Finding the *Whydah*

Although the general location where the *Whydah* went down was known, it took almost three hundred years for divers to find the wreck. Barry Clifford (1945–), a diver who grew up on Cape Cod, became fascinated by the *Whydah*'s story and spent years studying nautical charts and other clues about the precise whereabouts of the wreck. In 1984 he found it. He used electronic sensing technology to detect metal under the thick layers of sand that covered the wreck on the ocean floor. When he thought he knew the location, he organized an exploratory dive. After more than eighteen months of exploring, his team found cannons on the sandy ocean floor. The team also recovered numerous Spanish coins of gold, which were likely part of the loot that the pirates had stolen.

Clifford was certain that he had found Bellamy's prize ship when divers discovered a bronze bell inscribed with the words, "The Whydah Gally 1716." Some of the wooden crosspiece on which the bell hung, as well as a fragment of the bell rope, were also found. Divers have found thousands of other artifacts from the wreck, including a teakettle and eating implements, various weapons, brass measuring scales, a pure gold ring, and silver buttons and cuff links. Iron shackles from the *Whydah*'s earlier days as a slave ship were also among the items recovered from the wreck, as were hand grenades. And a leather shoe, a silk stocking, and a leg bone were identified as belonging to young John King.

The *Whydah* is the first pirate wreck ever found in North America. Artifacts that have been recovered from it are on display at the Whydah Museum in Provincetown, Massachusetts.

Spanish coins and a ring salvaged from the wreck of the Whydah, *Samuel Bellamy's pirate ship.* © RICHARD T. NORWITZ/CORBIS.

consent to marry her. Others suggest that Bellamy simply had economic motives and hoped to prey on vessels near Chesapeake Bay.

Sailing along the North American coast, Bellamy robbed several more merchant ships, including four off the coast of Virginia. Allegedly, he engaged in a spirited argument with one of the merchant captains. According to Angus Konstam in *Piracy: The Complete History*, Bellamy called the merchant captain "a sneaking puppy" and a coward for submitting to "laws which rich men have made for their own security." The wealthy ruling powers, continued the pirate, "rob the poor under the cover of law, ... and we plunder the rich under the protection of our own courage."

By April Bellamy was in command of a fleet of three or four vessels, with the *Whydah* as his flagship. The fleet continued northward toward New England. On the night of April 26, 1717, the pirates sailed into a tremendous storm off Cape Cod. It was the worst storm on record in the region, with wind gusts of more than 80 miles (129 kilometers) per hour. Only 500 feet (152 meters) from shore and in sight of land, the *Whydah* was driven into a sandbar. Pounded by waves 20 feet (6 meters) high, the ship's main mast snapped. Then the *Whydah* slipped off the sandbar and capsized. There were about forty cannons below decks, and when the ship tipped over, they crashed down through the decks and smashed the ship's hull, trapping many of the crew. Only 2 of the 145 men aboard the *Whydah* survived. Bellamy, as well as young John King, died in the wreck. According to Cape Cod legend, Maria Hallett witnessed the wreck and was so heartbroken at Bellamy's death that she withdrew from human contact and became a witch.

The people of Wellfleet, the village closest to the wreck, reported that more than one hundred corpses washed ashore. But Bellamy's body was never found. According to Konstam, the pirates might have been able to escape the storm or save their ship, but they were too drunk to respond to the danger in time.

Some of the *Whydah*'s treasure also washed onto the beach. A group sent by the Massachusetts governor to investigate the wreck reported that at least two hundred men had arrived to scavenge what valuables they could find.

Survivors stand trial for piracy

A second ship in Bellamy's fleet was wrecked farther up coast, and seven crew members survived. The two *Whydah* survivors, a Welshman named Thomas Davis and a part-Native American named John Julian, were brought to

Boston, Massachusetts, to be tried on piracy charges. Davis defended himself by saying that he had been forced into piracy and called a character witness to vouch for his good education, family, and behavior. He was acquitted. Julian was sent to jail but did not receive a trial and later disappeared. Historians believe he was sold into slavery.

The seven survivors from Bellamy's second ship also stood trial. Thomas South convinced the court that he had been forced to join the pirates. Like Davis, he was acquitted. But the others were found guilty and sentenced to death. They were hanged on November 14, 1717. Because their crimes had been committed at sea, their bodies were buried between the high tide and low tide markings on the shore.

When Bellamy's old shipmate Blackbeard received news of the *Whydah*'s fate, he declared that he would burn Boston to the ground if the survivors were hanged. The city was spared, however, when an English warship entered Boston harbor.

Bellamy's career as a pirate lasted only about one year, and he died at age twenty-nine. But in this short time, he and his pirates seized more than fifty ships. Although he did not live long enough to enjoy his plunder, Bellamy became one of the wealthiest pirates in the Americas.

For More Information

BOOKS

Clifford, Barry. *Real Pirates: The Untold Story of the Whydah*. Washington, DC: National Geographic, 2008.

Konstam, Angus. *Blackbeard: America's Most Notorious Pirate*. Hoboken, NJ: Wiley, 2006, p. 57.

———. *Piracy: The Complete History*. Oxford, England: Osprey, 2008, pp. 209–210.

Wren, Laura Lee. *Pirates and Privateers of the High Seas*. Berkeley Heights, NJ: Enslow, 2003.

PERIODICALS

Webster, Donovan. "Pirates of the *Whydah*." *National Geographic* (May 1999). Available online at http://nationalgeographic.com/whydah/story.html (accessed on January 3, 2011).

WEB SITES

Expedition Whydah. www.whydah.org (accessed on January 3, 2011).

"Real Pirates: The Untold Story of the Whydah from Slave Ship to Pirate Ship." *The Field Museum*. www.fieldmuseum.org/pirates (accessed on January 3, 2011).

Blackbeard

BORN: c. 1680

DIED: November 22, 1718 • North Carolina, United States

English pirate

"Some of Blackbeard's frolics of wickedness were so extravagant, as if he aimed at making his men believe he was a devil incarnate."

– Captain Charles Johnson
A GENERAL HISTORY OF THE ROBBERIES AND MURDERS OF THE MOST NOTORIOUS PIRATES.

The most notorious pirate in Western history was Edward Teach, better known as Blackbeard. He operated in the Caribbean Sea and along the Atlantic coast of North America in the early 1700s, preying on ships and terrorizing residents. Blackbeard's deeds became legendary and inspired many of the enduring images of piracy in the Americas. But ironically, Blackbeard was neither particularly successful nor especially violent. Many pirates captured more treasure than he did, and several others subjected their victims to crueler treatment. But Blackbeard excelled in provoking fear. He had a terrifying appearance and encouraged his victims and even his crew to believe that he had supernatural powers. Blackbeard developed such a frightening reputation that his victims would often surrender without a fight. Although his exploits were less spectacular than those of some other pirates, Blackbeard has continued to serve in the Western imagination as the perfect example of a ruthless pirate.

Blackbeard. © INTERFOTO/ALAMY.

Begins career as a privateer

Blackbeard was born around 1680, most likely in Bristol, England. Some accounts give his birthplace as London, but others say he was born in Jamaica or in Philadelphia, Pennsylvania. By 1702 he was reportedly operating in the Caribbean as a privateer. Privateers were commissioned by a state or government to attack the merchant ships of an enemy nation, and they were required to give a percentage of their plunder (goods stolen by force) to the government.

Considered a legal activity, privateering had been a common practice in the Caribbean since the late 1500s. The major European powers in the region, primarily Spain, England, and France, engaged in various rivalries and alliances, with frequent outbreaks of war. During periods of conflict, their treasure ships, loaded with wealth from the Americas, were ideal targets. Privateers could legally seize gold, silver, sugar, and other valuable cargo from enemy ships, and this treasure could make them extremely wealthy. But when wars came to an end, privateers had no legitimate way to earn income. In many cases, they simply continued raiding ships and stealing anything of value, keeping all their plunder for themselves. In other words, they became pirates.

Historians believe that Blackbeard followed this pattern. He most likely operated as a privateer until 1713 and soon afterward turned to piracy. It is generally believed that he began his criminal career under the pirate Benjamin Hornigold (d. 1719), who was based in the Bahamas. The first written reference to Blackbeard dates from the summer of 1717, when it was reported that he was given command of a small vessel that Hornigold had seized. Blackbeard named this ship the *Queen Anne's Revenge.*

Sails with Stede Bonnet

Blackbeard and Hornigold parted ways in 1717. That same year Blackbeard met **Stede Bonnet** (1688–1718; see entry), a gentleman from Barbados who had left his family to become the captain of a ten-gun pirate sloop, the *Revenge.* (A sloop is a fast vessel with a single fore-and-aft rigged mast, meaning that the mast was positioned for sails set lengthwise along the ship.) Bonnet had no seafaring experience and lacked the skills necessary to command a pirate crew. He had come into the port of New Providence, the largest pirate haven in the Bahamas, to recover from a devastating encounter with a Spanish battleship. (A pirate haven is a safe place for pirates to harbor and repair their ships, resupply, and organize raiding parties.) Bonnet agreed to allow Blackbeard to take over the *Revenge*. With Bonnet remaining onboard, Blackbeard added this vessel to his command.

The pirate band sailed northward, plundering several merchant ships near Philadelphia before turning back toward Barbados in November. By the spring of 1718, Blackbeard had made numerous raids. He commanded four vessels and more than three hundred men. He had parted ways with Bonnet and his ship the previous December, but Bonnet did not fare well on his own. When the *Revenge* and *Queen Anne's Revenge* met again soon after parting, Bonnet's crew deserted their captain and signed on with Blackbeard. He ordered Bonnet aboard the *Queen Anne's Revenge* and placed another officer in charge of Bonnet's ship.

Blockades Charleston

Blackbeard and his men then headed north. In May they reached the prosperous South Carolina port of Charles Town, later known as Charleston. At least ten merchant vessels were anchored in the harbor and others were approaching. In a move that Angus Konstam describes in *Blackbeard: America's Most Notorious Pirate* as "the most breathtakingly audacious piratical adventure of his short career," Blackbeard positioned his ships just outside the entrance to the harbor and began a blockade of the town.

The pirates easily seized every vessel that left the harbor or attempted to enter. They stole whatever the ships were carrying, including rice, lumber, rum, and slaves. The pirates also took the crews and passengers on these vessels as prisoners. Blackbeard knew that he could use these hostages to demand ransoms and to negotiate deals with local authorities. (A ransom is a sum of money demanded for the release of someone being held captive.)

Charles Town residents had considered themselves relatively safe from attack and were shocked and frightened by the blockade. Their fears worsened when Blackbeard sent some men ashore to demand that the colonial government give the pirates a chest of medicine. The pirate's message was clear: If the governor did not give him this chest, Blackbeard would kill all the prisoners he had taken and set fire to all the ships he had captured. Blackbeard also stated that if the men he had sent ashore were prevented from returning to their ships, he would sail into the harbor and burn any vessel anchored there.

Blackbeard's threats terrified the residents of Charles Town, who were already familiar with the pirate's fierce reputation. A tall man with a long, black beard that he sometimes wore in braids, he reportedly lit slow-burning matches under his hat during battles, to make it look as if he were surrounded by hellfire. According to an account by Captain Charles Johnson, author of *A General History of the Robberies and Murders of the Most Notorious Pirates*, Blackbeard wanted his crew to believe that he had special evil powers. On one occasion, the pirate closed his men up below decks and lit a smoky fire to create his version of hell on the ship. Blackbeard was very pleased when he was able to endure breathing the smoke longer than any of his men. The pirate also encouraged rumors that a mysterious figure sometimes seen aboard *Queen Anne's Revenge* was none other than Satan himself.

Intimidated by Blackbeard's reputation as well as his demands, the colonial government decided to hand over the medicine. But by this time, six or seven days had elapsed, and the pirate was growing worried that a force from the British Royal Navy might soon arrive to defend the city. On receiving the medicine, Blackbeard ordered the hostages released. But first the pirates took everything of value that the prisoners possessed, including any fine clothing they were wearing. It is estimated that this loot amounted to the modern equivalent of about four hundred thousand dollars.

Runs aground at Beaufort Inlet

With his medicines and treasure, Blackbeard left Charles Town and sailed up the coast to Beaufort Inlet, North Carolina. There he hoped to find a safe place to repair his ships. The *Revenge* and the smaller vessels made it into a protected harbor, but *Queen Anne's Revenge* ran aground on a sandbar and sustained heavy damage. Blackbeard ordered the crew of a smaller vessel, the *Adventure*, to sail close and attempt to free the flagship, but this resulted in the *Adventure* also running aground.

Unable to free the stricken vessels, Blackbeard and Bonnet decided to go to Bath, then the capital of North Carolina, and surrender to government authorities. The government had proclaimed a general pardon for any pirate who surrendered on or before September 5, 1718. But the pardon only covered crimes that were committed before January 5 of that year. Although the blockade of Charles Town had occurred in May, the pirate captains felt confident that the governor would overlook this detail and grant them pardons.

Blackbeard received his pardon immediately and returned to the waiting ships while Bonnet remained in Bath to try to obtain a privateering commission. But when Bonnet got back to Beaufort Inlet, he discovered that Blackbeard had stripped the vessels of their treasures and provisions and fled, abandoning most of the crew on an offshore island. Many historians interpret this as evidence that Blackbeard had deliberately run his ship aground in order to break up his pirate band, which had become too big, and to escape with a few of his best sailors. Bonnet rescued the stranded men and, without food or other supplies, returned to piracy to survive. He was captured soon afterward and hanged for his crimes.

Blackbeard, meanwhile, had established friendly relations with the colonial governor of North Carolina, Charles Eden (1673–1722). The governor declared that the pirate's ship, a vessel captured the previous year from the Spanish off the coast of Cuba, was a legitimate privateering prize and that Blackbeard had permission to keep it. The pirate renamed the vessel the *Adventure* and anchored it at his pirate base on Ocracoke Island, near Bath. (A pirate base is a place where pirates lived under their own rule and maintained their own defense system.) Blackbeard bought a lavish house in Bath and began living as if he had retired from his criminal adventures. He married the daughter of a local plantation owner, who allegedly became his fourteenth wife. According to local legend, he also tried to win the hand of Governor Eden's daughter, who spurned Blackbeard, because she was in love with another man. The pirate later captured a ship on which this man was a passenger. Seeing that the man wore Miss Eden's ring, the pirate killed the man and cut off his hand. He then sent the hand to Miss Eden, who was so heartbroken that she died of grief.

Many North Carolina residents believed that Governor Eden had an agreement with the pirate, offering him protection in exchange for some

The *Queen Anne's Revenge*

After the *Queen Anne's Revenge* ran aground off the coast of North Carolina in 1718, Blackbead abandoned the ship and it eventually sank. In 1996 the remains of a ship thought to be the *Queen Anne's Revenge* were found in about 20 feet (6 meters) of water in Beaufort Inlet, where the wreck had been buried in sand from the sea floor. Many of the ship's artifacts were recovered, including its bell, dated 1709 and thought to be of Spanish or Portuguese origin, as well as several cannonballs. The most unusual relic from the wreck is the brass barrel of a blunderbuss, a short musket with a flared muzzle. Engravings on the barrel prove that the gun was made in England sometime after 1672. These items, as well as the location of the wreck, strongly suggest that the wreck is indeed the remains of the *Queen Anne's Revenge*. More research is being done to prove that these objects came from the flagship of the notorious Blackbeard.

of Blackbeard's loot. According to local stories, the governor had ordered a secret tunnel dug, connecting his mansion to the creek where Blackbeard's ship was hidden. But no evidence of such a tunnel has been found.

The loot that Blackbeard and his men brought into the town of Bath boosted the economy and made the pirates quite popular. The pirate captain became a local celebrity, receiving invitations to the homes of the town's leading citizens. The man who had cultivated a demonic image as a pirate now became a charming personality, fascinating and delighting the residents of Bath. Soon he was boasting that there was not a single home in the entire colony where he would not be welcome as a dinner guest.

Dies in battle

Blackbeard's retirement did not last long. Within a few months, he was again raiding ships along the coast, attracting the attention of Virginia's governor, Alexander Spotswood (c. 1676–1740). Spotswood strongly disapproved of Eden's decision to tolerate Blackbeard's presence in Bath and believed that piracy had to be stamped out to protect the economy of England's colonies. Convinced that Eden would never take action against Blackbeard, Spotswood set out to defeat the pirate. In November 1718 he organized an expedition to apprehend Blackbeard and offered a reward one hundred pounds for the pirate's capture.

Spotswood sent an infantry force to surround Bath by land, and a naval force, consisting of two rented civilian sloops under the command of Robert Maynard (1684–1751), to hunt the pirates on the water. These forces expected to find the pirate at home in Bath. On the way, Maynard discovered that Blackbeard was not at his house but instead was aboard the *Adventure*, anchored at Ocracoke Island. Maynard reached the island just as night was falling on November 21. Blackbeard and his men were with the *Adventure* at the other end of the island, where they were hosting a party for sailors from another local vessel. Because many of the pirates had gone ashore, only part of Blackbeard's usual crew was aboard.

Ocracoke Island was a good hiding place for pirates. It was protected by a sandbar, and the twisting channel leading to the landing place was 1 mile (1.6 kilometers) long and shallow in some places, making navigation difficult. Perhaps because he felt so safe there, Blackbeard had not posted a lookout. Maynard's naval attack came as a complete surprise.

Maynard had ordered a rowboat to lead his two sloops into the place where the *Adventure* lay, reaching the spot at about 7:30 A.M. The pirates

Blackbeard and Robert Maynard duel for their lives. SUPERSTOCK/GETTY IMAGES.

had no idea where these vessels were from or why they had come. They began preparing their guns but did not have enough time to haul up their anchor. Needing to get into open water as swiftly as possible, Blackbeard ordered his men to cut the anchor cable.

Instead of heading northward, which offered a good chance of escape, the pirate positioned the *Adventure* for battle, waiting for the naval sloops to come within range for a broadside attack. As Maynard's vessels came closer, Blackbeard began moving the *Adventure* toward a beach on the island. His plan was to draw Maynard's unsuspecting men onto a hidden sandbar. In doing so, however, he risked running his own vessel aground. But with his expert knowledge of the waters, the pirate was willing to take this risk.

Once Maynard's sloops were close to the *Adventure*, Blackbeard ordered his men to fire. At least twenty men on one sloop, the *Jane*, were killed by the blast. The officers aboard the other sloop were also killed. The *Jane* fought on, however, and after a heated battle, the *Adventure* ran aground. But the tide eventually rose enough to refloat the stricken ship, and the fighting continued. The battle ended after fierce hand-to-hand combat, during which Maynard and Blackbeard dueled for their lives. In the end Blackbeard was killed. Maynard ordered the villain beheaded and threw his body into the water. Then he hoisted the severed head on his bowsprit, the pole at the forward end of the ship, and sailed with his gruesome trophy to Hampton, Virginia.

Blackbeard's death was seen as a triumph in the fight against piracy in the Americas. His exploits became infamous, and the pirate attained the status of an evil folk hero. In modern times, however, historians determined that Blackbeard's fearsome reputation did not match the reality of his deeds. He was ruthless in battle but is not known to have killed anyone simply for revenge or convenience, as some other pirates did. And some historians believe he may have been sincere in his efforts to start a new life as a legitimate seaman. But whatever the real details about Blackbeard may have been, he continues to be, for many people, the ultimate pirate, inspiring countless legends, songs, films, and other lore.

For More Information

BOOKS

Konstam, Angus. *Blackbeard: America's Most Notorious Pirate.* Hoboken, NJ: Wiley, 2006, pp. 130, 156–57.

Johnson, Captain Charles. *A General History of the Robberies and Murders of the Most Notorious Pirates.* London, England: Conway Maritime Press, 1998, 2002.

WEB SITES

"Blackbeard the Pirate." *North Carolina Maritime Museum.* www.ncmaritime.org/Blackbeard/default.htm (accessed on January 3, 2011).

"Historic Bath: Blackbeard the Pirate." *North Carolina Historic Sites.* www.nchistoricsites.org/bath/blackbeard.htm (accessed on January 3, 2011).

Kirkpatrick, Jennifer. "Blackbeard: Pirate Terror at Sea." *National Geographic.* www.nationalgeographic.com/pirates/bbeard.html (accessed on January 3, 2011).

Stede Bonnet

BORN: 1688 • Bridgetown, Barbados

DIED: December 10, 1718 • Charleston, South Carolina, United States

English pirate

Stede Bonnet. © CORBIS.

"The major was no sailor … and therefore had been obliged to yield to many things that were imposed on him … for want of a competent knowledge in maritime affairs. . . ."

– Captain Charles Johnson
A GENERAL HISTORY OF THE ROBBERIES AND MURDERS OF THE MOST NOTORIOUS PIRATES.

Stede Bonnet was one of the many pirates operating in the Atlantic Ocean in the early 1700s. Born a gentleman, he lacked seafaring experience and found it difficult to control his crew. He attacked merchant ships and stole cargoes but did not seem particularly interested in seizing wealth for himself. He agreed to give up his life of piracy in return for a government pardon, but need forced him to resume his raiding. Captured by the British colonial government of South Carolina, he was tried and hanged in 1718 after a pirate career that had lasted less than two years.

A respectable gentleman turns pirate

Unlike most pirates, Stede Bonnet came from a wealthy and distinguished family. He was born in 1688 in the English colony of Barbados, in the

Caribbean Sea, where his father, Edward, owned a plantation. Edward's father, Thomas Bonnet, had been one of the island's first settlers, and he had purchased more than 400 acres (162 hectares) of good fertile land. This property became one of the most extensive plantations in the colony in the mid–1600s, and when Thomas died, most of the estate went to Edward. Upon Edward's death, Stede inherited the property.

Stede received a good education and became a bookish and cultured man. At age twenty-one, he married Mary Allamby, daughter of a prosperous plantation owner. The couple had three sons and one daughter. Bonnet lived comfortably off the profits of his property, but was not considered extremely wealthy. He was a respected member of Barbadian society and became a major in the Barbados militia.

Why Bonnet turned to piracy is a question that continues to puzzle scholars. He did not need money, and he did not grow up in a seafaring family. In fact, he had no idea how to run a ship. But in the summer of 1717, Bonnet left his wife and family to become a pirate. According to some accounts, he went to sea to avoid his wife's constant nagging. Other accounts indicate he was hoping to avoid some kind of scandal or was simply looking for adventure. And some people in Barbados said that he was suffering from some kind of mental disorder. Whatever the reason, he purchased a ship and began a new life of robbery on the seas.

Outfits the *Revenge*

Bonnet was a very unusual pirate. Instead of capturing a ship and refashioning it for raiding, he simply bought one. He purchased a sleek, ten-gun sloop and renamed it *Revenge*. (A sloop is a fast vessel with a single fore-and-aft rigged mast, meaning that the mast was positioned for sails set lengthwise along the ship.) This name suggests that Bonnet may have been seeking revenge for something, but he never explained what his motives were for leaving home and going to sea. Unlike other captains, who had years of experience at sea and knew many skilled sailors who could serve as crew, Bonnet had to hire strangers to operate his ship. A pirate usually joined a ship's crew as a volunteer, with the understanding that he would receive a percentage of all the treasure seized, but no one would work on Bonnet's ship unless he promised to pay regular wages.

Leaving Barbados in the summer of 1717, Bonnet sailed toward the North American colonies. Along the coast of Virginia, he captured four merchant vessels in just a few weeks: the *Anne* and the *Young*, both from

Scotland; the *Endeavor*, from Bristol, England; and the *Turbet*, from Barbados. Continuing north, Bonnet reached the eastern end of Long Island, where he captured another merchant sloop. When he ran low on supplies, he allegedly surprised local residents by purchasing what he needed, rather than stealing from them as other pirates did.

Turning back south, Bonnet seized two ships heading into the harbor at Charleston, South Carolina: a small trading vessel from Boston, Massachusetts, which the pirates stripped and abandoned; and a vessel from Barbados, carrying slaves, sugar, and rum. Badly needing to do repairs on the *Revenge*, Bonnet took his ship and the Barbadian sloop to a secluded spot along the North Carolina shore. The pirates hauled the *Revenge* onto the beach, and replaced its rotted wood with timber from the captured sloop. Once the *Revenge* was again seaworthy, the pirates burned what was left of the stolen ship.

Meets Blackbeard

Bonnet then headed back to the Caribbean. On the way, he engaged in a skirmish with a Spanish battleship. It was unwise for one small pirate vessel to get into a fight with such a warship, and the encounter killed or wounded half of Bonnet's crew. It also left the *Revenge* seriously damaged. Bonnet was lucky to make it to the Bahamas, where he took refuge in the pirate haven of New Providence. (A pirate haven is a safe place for pirates to harbor and repair their ships, resupply, and organize raiding parties.)

In New Providence Bonnet met English pirate Edward Teach, known as **Blackbeard** (1680–1718; see entry). Bonnet still needed to recover from the Spanish attack and agreed to let Blackbeard take temporary control of the *Revenge*. Bonnet remained onboard, but Blackbeard ran the ship. They sailed northward again to Delaware Bay, near Philadelphia, Pennsylvania. Here they raided several merchant ships before heading back to Barbados in November.

In the Caribbean the pirates made several daring attacks and captured the *Concorde*, which Blackbeard renamed *Queen Anne's Revenge*. Sometime late in December 1717, Bonnet and Blackbeard separated. Once again captain of the *Revenge*, Bonnet sailed the ship into the western Caribbean. He had little luck, failing to capture a large merchant vessel off the coast of Honduras. When the *Revenge* and *Queen Anne's Revenge* met again soon after this failure, Bonnet's disgruntled crew deserted to Blackbeard's ship. Blackbeard placed an officer named Richards in charge of the *Revenge*, and Bonnet unwillingly joined Blackbeard on the *Queen*

Stede Bonnet met the pirate Blackbeard (pictured) in Barbados. © NORTH WIND PICTURE ARCHIVES/ALAMY.

Anne's Revenge. Although Bonnet appeared to live well under Blackbeard's control, he was shamed by the arrangement and grew depressed. He told the few crew members who remained sympathetic toward him that he would be happy to abandon piracy if he could find asylum in Spain or Portugal and never see another Englishman again.

Richards quickly captured another vessel, and Blackbeard directed this fleet of three ships toward South Carolina. Reaching Charleston by the spring of 1718, the pirates blockaded the city, raiding any ship that approached. They plundered (robbed of goods by force) at least five merchant vessels and took hostages from the city, receiving a handsome ransom for the captives' return. (A ransom is a sum of money demanded for the release of someone being held captive.)

Regains the *Revenge*

Blackbeard then led the pirate fleet up the coast toward Beaufort Inlet, North Carolina, where he hoped to find a suitable place to do repairs on the ships. The *Revenge* and the smaller vessels were able to enter Beaufort Inlet's protected harbor, but the *Queen Anne's Revenge* ran aground on a sandbar and could not be saved. Leaving the remaining ships there, Bonnet and Blackbeard went ashore to Bath, then the capital of the colony, to obtain an official government pardon in return for renouncing piracy. Blackbeard then returned to Beaufort Inlet. Bonnet remained in Bath to persuade the governor to grant him a license to raid Spanish ships as a privateer, a private ship owner commissioned by a state or government to attack the merchant ships of an enemy nation.

Privateering license in hand, Bonnet planned to sail to the Caribbean and prey on Spanish trade vessels there. But when he returned to Beaufort Inlet, he discovered that Blackbeard had abandoned most of his crew on an offshore island and fled with all the treasure. Bonnet resumed command of the *Revenge* and rescued the marooned sailors. But he had no food or money to obtain the desperately needed supplies. And he had only a short time to make it back to the Caribbean before the hurricane season began.

Realizing he would have to resort to pirate raids to get food for his men, Bonnet disguised his activities by calling himself "Captain Thomas" and changing the name of his ship to *Royal James*. He did not want any news of his piracy reaching the governor, for this would cancel Bonnet's pardon. Coming upon a couple of merchant ships, Bonnet took several barrels of food from them but was careful to give something in return to make it look like he was operating as a legitimate trader. Before long, though, he stopped bothering with this and simply attacked ships.

Within two months, Bonnet had seized the cargoes of thirteen ships carrying goods such as tobacco, molasses, and hides. Not eager to fight, as some pirates were, Bonnet tried to get his victims to surrender without having to resort to violence.

Attacks the *Fortune* and the *Francis*

On July 29, 1718, Bonnet saw the sloop *Fortune* off the coast of Cape May, New Jersey. He sent his quartermaster, Robert Tucker, to board the sloop with a small party of men. In doing so, however, Tucker attacked several of the *Fortune's* crew for no reason. When the authorities learned of this attack, Bonnet was blamed for Tucker's violence. Bonnet decided to keep the sloop as a supply ship and took its captain, Thomas Read, aboard the *Royal James*. Two days later, another sloop, the *Francis*, anchored in the area. A rowboat carrying five of Bonnet's men approached the *Francis*, and the men, pretending to be from merchant vessels, asked permission to come aboard. Once on deck they seized the captain, Peter Mainwaring, and took him back to the *Royal James*. Then Bonnet's crew raided the *Francis*, transferring its cargo of sugar, molasses, cotton, and rum to the *Royal James*. The pirates got so drunk and rowdy that, to restore order, Bonnet ordered two of the men whipped. He also sent Captain Read's wife and son ashore, to be taken to safety.

Bonnet then led the four ships south. The *Francis* kept so far to the rear that the pirate feared its crew would try to escape. He shouted out to the men that, if they did not stay closer to the *Royal James*, he would fire on them. The crew took this message seriously and obeyed. The four vessels reached Cape Fear, North Carolina, on August 12 and found a safe harbor in the Cape Fear River where they could stop and repair leaks to the *Royal James*.

By now, word of Bonnet's activities had reached Charleston, and the governor sent out two heavily armed patrol ships, commanded by Colonel William Rhett, to hunt for pirates in the area. The patrol found Bonnet on the evening of September 26 and planned an attack for the next morning. But Bonnet made the first move, sneaking the *Royal James* out of the river and toward the patrol before dawn. He was hoping to take Rhett by surprise and escape into the open sea before the colonel could fire, but he ran aground. Rhett followed, but his two vessels also ran aground.

Stuck, Bonnet and Rhett engaged in an hours-long musket battle. Twelve of Rhett's crew were killed, and eighteen were wounded, while only nine of Bonnet's men were wounded. Finally one of Rhett's vessels managed to get free and position itself in range to hit the *Royal James* with its cannons. With no way to escape, Bonnet was forced to surrender.

Trial and execution

Rhett took the pirates to Charleston, where the crew was put in jail. Bonnet, as a gentleman, was allowed to lodge as a captive in the comfortable private home of the city's marshal. His two officers, David Heriot and Ignatius Pell, joined him there as prisoners. But the house was not well guarded, and on October 24 the three men escaped. Stealing a canoe, they tried to make it into the Atlantic Ocean, but a storm blew them onto Sullivan's Island, near the city's harbor.

The colonial governor offered a huge reward for Bonnet's capture, and several men went looking for the fugitive. He was found on November 5 and taken to the Charleston jail, where his crew was still imprisoned. All of the men were charged with piracy. At their trial, all but two pleaded innocent, arguing that they had been forced against their will to join Bonnet. But twenty-nine of the thirty-three accused men were found guilty and sentenced to death. Twenty-four were hanged on November 8.

Then Bonnet's trial was held. He was charged with piracy against the *Francis*. Prosecutor Thomas Hepworth, quoted in the book *Pirates, Privateers, and Rebel Raiders of the Carolina Coast* by Lindley S. Butler, called Bonnet "the great *Ringleader* of [the pirates] who has seduced many poor ignorant Men to follow his Course of Living and ruined many poor wretches." Bonnet pleaded innocent. He also stated that he had never forced anyone to join his crew. In fact, he blamed his men for piracy, saying that they had acted without his orders. He emphasized that he had not consented to the plundering of the *Francis* and had actually been asleep when the assault took place. But these arguments did not persuade the jury, and Bonnet was found guilty.

Immediately following the verdict, Bonnet was tried again. This time the charges were related to the capture of the *Fortune*. When Bonnet pled guilty to thirteen acts of piracy and eighteen counts of murder in the battle with Captain Rhett at Cape Fear, Judge Nicholas Trott (1663–1740) subjected Bonnet to a harsh lecture. As quoted by Butler, Trott stated, "Their *Blood* now cries out for *Vengeance* and *Justice*." He sentenced Bonnet to death, adding that the pirate should suffer for his crimes "in the Lake which burneth with Fire and Brimstone."

Judge Nicholas Trott

Nicholas Trott, who presided over the trial of Bonnet and his crew, was a distinguished figure in South Carolina. He was born in London, England, where he studied law before being appointed attorney general of Bermuda in 1693. In 1699 he moved to Charleston, South Carolina, where he was named attorney general and naval officer. Four years later, he became the colony's chief justice. Trott took piracy seriously and used the Bonnet trial to clarify laws and punishments for the offense. In 1719 Trott published *The Tryals of Major Stede Bonnet and Other Pirates*, a transcript of the court proceedings. The book included detailed and thorough definitions of piracy from ancient scholars through the seventeenth century and presented a comprehensive analysis of piracy and the law. According to L. Lynn Hogue's biography of Trott in *American National Biography*, Trott's book was extremely influential and "continued to be cited in the literature of public international law into the nineteenth and twentieth centuries." Trott wrote several other books as well, including an essay about what kinds of evidence could be used in trials for the crime of witchcraft. He argued that use of spectral evidence (a claim by a witness that the accused's evil spirit appeared to the witness in a dream and said or did certain damaging things) should not be considered reliable evidence.

As Bonnet waited for his execution, he did what he could to gain sympathy from the people of Charleston. The city's young women, in particular, urged the governor to take pity on the pirate and spare his life. As time ran out, Bonnet sent the governor a desperate letter asking him, as quoted by Butler, "to look upon me with tender Bowels of Pity and Compassion; and believe me to be the most miserable Man this Day breathing." But the governor refused to lessen the sentence, and Bonnet was executed on December 10, 1718, in front of a jeering crowd on the Charleston waterfront.

For More Information

BOOKS

Butler, Lindley S. *Pirates, Privateers, and Rebel Raiders of the Carolina Coast.* Chapel Hill: University of North Carolina Press, 2000, p 70.

Konstam, Angus. *Piracy: The Complete History.* Oxford, England: Osprey, 2008.

Hogue, L. Lynn. "Nicholas Trott" in *American National Biography*, edited by John A. Garraty and Mark C. Carnes. Oxford University Press, 1999. Available online at http://law.gsu.edu/lhogue/spring05/Handout1.pdf (accessed on January 3, 2011).

Johnson, Captain Charles. *A General History of the Robberies and Murders of the Most Notorious Pirates.* London, England: Conway Maritime Press, 1998, 2002.

Anne Bonny and Mary Read

Anne Bonny

BORN: c. March 8, 1700 • County Cork, Ireland

DIED: April 25, 1782

Irish pirate

Mary Read

BORN: c. 1690 • England

DIED: 1721 • Jamaica

English pirate

"[Bonny and Read] were both very profligate [immoral], cursing, and swearing much, and very ready and willing to do any Thing on board."

– Thomas Dillon, testifying about an attack on his merchant vessel by Bonny and Read's ship
QUOTED IN *THE PIRATE TRIAL OF ANNE BONNY AND MARY READ* BY TAMARA J. EASTMAN AND CONSTANCE BOND.

Anne Bonny. © THE PRINT COLLECTOR/HIP/THE IMAGE WORKS. REPRODUCED BY PERMISSION.

When a crew of ruthless pirates was brought to trial in Jamaica in 1720, the public was astonished to learn that two of these sea bandits were women. Disguised as men, Anne Bonny and Mary Read had fought alongside their male comrades to attack ships and steal their cargoes. They lived as they pleased at sea, defying the law and the expectations of society until their eventual arrest. At a time when few women in the Western world ever set foot on a ship and were expected to live quiet lives as wives and mothers, Bonny and Read proved that women could act as bravely and as independently as any man.

Anne Bonny

Born in 1700 (some sources say 1697) in County Cork, Ireland, Anne Bonny was the out-of-wedlock daughter of William Cormac, a lawyer, and Peg Brennan, a servant who had been fired by Cormac's wife for stealing some silver spoons. After Bonny's birth, which reportedly occurred when Brennan was in prison, Cormac left his wife and tried to raise the child on his own. He dressed her as a boy and told people that the child was the son of relatives who had asked him to train the boy as a clerk. But the disguise was eventually discovered, causing a scandal. After this, Cormac and Brennan immigrated to the American colonies with their daughter. They settled in South Carolina on a small plantation near the city of Charles Town (present-day Charleston).

Bonny's mother died when the girl was still young, and Cormac had a difficult time disciplining the child. There are many colorful stories about Bonny as a young woman. She is said to have once stabbed and killed a servant in a quarrel and also severely beat a man who tried to rape her. Bonny thrived on excitement, and enjoyed visiting Charles Town when sailors and pirates were in port. She listened to their stories and yearned to have the kinds of adventures that they described. She reportedly came upon the pirate **Blackbeard** (1680–1718; see entry) one day, and his strange appearance and behavior were so fascinating that Bonny decided then and there that she, too, would become a pirate and lead a life of adventure at sea.

Among the sailors whom Bonny met in Charles Town was the handsome young James Bonny. The couple fell in love, but Bonny's father objected to her wish to marry James. Instead, Cormac wanted his daughter to become the wife of a local medical student. But Bonny knew she would be bored as a doctor's wife and eloped with James in 1716. The couple then sailed to Nassau, a busy port on New Providence Island in the Bahamas.

In the early 1700s Nassau was one of the busiest ports in the Caribbean Sea. The huge volume of shipping in the region had attracted pirates to these waters since the early 1500s. Pirate activity here had increased so dramatically that the period from about 1690 to 1730 became known as the golden age of piracy. The major center of piracy in the Caribbean was Nassau. Some fifteen hundred pirates were based in the town in 1710, making it the largest pirate settlement in the Americas.

Expecting to join her husband in various pirate adventures, Bonny was disappointed to discover that James wanted to retire from his earlier life at sea. He took advantage of a government deal offering amnesty to pirates who promised to become law-abiding citizens, and he even gave information to the authorities about his mates who were still plundering ships. Disgusted by James's behavior, Bonny started spending her time in Nassau's taverns, where she met John "Calico Jack" Rackham (1682–1720). The two soon fell in love, but James refused to give Bonny a divorce and even threatened her with a public whipping if she did not return to him. Defying marriage laws, Bonny decided simply to run away with Rackham. She helped him steal a fast ship, the *Curlew*, which was anchored in Nassau harbor, and together they sailed off to begin a life of raiding. In 1718 Bonny gave birth to an infant girl who did not survive.

Mary Read

Mary Read was born in England, possibly in 1690. Her mother, Polly, became pregnant with Mary after her husband, Alfred Read, had disappeared at sea. Needing help to support the child, Polly turned to her husband's mother. Since Polly's first-born child, a son, had died, Polly hoped that her mother-in-law would want another grandson to pass along the family name. So she dressed Mary as a boy and told her mother-in-law that she had given birth to another son. The mother-in-law agreed to send Polly a weekly allowance for the child.

Read's grandmother died when she was thirteen, but she continued to dress like a boy. She was sent to work as a footboy, a type of servant, to a French lady, but she hated this work and ran away to join the crew of a naval warship. Later, she went to the Netherlands and served as a soldier. Throughout this time, she succeeded in keeping her gender secret. But when she fell in love with a fellow soldier, Corporal Jules Vosquon, she had to tell him the truth. He returned her love, and they were married after being discharged from the military.

For a few years, the couple ran a dining house called the Three Horseshoes, near Breda castle in the Netherlands. It was a popular place, but after Vosquon's death in 1716, the business began to fail. Read decided to disguise herself as a man again and join another army. But because it was peacetime and there was little need for soldiers, she chose instead to sign on with a Dutch ship preparing to sail to Jamaica. When this vessel reached the Caribbean, it was attacked by pirates. Preferring to take her chances with these sea bandits, Read joined the pirate band and soon gained her crewmates' respect as a brave fighter. According to

Calico Jack Rackham

John Rackham, known as Calico Jack, got his nickname because of the cotton calico clothing he liked to wear. Rackham was born in England in 1682. He served as a junior commander of a vessel captained by English pirate Charles Vane (died 1720) in the Caribbean. In this position, Rackham learned to deal with disputes among men, maintain discipline, and manage questions such as how stolen goods should be fairly divided. Rackham's crewmates came to trust him more than their captain. When Vane confronted a larger French vessel and ordered his men to retreat from battle, Rackham objected and said that they should stay and fight. Although the men overwhelmingly agreed with Rackham, Vane ignored their protests and insisted on retreat. Disappointed that they had lost an opportunity to capture a great deal of treasure, the crew later voted to remove Vane as captain and put Rackham in his place.

Unlike some pirate captains who had problems with mutinous crews, Rackham's pirates seemed to respect him as a good leader.

Because Rackham focused most of his attention on relatively small vessels close to shore, he never stole huge treasures. But he harassed so many vessels that the Jamaican authorities decided to make an example of him. He was captured in 1720. After he was tried and convicted of piracy, he was hanged. Then his body was smeared with tar, a preservative, and placed in a metal cage that was hung on a small island at the entrance to the Jamaican capital, Port Royal. It was one of the first things people saw when they sailed into the city. Governments used the punishment of death to frighten would-be pirates away from a life of crime. The island where Rackham's body was displayed later became known as Rackham's Cay.

Rackham is perhaps most famous for his version of the Jolly Roger, or the pirate flag.

some accounts, the pirate who captured the Dutch vessel was none other than Anne Bonny's love, Jack Rackham.

In 1718 Read decided to accept the same amnesty bargain that Bonny's husband, James, had accepted. Under Jamaica's new colonial governor, **Woodes Rogers** (c. 1679–1732; see entry), she became a privateer. This meant that she had legal authority to raid merchant ships belonging to England's enemy, Spain. Although privateering licenses did not permit sailors to attack any vessels except those belonging to an enemy nation, few privateers bothered to honor this technicality.

Bonny and Read sail with Calico Jack

By the summer of 1719, Read had joined Rackham's pirate ship and began serving alongside Bonny. The women continued to dress as men,

This flag is black, and typically shows a white skull with two long bones crossed beneath it in the shape of an X—an emblem that became known as the skull and crossbones. Although most pirate ships in the eighteenth and nineteenth centuries actually flew plain black flags, the Jolly Roger became part of the popular conception of piracy, and its pirate symbolism is instantly recognizable.

Many pirates had their own version of the Jolly Roger. For example, **Henry Every** (c. 1653–1699; see entry) flew a Jolly Roger with a red background and a skull in profile. The skull appeared to be wearing a pirate kerchief and a large earring. Another Jolly Roger design, associated with the pirate Blackbeard, showed a white devil on a black background, stabbing a red heart with a spear. Rackham's version features a skull with crossed cutlasses (short, heavy, single-edged swords) on a black background. This is the flag used by Captain Jack Sparrow in the *Pirates of the Caribbean* films.

Captain John Rackam, also known as Calico Jack. © THE PRINT COLLECTOR/HERITAGE/THE IMAGE WORKS. REPRODUCED BY PERMISSION.

and their disguises were so successful that, according to some accounts, Bonny believed Read to be a man and tried to seduce her. Bonny was astonished to learn that the object of her affection was, in fact, another woman. They became close friends.

Aboard Rackham's ship, the women often acted with more courage and daring than the men. When Read's lover, a sailor named Tom Deane, was challenged to a duel on shore to settle an argument with another pirate, Read was terrified that Tom would be killed. She picked her own fight with the pirate and got him to agree to fight a duel with her before his scheduled encounter with Tom. Still dressed as a man, Read was put ashore with the other pirate. After shooting their pistols and missing, the two drew their swords. Using the skills she had perfected during her soldiering days, Read outfought the pirate and fatally wounded him. As

Mary Read fights a duel with another pirate to save her lover's life. PRIVATE COLLECTION/PETER NEWARK HISTORICAL PICTURES/THE BRIDGEMAN ART LIBRARY.

he lay dying, she reportedly opened her shirt to show her breasts, jeering that the man had let himself be killed by a mere woman.

After this, Rackham's crew accepted the fact that two of their ship-mates were women. Bonny and Read began to wear skirts on deck and to let their long hair hang loose. When they approached other ships, how-ever, the women put on men's clothing again, which gave them greater freedom of movement.

Arrested and tried

In 1720 Rackham and his crew made several small raids before capturing a schooner belonging to James Spenlow. This captain had been robbed just a short time previously and was furious about being robbed again. He went to Governor Rogers with a detailed description of the pirates and their ship, demanding justice. Rogers assigned Jonathan Barnet the task of stopping Rackham once and for all.

Barnet, on his warship the *Albion*, found Rackham's ship and slowly drew close. But the naval officer saw only two men on deck. The men, it turned out, were Bonny and Read. The women were the only pirates to notice the *Albion*'s approach, because the rest of the crew, including Rackham, were below decks, drinking. The women shouted an alarm, but their crewmates were too drunk to notice. Finally Bonny fired her gun down the ladder. The blast got the pirates' attention, but killed one man and injured several others.

Meanwhile, Bonny and Read stood side by side on deck, prepared to defend their ship alone against the assault. Although they fought bravely, they were quickly overrun by Barnet's men. They, along with Rackham and his entire crew, were arrested and taken to Jamaica to stand trial for piracy.

At the trial, which took place in November that year, Bonny and Read both appeared in men's clothing. But it soon became public knowledge that these two pirates were actually women. Read defended herself by saying that she had never willingly chosen a pirate's life, but had been forced into it out of financial desperation. However, several of her crewmates testified that she and Bonny had been among the most ambitious and resolute of the pirates, ready to do whatever was required to gain riches.

All of the pirates were found guilty and condemned to death. The male pirates were executed on November 28. But the women escaped the gallows when it was discovered that both were pregnant. For the sake of their unborn children, their lives were spared. Soon after the trial, Read contracted a fever. She died in prison on December 4, 1721. Some accounts say that Bonny gave birth to a child in prison and was then released. It is not known whether this infant survived. How Bonny lived the rest of her life is also not known, but she reportedly died around 1782.

Bonny and Read's legacy

The story of Anne Bonny and Mary Read caused a sensation in the Americas and in Europe. In 1724 *A General History of the Robberies and Murders of the Most Notorious Pirates* by Captain Charles Johnson was published. It provides a detailed account of the women's adventures. The book was so popular that it was immediately translated into Dutch,

French, and German. It was republished several times in London, Amsterdam, Dublin, Paris, and other cities. Popular ballads and songs also recounted Bonny's and Read's exploits, and their stories were repeated in popular literature throughout the eighteenth, nineteenth, and twentieth centuries.

The fame of these female pirates did not lead to any changes in the place of women in the eighteenth century, but it did bring attention to some of the era's social problems. Born without comfortable status or income and without much education, Bonny and Read chose to live outside the law as pirates, rather than accept a life of drudgery and servitude. This shocking decision showed society the limited, legitimate choices that were available to most women and low-income people of that time.

For More Information

BOOKS

Eastman, Tamara J., and Constance Bond. *The Pirate Trial of Anne Bonny and Mary Read*. Fern Canyon Press, 2000.

Konstam, Angus. *Piracy: The Complete History*. Oxford, England: Osprey, 2008.

Rediker, Marcus. *Villains of All Nations: Atlantic Pirates in the Golden Age*. Boston, MA: Beacon Press, 2004.

Sharp, Anne Wallace. *Daring Pirate Women*. Minneapolis, MN: Lerner, 2002.

Travers, Tim. *Pirates: A History*. Briscombe Port Stroud, England: The History Press, 2009.

Weatherly, Myra. *Women Pirates: Eight Stories of Adventure*. Greensboro, NC: Morgan Reynolds, 1998.

Yolen, Jane. *Sea Queens: Women Pirates Around the World*. Watertown, MA: Charlesbridge, 2008.

Cheng I Sao

BORN: 1775 • Canton, China

DIED: 1844 • Canton, China

Chinese pirate

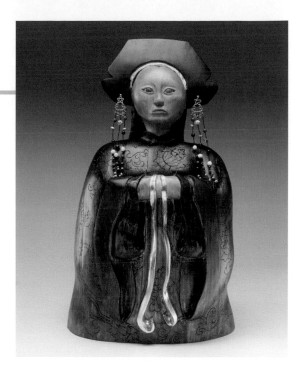

"In their attacks [Cheng I Sao's pirates] are intrepid [fearless], and in their defence [sic] most desperate, yielding in the latter instance to no superiority of numbers. . . . They are taught to be fearless in danger."

– Richard Glasspoole, captive of Chinese pirates
QUOTED IN *BANDITS AT SEA: A PIRATES READER*, EDITED BY C.R. PENNELL.

One of the most successful pirates in history was a Chinese woman named Cheng I Sao. She controlled a vast fleet of pirate vessels along China's coastal waters. The fleet preyed on merchant vessels in the area, stealing valuable cargos of silks, tea, spices, and other treasures. It also raided coastal villages and towns. With more boats and sailors under her command than many countries had in their entire navies, Cheng I Sao dominated events in China's seas for almost a decade.

Although China's rulers attempted to defeat Cheng I Sao, she was able to evade capture until 1810. She negotiated a surrender that spared the lives of most of her pirates and allowed her to live the rest of her life in comfort.

Cheng I Sao. © WOODCARVING BY JENNIFER MARLOW/PHOTO BY ROBERT GEORGE YOUNG.

Early life

Cheng I Sao was born in Canton, China, in 1775. Almost nothing is known about her childhood and early life except that she worked as a prostitute before her marriage to the pirate chief Cheng I (1765–1807). Before her marriage, she was known by several names, including Ching Shih, Shih Hsiang-ku, and Shih Yang.

According to one account, the couple met after Cheng I captured a merchant ship and was surprised to learn that a group of Chinese prostitutes was also onboard. He ordered the women to be brought to him. He was immediately attracted to one woman whose beauty and confidence were evident in the way she stood. But when she was brought face to face with the pirate chief, she attacked him so ferociously that she almost gouged out his eyes. This bravery impressed Cheng I, and he offered to marry the woman. He was astonished when she refused. Even the promise to give her gold and jewels did not change her mind. Finally Cheng I asked what would make the woman consent to become his wife. She demanded that he give her joint command of his fleet, and he agreed.

Historians are not certain whether this account of the couple's first meeting is accurate. But in 1801 the woman did marry Cheng I and from that time became known as Cheng I Sao, which means "wife of Cheng I." Together the couple amassed a large and powerful pirate fleet. They had two sons, Cheng Ying-shih (born 1803) and Cheng Hsiung-shih (born 1807).

Cheng I's pirate empire

Cheng I was the son of a Chinese pirate whose operations were centered in the waters off the coast of Vietnam. Because of political unrest in Vietnam in the late 1700s, the government was preoccupied with rebellion and did not have the resources to control piracy. With the support of the dominant political faction, Cheng I was able to prey on ships near this coast without having to worry about government interference. In time he became the most formidable pirate in the area. But by 1800 a new order had taken over in Vietnam, making Cheng I's position there less secure. In 1801, the year he married Cheng I Sao and made her his co-commander, he shifted his base of operations to southern China, off the coast of Kwangtung province.

This region was the center of the lucrative opium trade. Using opium, a powerful narcotic, was technically illegal in China, but British merchants managed to create loopholes in the law for themselves, and by

Opium

While the first European merchants who traded with Asia dealt in goods such as tea, spices, and silk, by the 1700s one of the most important trade commodities from the region was opium. Opium is a highly addictive narcotic drug that is made from the seeds of opium poppies. Many ancient people, including the Greeks, the Romans, the Egyptians, and the Persians, grew poppies in order to make and use opium for medical purposes. It was used for pain relief and sometimes to help with symptoms of depression. Opium may even have made it possible for people to endure surgical procedures in ancient times.

Recreational use of opium in China began in the fifteenth century, but was rare. In the early 1700s, however, trade in opium increased, in large part because of the British, who brought it into the country from India. The drug was mixed with tobacco, a product that Great Britain was importing from its North American colonies, and then smoked in a pipe. More and more people began using the drug this way. At the same time, Chinese officials could see that opium was addictive and caused serious negative health effects. In 1729 the emperor prohibited the sale

and smoking of opium but allowed licenses for its medical use. Despite this trade restriction, however, Britain continued to bring large amounts of opium into China, prompting the emperor to ban the drug outright in 1799. Yet Britain insisted on its right to continue this trade, a stance that led to two bitter trade wars in the 1800s.

Despite efforts to control it, by the mid–1800s opium use had spread throughout much of the world, including Europe and the United States. As of the twentieth century, most opium was sold to be processed into heroin, an illegal narcotic drug that is most often injected intravenously. In the early twenty-first century trade in opium remained an extremely profitable business that fostered political violence and other social harms. With an estimated fifteen million heroin users in the world as of 2010, opium remains in great demand and sells for extremely high prices on the black market. Opium poppies are the major crop in Afghanistan. The Taliban, a militia group who oppose Western lifestyles and seek a return to a strict tribal form of Islam, fund their militant campaigns with the hundreds of millions of dollars they reap annually on opium profits.

the late 1700s they were making huge profits from this business. Portugal, too, wanted to carve out a share of this trade, and British and Portuguese merchant ships frequented the waters along the Kwangtung coast, where the Europeans had built trade colonies. The Chengs decided to attack the Portuguese, and in 1804 imposed a blockade on Portugal's colony, Macau. After this, Britain began sending Royal Navy vessels to escort British merchant ships sailing near Hong Kong. But this move did not weaken the Chengs; in fact, their power grew. In 1805 Cheng I created a huge federation of pirates, uniting different fleets in one huge organization totaling some twelve hundred junks. (Junks are Chinese sailboats.)

He divided this federation into six fleets, each sailing under a different color and assigned to a particular geographic area. Cheng I commanded the Red Flag fleet, which in 1805 consisted of about two hundred pirate junks. By 1807 the Red Flag fleet had tripled in size.

Assuming command

In 1807 a typhoon hit the Red Flag fleet, and Cheng I was killed, most likely swept overboard in the storm. Cheng I Sao quickly convinced the Red Flag fleet to accept her as their chief. She was able to maintain general control over the larger federation, as well. It was quite unusual at that time for a Chinese woman to assume such a powerful role. Women often helped run their family's business but rarely enjoyed a position of full control. Important decisions were left entirely to the men. Among pirates, though, the situation was different. Whole families lived together on pirate junks and helped with the daily tasks of operating the boats. Although women were still expected to be submissive to their husbands or male relatives, many fought alongside their husbands during pirate attacks and even took charge of a junk if necessary. Even so, Cheng I Sao's success in taking over command of the entire pirate empire was a rare feat.

Earlier in his life, Cheng I had attacked a fishing boat and killed most of its crew. But one young man on the boat, Chang Pao (also known as Chang Po Tsai; died 1822), caught his interest, and Cheng I and his wife adopted the boy. Chang Pao joined Cheng I aboard his junk and grew up learning the business of piracy. Shortly after taking command of the pirate empire after her husband's death, Cheng I Sao named Chang Pao commander of the Red Flag fleet. While Cheng I Sao focused on general goals and strategies, Chang Pao oversaw the day-to-day business of running the fleet. Within a few years, Cheng I Sao and Chang Pao were married. She later bore him a son.

Cheng I Sao's pirate code

One of Cheng I Sao's major achievements as head of the pirate empire was that she imposed a code of laws that all of her pirates were expected to obey. Many accounts say that Cheng I Sao drew up these laws herself, but historians believe that they were actually created by Chang Pao. Cheng I Sao, however, was the one who made the code more formal, and used it to unite the various pirate fleets and to make the federation operate more smoothly. She saw to it that any violation of the code resulted in swift punishment. For this reason, the code is often attributed to her.

The code established rules about how treasure would be divided among the pirates. Anyone who took more than his share was beheaded. Disobeying orders was also a capital offense, as was rape of female captives. Those who committed lesser offenses, such as desertion, could have an ear, thumb, or entire limb cut off. A second offense resulted in death.

Although these rules were harsh, Cheng I Sao enforced them fairly. As a result, discipline among the pirates improved. This helped to make them a more efficient fighting force. They attacked any boat they encountered. If it was a merchant ship, the pirates killed the officers and stole the cargo. They took women and children as captives, selling them later as slaves. Then they offered the crew a choice: join the pirates or be put to death. If the pirates captured a vessel belonging to the emperor, though, they killed everyone onboard.

Cheng I Sao was very religious and kept a family shrine onboard her junk. She honored the gods and asked them for advice whenever she had to make a decision. She believed that her guardian spirit spoke to her through dreams and mystical experiences, and she never disobeyed the spirit's orders. Whether the spirit said to attack or to flee, Cheng I Sao did as it commanded—even if the order seemed to place the pirates in danger.

Terrorizing the coast

When their food and supplies ran short, the pirates raided villages near the coast. If the residents fought back, the pirates showed no mercy. They ransacked homes, taking women and children as prisoners and beheading the men. Then they burned the village to the ground. The pirates announced that any villages that wanted to be spared would have to pay protection money. Many were willing to do this, but some resisted. San Shan was one village that refused to pay what the pirates demanded. The pirates over-whelmed the village and spent three days plundering (robbing of goods by force) every home. They beheaded eighty men, and hung the heads on a nearby tree to frighten other local people. Then they took all the women and children onto the pirate junks to be sold into slavery.

The pirates offered safe-passage documents to fishermen and mer-chant sailors for a steep price. They even set up financial offices along the coast where these fees could be collected. In effect, the people bribed the pirates not to attack them.

Battles against the Chinese navy

As Cheng I Sao's federation increased in size and conducted more frequent raids, any merchant ship in China's waters was vulnerable to attack. Trade suffered to such an extent that China's export business seriously declined. This was a serious blow to China's economy. The emperor knew that the country's prosperity depended on putting an end to piracy.

But this proved to be an exceedingly difficult task. In 1808 the chief commander of Chekiang province, Li Ch'ang-keng, launched a special assault against the pirates along the coast of Kwangtung. However, the pirates fought back, killing Li Ch'ang-keng and destroying half of his fleet. Officials in Canton, the capital of Kwangtung province, asked the British for assistance. The British lent them the *Mercury*, a ship carrying twenty cannons that was used to escort merchant vessels. The Cantonese also obtained permission from Portugal to lease six man-of-war ships, which sailed with China's imperial navy in 1809. (A man-of-war is a powerful war ship armed with cannons and propelled primarily by sails.)

The Chinese government hoped to conquer the pirates, but Cheng I Sao was a brilliant military tactician. In many cases she outsmarted the admirals sent to destroy her. In a battle against Admiral Kwo Lang in 1808, Cheng I Sao engaged only some of her junks, hiding most of her boats behind a high spit of land. Just as the admiral thought he had won the battle, the rest of the pirate junks appeared and fought to victory. Disgraced, the admiral committed suicide.

In another battle, Admiral Tz'eun Mao Szun almost succeeded in defeating Cheng I Sao. His ships surrounded her fleet during the night. He ordered one of his vessels to be filled with explosives and set on fire. This boat was then aimed at the pirate junks, which were all anchored close together. When the fire ship reached its target, it caused an explosion that ignited a huge blaze among the junks. Riggings and sails caught fire, and the pirates were desperate to put out the flames. Cheng I Sao ordered the fleet to withdraw. The admiral thought his plan had worked. But when he least expected it, the pirate leader ordered a counterattack. She turned her junks around and assaulted the naval force. A soldier who participated in the battle, quoted by Laura Lee Wren in *Pirates and Privateers of the High Seas*, said, "Everyone fought to save their own skins" and that "only scarcely a hundred people survived."

Cheng I Sao in battle. PRIVATE COLLECTION/PETER NEWARK HISTORICAL PICTURES/THE BRIDGEMAN ART LIBRARY INTERNATIONAL.

Surrendering

By this time, the Chinese government realized it needed a new approach. Instead of trying to defeat the pirates outright, it focused instead on subduing them. The government let it be known that it would consider negotiating with pirates who wished to give up sea raiding and pursue a new life.

Some of Cheng I Sao's commanders saw this as a good opportunity. The leader of her Black Flag fleet, for example, had grown increasingly resentful of Chang Pao. According to some accounts, this man was secretly in love with Cheng I Sao and was jealous of her marriage to Cheng's adopted son. The Black Flag commander led an attack on part of the Red Flag fleet, sinking sixteen of Chang Pao's junks and killing about three hundred of his men. Then he asked the governor of Macau for protection. The governor agreed not to prosecute the man, and he surrendered.

Cheng I Sao realized that times were changing. The era of vast pirate power in China was coming to an end, and continuing to defy the Chinese navy would only worsen the growing disagreements among the pirate federation. She and Chang Pao decided to surrender. But Cheng I Sao insisted that it had to be on her own terms.

On April 18, 1810, Cheng I Sao and many women and children from her fleet boarded a ship belonging to the governor-general of Canton. She was greeted like royalty, and she acted with queenly confidence. She demanded, and won, excellent terms from the government. Fewer than 400 of her pirates were punished. Of these, 60 were banished for two years, and 151 were permanently exiled. Another 126 were put to death. But more than 17,000 pirates who gave up their weapons and their junks were allowed to keep the goods that they had stolen. The governor even allowed some pirates to join the military. Chang Pao decided to do this, and was given command of a fleet of twenty naval junks, with the rank of lieutenant. He died in 1822 at age thirty-six

Allowed to keep her wealth, Cheng I Sao received honors and was even given a palace from the governor. She was able to retire comfortably in Canton, where she went into business running a brothel and gambling house. The rest of her life was uneventful. She died in 1844 at age sixty-nine.

Once Cheng I Sao retired, the rule of the pirates in China was broken. She had held her vast fleet together largely by the force of her strong personality, and no other individual pirate after her had the personal magnetism to continue in her footsteps. While Chinese piracy did not completely disappear after 1810, it never regained the size and strength it had enjoyed under the command of Cheng I Sao.

For More Information

BOOKS

Konstam, Angus. *Piracy: The Complete History*. Oxford, England: Osprey, 2008.

Pennell, C.R., ed. *Bandits at Sea: A Pirates Reader*. NY: New York University Press, 2001, p. 273.

Sharp, Anne Wallace. *Daring Pirate Women*, Minneapolis, MN: Lerner, 2002.

Travers, Tim. *Pirates: A History*. Brimscombe Port Stroud, England: The History Press, 2009.

Wren, Laura Lee. *Pirates and Privateers of the High Seas*. Berkeley Heights, NJ: Enslow, 2003, p 91.

WEB SITES

Vallar, Cindy. "Cheng I Sao ('wife of Cheng I')." *Pirates and Privateers: A History of Maritime Piracy.*. www.cindyvallar.com/chengsao.html (accessed on January 3, 2011).

William Dampier

BORN: June 1651 • East Coker, Somerset, England

DIED: 1715 • England

English pirate, explorer, naturalist, writer

"It is not easy to name another voyager or traveler who has given more useful information to the world; to whom the merchant and mariner are so much indebted; or who has communicated his information in a more unembarrassed and intelligible manner."

– Admiral James Burney, English explorer and author
QUOTED IN *A PIRATE OF EXQUISITE MIND: EXPLORER, NATURALIST, AND BUCCANEER: THE LIFE OF WILLIAM DAMPIER* BY DIANA AND MICHAEL PRESTON.

William Dampier was not very good at being a pirate. He never made a fortune at raiding. But wherever he went, Dampier enjoyed observing his surroundings. He wrote down details about plants, animals, and the patterns of winds, tides, and ocean currents. He described the customs of the different people he encountered. The books he wrote about his travels provided readers with valuable information about parts of the world that they had never seen.

Scientists used Dampier's writings to increase their knowledge of biology, geography, and weather. Sailors and merchants relied on his

William Dampier. © LEBRECHT MUSIC AND ARTS PHOTO LIBRARY/ALAMY.

information to plan sea voyages. Dampier's writings also inspired other writers. Because he wrote about what he saw while traveling, Dampier is considered one of the creators of the genre of travel writing.

Early life

The son of a tenant farmer, William Dampier was born in East Coker, a village in Somerset, England, in June 1651. The family was not poor, but they were not wealthy enough to own their own land. Unlike many boys in rural England at this time, Dampier went to school. He learned basic subjects as well as some Latin.

Both of his parents had died by the time he was fourteen, and the young Dampier apprenticed himself to a shipmaster in Weymouth, a port in southern England. During this time, he went on a few short trading voyages to France and to Newfoundland, Canada, a trip that gave him a lifelong hatred of cold weather. In 1670 Dampier was part of a trading crew that sailed around Africa into the Indian Ocean. Along the way, Dampier made careful observations about the weather and learned the skill of navigation.

Travels to Jamaica

After a brief stint in the English navy, Dampier went to Jamaica in 1674 to take a job on a sugar plantation. Jamaica had once been a possession of Spain, which together with Portugal had been granted sole control of the Americas in 1494 by the Treaty of Tordesillas. Since then, silver and gold from Mexico and Peru had made Spain the wealthiest country in the world. England, a small and relatively poor country at this time, wanted to expand its economy and felt that it was being unfairly excluded from essential markets in the Americas. In 1655 an English force seized Jamaica from the Spanish. This gave England a valuable trading base in the Caribbean.

Soon after arriving in Jamaica, Dampier quarreled with the plantation overseer. When Dampier quit, according to Diana and Michael Preston in *A Pirate of Exquisite Mind: Explorer, Naturalist, and Buccaneer: The Life of William Dampier*, the overseer complained that Dampier was "a self-conceited young man" who was "given to rambling and could not settle himself to stay long in any place."

Logwood cutting in Campeachy

In February 1676 Dampier sailed to Campeachy, later known as Campeche, a part of the southern Gulf of Mexico near the Yucatán Peninsula. Along this hot, swampy shore were groups of men who cut and sold logwood for export to Europe. Many had once been pirates with **Henry Morgan** (1635–1688; see entry). When the English government decided to rid Jamaica of pirates in 1671, many found a new life as loggers.

Dampier enjoyed the hard work and comradeship at Campeachy and hoped that logging would make him rich. But bad luck wiped out all his efforts when a severe hurricane struck Campeachy that June. The storm destroyed everything—the cut wood; the men's huts, food, and tools; and the boats in the harbor. Dampier and a few others were lucky to escape the settlement, which was flooded, in one surviving canoe. They paddled to a nearby island. Once again penniless, Dampier decided to join the buccaneers, or seventeenth-century sea raiders based in the Caribbean.

Life with the buccaneers

Buccaneer communities had sprung up by the early 1600s on Tortuga Island, near Hispaniola (present-day Haiti and the Dominican Republic). Desperate men, such as ex-convicts, runaway servants, and escaped slaves from Hispaniola, found refuge on Tortuga. They survived by hunting and kept to themselves. But Spain objected to their presence, and in 1630 began efforts to drive them out. Determined to fight back, the buccaneers became pirates and attacked the Spanish at sea and on land. Unlike privateers, who held official letters from the government giving them permission to raid Spanish ships, the buccaneers were outlaws. But the English government tolerated them, because they weakened England's major rival, Spain.

In the books he later wrote about his adventures, Dampier tried to make it sound as if he had joined the buccaneers without realizing that they were actually pirates. But he knew that the buccaneers often operated outside of the law. He was looking for gold, and he was willing to do whatever it would take to find it.

In his books Dampier describes only one actual pirate raid from this time. The buccaneers attacked a town on the Mexican coast, only to discover that the residents had fled with all their valuables. All that was left behind was a large number of tame parrots. The buccaneers loaded the birds onto their boats but had to throw almost everything they were carrying—including crates of supplies—overboard when Spanish ships

A seventeenth-century illustration of a buccaneer. William Dampier joined the buccaneers of Hispanola, hoping to make his fortune.
© LORDPRICE COLLECTION/ALAMY.

chased them as they left. After about two years of buccaneering, Dampier had not made much money. He returned to England in 1678 and soon afterward married a woman named Judith, who was a servant in the household of a noblewoman.

With money that he likely obtained from his wife's dowry Dampier left for sea again only a few months later. (A dowry is money or property provided to the groom by the bride's parents.) He had purchased goods in England that he intended to sell for a profit in the Caribbean. He sailed in 1679, expecting to return to England within a few months.

Raiding in Panama

The trip to the Caribbean did not go as planned. Dampier sold his goods in Jamaica and used the profits to buy property in England. But instead of returning home, he decided to stay in the Caribbean to look for more trade opportunities. On a voyage to the coast of Nicaragua, he encountered a large band of buccaneers. He and all his shipmates voted to join these pirates.

After a successful raid on the city of Portobelo, on the coast of Panama, the buccaneers planned an audacious feat. They would make their way across the isthmus, the narrow land of Panama from the Caribbean to the Pacific, and attack Spanish cities on the Pacific coast. This would take the Spanish completely by surprise. Few English ships dared to sail all the way around South America into the Pacific; such a long journey made it necessary to go ashore for fresh supplies, and Spanish ports in South America were not friendly. Nor was it thinkable that the English would attempt to reach the Pacific coast on foot, because this would make them vulnerable to Spanish troops. The Spanish were confident that their territory was safe.

But with the help of local Kuna Indians, who hated the Spanish for treating them brutally, the buccaneers began their journey. Having hidden their ships in a harbor on the Caribbean coast, the men hiked through dense jungle, enduring oppressive heat, thirst, and hunger and carrying a few canoes, which they paddled along networks of rivers. Finally reaching the town of Santa Maria, the exhausted buccaneers were furious to discover that the residents had already run away, leaving no riches behind. Greedy for treasure, they decided to continue to the wealthy port city of Panama.

Failure and retreat

Before attacking Panama, the buccaneers first needed to get bigger ships. In the harbor outside Panama's city walls they were able to capture five large Spanish vessels, taking three for themselves and burning the others. They also captured a boat carrying all the wages for Panama's soldiers, as well as fourteen hundred jars of wine and brandy. But these attacks used up almost all of their ammunition, and they did not have enough fire-power left to attack the city itself.

Then the buccaneers tried to trick the governor of the city into surrendering the town without a fight. They pretended to be on a friendly assignment in the region, and asked the governor to pay them a bribe so that they would leave in peace. But he refused. Raiding a neighboring town instead, the buccaneer leader was killed. After this, the group argued and eventually agreed to separate. Dampier's group chose to try raiding ports in Ecuador, Peru, and Chile, but their supplies of food and water were low, and they had little success against these well-defended towns. Finally, they tried to invade Arica, a port in northern Chile. But the Spanish fought back, capturing and beheading the captain. The buccaneers were forced to withdraw; only Dampier and about half of the men were still alive. After a difficult sea journey back to the coast of Panama, they trekked across the isthmus once again to reach the Caribbean.

Adventures in the Pacific

Immediately joining another group of buccaneers, Dampier made a voyage to the coast of Virginia before meeting John Cook, a buccaneer who was planning a voyage around the South American continent. Eager to see more of the Pacific, Dampier decided to sign on with Cook. They left Virginia on August 23, 1683, first sailing to the Cape Verde Islands, located off the west coast of Africa, for supplies. Near there the buccaneers seized a Danish ship, which they renamed the *Bachelor's Delight*. In this vessel they set out for the coasts of Chile and Peru.

Sailing through the treacherous seas off the southern tip of South America, they reached the Pacific Ocean, but encountered one of the worst storms that Dampier had ever experienced. After more than two weeks of this tempest, the *Bachelor's Delight* was blown far to the south—farther, according to the ship's navigator, than any sailor had gone before. Finally the weather improved and the buccaneers headed north.

To their surprise, they came upon an English ship, the *Cygnet*, under the command of Charles Swan (died 1690). Joining forces with Swan, the buccaneers continued up the coast to seek treasure. But once again, Dampier and his companions had bad luck. The Spanish had received word that the pirates were in the area and had arranged to move any precious cargo off their ships. Because the buccaneers did not have enough men and ammunition to attack cities on the mainland, which were well guarded, they sailed to the Galapagos Islands, located about 600 miles (965 kilometers) off the coast of Ecuador to get fresh food and water and make new plans.

Dampier was fascinated by the geography and wildlife of these uninhabited islands, which contain numerous species found nowhere else on Earth. He watched animals as they hunted, mated, and raised their young and made careful notes about what he observed. He was able to develop a basic notion that creatures might be shaped by their environment and pass changes on to future generations. Although his ideas were only partially developed and not scientifically tested, Dampier was writing about evolution some 150 years before English naturalist Charles Darwin (1809–1882) published his groundbreaking book on the subject, *On the Origin of Species*, in 1859.

Sailing back toward Panama, the buccaneers joined a group of English and French pirates who had crossed the isthmus, creating a force of about six hundred men. Their goal was to wait along the coast for Spanish treasure ships, which they would then attack. They also raided coastal villages, sometimes torturing survivors into revealing where they had hidden their valuables. Dampier, however, hated such cruelty and usually refused to take part. The buccaneers got food and other goods this way, but little gold.

In May 1685 the buccaneers finally saw what they had been waiting for: a fleet of fourteen Spanish treasure ships, with a force of about three thousand men. Although the buccaneers numbered only about three hundred, they planned to assault the ships. But the Spanish outwitted them. The night before the battle, the Spanish lit their lanterns on one side of the ship, and then blew them all out. Then they moved the lanterns to the other side, and lit them again. This made it look as if the Spanish ships had changed their position. When the buccaneers woke up the next morning, they were surprised to find the enemy ships sailing straight at them. The pirates were not prepared for such an assault, and were forced to flee. Later they learned that the Spanish had secretly put their treasure on other boats and taken it to a port city. Even if the pirates had won the battle, they would not have found any gold.

Around the world

Shortly after the seafarers had left the Galapagos, Cook suddenly died. A few months later, in August of 1685, the band of buccaneers split up. Dampier moved from the *Bachelor's Delight* to the *Cygnet*. He had given up any hope of making his fortunes as a pirate. The challenge for the sailors now was how to get back to England. Rather than risk a return to enemy waters off South America, the men chose to make the perilous journey across the Pacific to Southeast Asia. They would have to sail nearly 7,000 miles (11,000 kilometers) before reaching land on the island of Guam, east of the Philippines. Although they stocked up on as much food and water as their ship could hold, they knew it would not be enough and they would suffer thirst and malnutrition along the way. Their safety and their lives depended on a quick voyage.

After fifty-one days on the open sea, the sailors finally reached Guam. There was only enough food and water left for three days, and the men had secretly decided that when the food ran out they would kill and eat Swan, as well as those who had devised the Pacific plan. Finding out about this plan later, Swan joked that Dampier was too thin and bony to make a decent meal for the men.

From Guam the buccaneers sailed to the Philippines and to the coast of China. On January 4, 1688, they became the first English people to reach the mainland of Australia. Dampier eventually quarreled with the *Cygnet's* crew and, at his own request, was marooned (abandoned on a deserted shore) on one of the Nicobar Islands, southeast of India. He escaped to the island of Sumatra by canoe. Dampier remained in Southeast Asia for a few more years, serving on merchant ships and briefly as a gunner for the East India Company on Sumatra. Dampier finally made his way to Africa and then to England. He reached London in 1691, more than twelve years after his departure.

Literary career

Throughout his adventures Dampier took pains to protect his notes from any damage. He always carried a notebook and stored his papers in a hollow piece of bamboo, which he sealed at each end with wax to keep out moisture. His notes described not only wild animals and plants but also the peoples he encountered. Unlike many Europeans of his time, he did not feel that other cultures were inferior to his. It did not bother him to meet people who wore little or no clothing, ate strange foods, or worshipped different gods. Dampier respected others' customs and often admired their way of life.

Back in England Dampier published *A New Voyage Round the World* in 1697 and *Voyages and Descriptions* two years later. Naturalists valued these books for their important information about species, habitats, and climate. Merchants and navigators also admired the books for their information about tides, currents, and other topics important to sailing. And ordinary readers enjoyed Dampier's accounts of exotic places. He was the first person to write in English about many foreign items, including chopsticks, barbecues, and avocados, and he described his experiences in language that was vivid and detailed yet also plain and easy to understand.

Dampier did not make much money from his books, but he gained the respect of England's leading scientists. He was hired to make two more trips around the world to gather additional data, the first of which as captain of a British Royal Navy vessel. It was not until the second of these research voyages in 1710 that Dampier finally achieved his dream of capturing a Spanish treasure ship. He had not set out to find treasure, but he had legal authority to raid this vessel, because England was then at war with Spain. Disagreements about how the treasure should be divided among the privateers, however, soured Dampier's victory. He returned to England in 1711 and died in early 1715.

Differing views on Dampier

Many of the men who had sailed with Dampier over the years did not like him. He was more intelligent and observant than they were, and they resented him for telling them so. The naval officer assigned as Dampier's first mate on his second research voyage, quoted by Diana and Michael Preston in *A Pirate of Exquisite Mind*, declared that "he did not care a fart" for Dampier, whom he considered an "old pirate dog" who would steal the naval ship for his own use. The crew on this same vessel refused to obey many of Dampier's orders. When Dampier returned from this voyage, the Royal Navy stripped Dampier of his command and said that he was unfit to captain a ship.

But others admired Dampier for his enthusiasm for learning, knowledge about navigation, and literary skill. Writers, including Daniel Defoe (1659–1731), Jonathan Swift (1667–1745), and Samuel Taylor Coleridge (1772–1834), as well as Darwin and other naturalists, hailed him as

Pirates and Books

Although many pirates were not well educated, seafarers in the eighteenth century were more literate than many other groups. About 70 percent of sailors could read and write well enough to sign their own names on documents, instead of just making a mark. This placed seafarers well above the average literacy rate in England, which was only about 45 percent in 1700 and 65 percent by the end of the century.

Many workers in England were illiterate compared to sailors. Only about 33 percent of men who worked along the Thames River in England in the early 1700s could read and write; the literacy rate among carpenters was about 60 percent.

One explanation for the relatively high rate of literacy among sailors may be that the seafaring life tended to attract people who were intelligent and curious about the world, as Dampier was. While many crew members did not need literacy skills to do their jobs, navigators had to be able to read charts and maps in order to set safe courses for their ships. For other reading, seafarers sometimes chose inspiring works, such as the Bible. More often, though, they preferred adventure stories or pornography.

a major influence. His account of rescuing a shipmate who had been abandoned on a remote island and had learned to adapt to harsh conditions, for example, was the inspiration for Defoe's book, *Robinson Crusoe.*

Later in life Dampier wrote that he regretted things he had done as a buccaneer, observing that he "look'd back in Horror and Detestation, on Actions which before I disliked, but now I trembled at the remembrance of," as quoted by Tim Travers in *Pirates: A History.* But Dampier also retained his keen appetite for knowledge. Through that inquisitiveness, he contributed to a greater understanding of the natural world.

For More Information

BOOKS

Preston, Diana, and Michael Preston. *A Pirate of Exquisite Mind: Explorer, Naturalist, and Buccaneer: The Life of William Dampier.* New York: Walker, 2004, pp. 253, 329.

Travers, Tim. *Pirates: A History.* Brimscombe Port Stroud, England: The History Press, 2009, p. 156.

WEB SITES

"William Dampier: Pirate, Explorer and Naturalist." *BBC.* www.bbc.co.uk/dna/h2g2/A15883374 (accessed on January 3, 2011).

"William Dampier." *Notable Names Database,* www.nndb.com/people/943/000096655/ (accessed on January 3, 2011).

Dragut Reis

BORN: 1485 • Turkey

DIED: June 23, 1565 • Malta

Turkish admiral, pirate

"No one was more worthy than he to bear the name of king."

– A French admiral, describing Dragut
QUOTED IN *THE SIEGE OF MALTA, 1565* BY FRANCISCO BALBI DI CORREGGIO.

Known as "the Drawn Sword of Islam," Dragut Reis was one of the greatest of the Barbary corsairs, the pirates who dominated the Barbary coast in the Mediterranean Sea. In the service of the Ottoman Empire, he won numerous battles against European nations and expanded the power and reach of the Ottoman navy. He became chief admiral of the Ottoman fleet and was also appointed ruler of the North African city of Tripoli. Still actively fighting for the Ottomans at age eighty, Dragut Reis died at the Siege of Malta in 1565.

Trained by an Ottoman general

Dragut Reis, also known as Turgut Reis, was born in 1485 to a Greek family in a village on the Aegean coast of Turkey. ("Reis," also spelled "Rais," means "captain" or "chief" and was used as part of many corsair leader's names.) As a youth, he was captured by corsairs and converted to Islam. At age twelve, he was noticed by an Ottoman general who recognized the boy's

Dragut Reis. DANITA DELIMONT/
GALIO IMAGES/GETTY IMAGES.

Janissaries

Dragut Reis's early experiences bore some remarkable similarities to those of *janissaries*, the corps of specially trained soldiers who made up the sultan's elite army. Ottoman rulers in the eastern Mediterranean obtained janissaries through the practice of *devshirmeh*. This was the systematic abduction of young Christian boys from lands that the Ottomans conquered. It was a type of tax due to the sultan, paid not with money but with human beings. The abducted boys were required to convert to Islam, and they received extensive military training, particularly in archery and other kinds of shooting. As muskets and rifles became more commonly used in warfare in the 1700s, the janissaries became renowned marksmen.

Their expert skills made the janissaries an indispensable part of the sultan's forces. They were given good living quarters, food, and clothing, and were highly respected by the generals under whom they served. They also received regular pay in cash, during peacetime as well as during war. But they were slaves. And because they were slaves, they owed the sultan their complete loyalty. This meant that he did not fear them as rivals to his power, as was sometimes the case with the bands of tribal fighters that joined in Ottoman military campaigns.

By the late 1600s, service as a janissary was considered a highly desirable career. In 1683 the sultan did away with the devshirmeh system, allowing free Muslim and Christian men to apply.

A janissary captain. PRIVATE COLLECTION/THE STAPLETON COLLECTION/THE BRIDGEMAN ART LIBRARY.

Many families were happy to send their sons to janissary training schools. Circumstances changed as the janissaries gained more freedom, however. They were drawn into political plots and participated in rebellions against the Ottoman court. By the early 1800s the empire found it increasingly difficult to provide the financial support necessary to keep the janissaries going. The janissary corps was abolished in 1826, after a failed revolt against the sultan.

military potential, particularly his talent at archery. This general became the boy's master. (Once he converted to Islam, Dragut was no longer a slave of the corsairs, but he still owed service to his master.) The boy received extensive naval training, becoming an expert sailor and ship's gunner. He was also trained in artillery, or the use of cannons in warfare.

In 1517 Dragut participated with his master in the Ottoman conquest of Egypt, where the young man gained valuable battle experience. After his master's death, Dragut joined the fleet of the corsair Sinan Reis (d. 1553) at the Egyptian port of Alexandria. He was so successful at calculating artillery attacks against enemy ships that he was soon made captain of his own vessel. Later he also acquired a galiot (a small, fast galley using both sails and oars) and outfitted it with the most modern guns available.

Dragut began operating on his own as a corsair in the eastern part of the Mediterranean. He focused primarily on trade ships sailing between the city of Venice, in northeastern Italy, and its islands off the coast of the Balkan Peninsula. The Mediterranean at this time was the site of an ongoing struggle between Christian nations and the Muslim Ottoman Empire, and Venice was among the Ottoman Empire's main rivals in the eastern Mediterranean. The city-state was a stronghold of Christianity and an ally of several Christian kingdoms. Because Venice and its allies were the Ottomans' enemies, it was accepted practice for corsairs to attack the city-state's merchant vessels as well as its battleships and to make raids on its territory. Corsairs stole valuable cargoes, captured or burned enemy ships, and kidnapped sailors and men, women, and children living in coastal villages and towns to be sold into slavery or to work on corsair vessels as galley slaves.

Joins Barbarossa

In 1520 Dragut joined the fleet of the famous corsair **Barbarossa** (c. 1478–1546; see entry). The men became close friends. Barbarossa, who was well-respected by the sultan and was named admiral-in-chief of the Ottoman navy in 1533, helped Dragut advance his career. Barbarossa made Dragut a chief lieutenant of his fleet, which was part of the larger navy, and gave him command of twelve galiots. From 1526 to 1533, Dragut launched several attacks at ports in Sicily, Italy, capturing the fort at Capo Passero in 1526. He also raided ports along coast of Italy near Naples and harassed merchant ships sailing between Spain and Italy, seizing several and adding to his fleet.

After several Ottoman successes, in 1538 the pope (the head of the Catholic Church) created the Holy League, an alliance of various Christian states that hoped to defeat the Ottomans once and for all. Admiral Andrea

Doria (1466–1560) led the league's fleet, which consisted of vessels from Genoa, Spain, Portugal, the Vatican, and the Knights of Malta. In the summer of 1538, Dragut sailed with Barbarossa into the Adriatic Sea, which separates Italy from the Balkan Peninsula, to do battle with Doria.

Battle of Preveza

The two forces met at Preveza, Greece, on September 28, 1538. Dragut and a few other captains commanded the rear as Barbarossa led a bold attack. Doria's force had superior numbers, but he was ultimately defeated. It was a brilliant victory for the Ottomans and a disgraceful defeat for the Holy League. The Ottomans destroyed thirteen enemy ships and captured another thirty-six, taking some three thousand prisoners. Dragut captured a Vatican galley, taking custody of its captain and entire crew. Although the Ottomans suffered extensive casualties, they did not lose a single vessel.

Leading his own fleet, Dragut continued to do battle along the Adriatic coast, retaking the Balkan port of Castelnuovo from the Venetians in 1539. Later that year he encountered twelve Venetian galleys near Corfu, capturing one. After this, he landed at Crete, battling with Venetian cavalry troops.

Near the end of 1539, Dragut became governor of Djerba, a North African island off the coast of Tunisia. This gave the corsair an excellent base from which to launch attacks on enemy territory. He landed at Gozo, part of Malta, in April 1540, ransacking the entire island. He terrorized ports along the coasts of Sicily, Spain, Italy, Corsica, and other Mediterranean islands. His activities almost paralyzed the region's trade economy, and much of the population lived in fear of being kidnapped and sold into slavery. According to an account written by a French bishop in 1561 and quoted by Roger Crowley in *Empires of the Sea: The Siege of Malta, the Battle of Lepanto, and the Contest for the Center of the World*, "[Dragut] has held the kingdom of Naples in such a noose … [that the galleys] of Malta, of Sicily, and other neighbouring ports are so harassed and confined by [him] that not one of them can pass from one place to another."

Captured and imprisoned

Dragut's good fortune soon changed. Having stopped for repairs at Girolata, on the western coast of Corsica, in 1541, the corsair was attacked and captured by forces led by Giannettino Doria, Admiral Andrea Doria's nephew. Dragut spent nearly four years working as a galley slave on

Giannettino Doria's ship. Many men forced into this life did not survive one year. Slaves were chained to their oars and often required to row for hours at a time. They received little food and were severely beaten if they disobeyed. In one way, Dragut was lucky. He was extremely valuable to the Ottoman navy, and Ottoman leaders were willing to pay a substantial ransom for his release. (A ransom is a sum of money demanded for the release of someone being held captive.)

Barbarossa approached Admiral Andrea Doria with a ransom deal, but the admiral refused. By this time, Dragut had been released from the galleys and thrown into a dungeon in the city of Genoa. In 1544 Barbarossa returned to Genoa with a large fleet. This time, he besieged the city until Doria was forced to agree to a ransom deal. Barbarossa paid thirty-five hundred gold ducats, an amount worth the modern equivalent of about $1.25 million, and Dragut was set free.

Dragut immediately received a new flagship from Barbarossa, as well as a substantial fleet, and resumed his battles against his European enemies. He raided Gozo again, invaded Liguria and other areas along the coast near Genoa, and attacked ships in the Tyrrhenian Sea, which separates Corsica and Sardinia from mainland Italy.

Commander-in-chief of the Ottoman navy

When Barbarossa died in July 1546, Dragut replaced him as commander-in-chief of the Ottoman navy in the Mediterranean. The following year he led another attack on Malta, as well as raids on Sicily and other islands. When he approached Calabria, in southern Italy, the desperate inhabitants fled to the mountains to prevent being taken into captivity.

In 1548 Dragut was appointed chief governor of the North African port of Algiers. Enjoying great wealth, power, and esteem, the corsair ordered the construction of a quadrireme galley, a galley that has four tiers of oars instead of the usual two or three, for his new flagship. He intensified his attacks on enemy possessions, conducting raids on Liguria and other Italian territories, as well as the coast of Spain.

Dragut was back in Djerba in October 1550, and he pulled his vessels onto the beach to make repairs. There, he was surprised by Admiral Doria, whose fleet blocked Dragut's exit. The corsair's defeat looked certain. But Dragut had no intention of surrendering to the Christian admiral. He ordered his men to quickly dig a series of shallow channels, through which they dragged their ships on greased planks to the other end of the island. There they put out to sea and sailed to Istanbul, the Ottoman capital, capturing two ships along the way that had been sent to provide assistance to Doria.

In Istanbul Dragut received the sultan's permission to gather a fleet of 112 galleys, two larger ships, and twelve thousand elite fighters called *janissaries*. With this huge force, he set out in 1551 to battle enemy forces in the Adriatic. After bombarding Venice, he attacked Sicily and invaded Malta once again. Landing on the island of Gozo, Dragut bombarded its fortress and, after forcing the governor to surrender, he took some five thousand men, women, and children—almost the entire population—as captives.

Seizes Tripoli

Dragut's next major victory was the capture of Tripoli, which had been under the control of the Knights of Malta for twenty years. Previously known as the Knights Hospitaller, this Christian order had been fighting Muslims for centuries. Founded five hundred years earlier in Jerusalem, its original mission had been to provide care for Christians visiting that city's holy sites. But after Christian armies conquered Jerusalem in the First Crusade (1099), the Knights became a military order. Expelled from Jerusalem after Muslim armies took control in 1291, the Knights established a new base on the island of Rhodes. They were eventually expelled from Rhodes in 1522 and went to Sicily. In 1530 King Charles V (1500–1558) gave them territories that included Malta, a group of Mediterranean islands south of Sicily and close to the port of Tunis. From Malta, the Knights were within easy reach of some of the busiest pirate ports in North Africa, and they seized Tripoli in 1530.

Dragut attacked Tripoli in August 1551, capturing the commander of the fortress as well as other high-ranking knights. Their release, however, was soon negotiated through the intervention of the French, who at that time were on friendly terms with the sultan. In honor of his service, Dragut was made ruler of Tunis.

The following year, Dragut was named commander-in-chief of the entire Ottoman fleet. Again, the corsair sailed toward Italy, conducting several raids before engaging with Admiral Doria's forces at Ponza on August 5, 1552. It was another resounding victory for the Ottomans and won Dragut the position of regional governor-in-chief of the entire Mediterranean Sea.

Advancing age did not slow Dragut's military activities. He conducted ruthless attacks in the Aegean, the Tyrrhenian, and the Adriatic Seas, as well as the western regions of the Mediterranean. He captured the cities of Paola and Santo Noceto, in southern Italy, and took some six thousand prisoners at the town of Bastia, on Corsica. He invaded southern Spain, taking four thousand captives from Granada. In 1560 he defeated a huge Christian force led by Spain at Djerba, destroying or capturing half of the Christian fleet in a battle that further strengthened Ottoman power in the region.

Final battle and death

In 1565 the sultan ordered Ottoman forces, numbering around forty-eight thousand men, to invade Malta and conquer the island. Although Dragut was eighty years old by this time, he joined the Ottoman forces to help direct the fighting. It should have been an easy victory for the Ottomans. Instead, it became one of the bloodiest and hardest-won sieges in history and a decisive victory for the Christians, led by the Knights of Malta.

The Ottomans arrived on May 18 and set up their artillery so that they could bombard and destroy Fort Saint Elmo before continuing the invasion. The attack had already begun before Dragut arrived, and he was furious that the guns had been placed before he could check their position. He joined the artillery forces, giving orders to improve the guns' aim and reach. According to Francisco Balbi di Correggio in *The Siege of Malta, 1565*, written only three years after the battle, Dragut was accidentally killed by his own troops. Reviewing the artillery placements, he saw that the Ottomans were aiming their cannons too high. Standing in a trench, he gave an order to adjust the guns' position. A shot from one of the cannons hit the side of the trench and hurled a sharp rock at the corsair's head. Bleeding profusely, he died a few hours later.

Dragut's death was a significant blow to the Ottomans. But they succeeded in capturing Fort Saint Elmo. However, the engagement took more than once month and cost the Ottomans six thousand men as well as vast stores of ammunition. Weakened after the battle at Fort Saint Elmo, the Ottomans ultimately failed to subdue the rest of the island. After four months of siege, the Ottomans left in defeat. They failed in their mightiest attempt to capture Malta and never invaded the island again.

For More Information

BOOKS

Balbi di Correggio, Francisco. *The Siege of Malta, 1565.* Translated from the Spanish edition of 1568 by Ernle Bradford. London, England: Folio Society, 1965. New edition, Woodbridge, England: Boydell Press, 2005, p. 64.

Crowley, Roger. *Empires of the Sea: The Siege of Malta, the Battle of Lepanto, and the Contest for the Center of the World.* New York: Random House, 2009, p. 70.

WEB SITES

"Janissary." *Encyclopedia of the Middle East,.* www.mideastweb.org/Middle-East-Encyclopedia/janissary.htm (accessed on January 3, 2011).

Francis Drake

BORN: 1541 • Tavistock, Devon, England

DIED: January 28, 1596 • Puerto Bello, Honduras

English privateer, explorer

"I know many means to do her Majesty good service and to make us rich, for we must have gold before we see England."

Francis Drake was the most famous, and the most notorious, English seafarer of the 1500s. He sailed as a privateer for England and gained wealth and glory by raiding Spanish possessions in the Americas. (A privateer is a private ship owner commissioned by a state or government to attack the merchant ships of an enemy nation.) Daring to sail around the southern tip of South America, he launched assaults at will on unprotected Spanish possessions in the Pacific Ocean. From the western shores of the Americas he sailed across the Pacific and returned to England, becoming the first English seaman to circumnavigate, or sail around, the globe. While the Spanish denounced him as a pirate and a criminal, England honored Drake as a hero for enriching the royal treasury with plunder, or goods stolen by force. His actions against Spain contributed to crucial power shifts among rival European countries and helped England challenge Spain's dominance at sea.

Francis Drake. © THE PRINT COLLECTOR/ALAMY.

Early life

Francis Drake was born into a humble family in Tavistock, a town in Devon, England, in 1540. His father, Edmund Drake, was a Protestant preacher who left the family when Francis was young. The boy received little formal schooling. As a young child, he was sent to live with William Hawkins, a relative, in the nearby town of Plymouth.

Hawkins ran a successful shipping business, and in his household Drake learned about sailing, exploring, trading, and piracy. Although piracy was illegal, it was quite common. And under some circumstances it was even tolerated. Governments generally allowed sailors to raid the ships of enemy countries, a practice known as privateering. Privateering allowed countries to harass their enemies without bearing any responsibility for planning, executing, or financing the attacks. If privateers were able to seize any treasure, they were allowed to keep a portion but were expected to the rest over to the government.

Joins John Hawkins on slaving voyages

As a young man Drake joined his cousin, **John Hawkins** (1532–1595; see entry), on trading voyages along the coasts of France and other parts of Europe. Hawkins knew that there was much money to be made in the Americas, particularly in the slave trade. Spain and Portugal had begun selling African slaves in the Americas in 1502, and demand for slaves kept growing. It was a highly profitable business, and Hawkins decided to try to break into it. He made two successful slaving voyages, in 1562 and in 1564, and historians believe that Drake sailed with him on both.

In 1567 Hawkins organized a third slaving voyage, giving command of one of the vessels, the *Judith*, to Drake. But before they were able to sell all their cargo, a huge storm forced them to land at San Juan de Ulúa, near Veracruz, Mexico, to repair extensive damage to their ships. Here the Englishmen encountered serious trouble. In 1494 Spain and Portugal had been granted sole rights to trade in the Americas by the Treaty of Tordesillas, and Spain had become the dominant force in the Caribbean Sea. Any ship wishing to enter these waters was required to obtain official permission first. But Hawkins had never bothered to do so. Spain considered these actions illegal. After learning about Hawkins's plans for this third voyage, Spain sent word that ships in the Caribbean should look out for him and confront him. The day after the Englishmen reached San Juan de Ulúa in September of 1568, a large fleet of Spanish ships entered the harbor and fired on Hawkins's ships. After a furious battle in which the Spanish captured or destroyed four of the pirates' vessels and most of their plunder, Hawkins and Drake barely escaped. When Hawkins finally made it back to England three months later with a surviving handful of famished men, he claimed that Drake sailed for England on the *Judith*, leaving Hawkins and his crew to make their own way home in a damaged vessel with inadequate food. Hawkins accused Drake of desertion and cowardice. Drake denied this charge, stating that he had returned to England on Hawkins's orders. But the episode created a permanent stain on Drake's reputation.

Attacks on Panama

The defeat at San Juan de Ulúa made Drake intensely bitter toward Spain. In his view, the Spanish had stolen his rightful property in the attack, and he wanted revenge. Drake would spend the rest of his life attacking the Spanish at sea. First, he sought a privateering license, which the English monarch, Queen Elizabeth I (1533–1603), granted him in 1572. In May of that year Drake sailed for the Caribbean with two small ships. His first target was the Spanish port of Nombre de Dios, Panama, which held stores of silver and gold waiting to be taken to Spain. Drake launched his attack on a July night. His men entered the city in two groups, making lots of noise in an attempt to make the residents think they were being attacked by a much larger force. But Drake was injured, shot in the thigh when a group of Spaniards fired their muskets at the attackers. His crew carried Drake back to the ship.

Despite his failure at Nombre de Dios, Drake decided to continue his search for treasure. The jungles of Panama had become home to many Cimarrones, African slaves who had escaped their Spanish masters. Drake made contact with the Cimarrones, who shared his hatred of the Spanish, and they agreed to help with his next raid. In the spring of 1573 Drake met French privateer Guillaume Le Testu (c. 1509–1573), who told Drake about a mule train that was poorly defended. The gold and silver that the Spanish took from Peruvian mines was hauled across the isthmus, the narrow strip of land separating Panama's Caribbean coast, to Nombre de Dios, where it was loaded into treasure ships and sent to Spain. These ships were heavily guarded against attack, but the land route was not. The Spanish were confident that no invaders could make an attack by land. Knowing that the Spanish would not expect this, Drake ordered his ships to wait in a safe harbor while he took an expedition across land.

Francis Drake is wounded during his attack on Nombre de Dios, Panama. MARY EVANS PICTURE LIBRARY/EVERETT COLLECTION.

With the help of the Cimarrones and Le Testu's crew, Drake's party ambushed a treasure caravan with almost two hundred mules, carrying almost 30 tons (27 metric tons) of silver. The privateers fought off the small military guard accompanying the silver train but a few soldiers escaped, and fearing that these men would soon return with reinforcements, Drake ordered his men to take only as much silver as they could carry and bury the rest. Burdened with their heavy load of silver, the English struggled through the jungle back to the Caribbean coast, only to find that their ships were not waiting there as expected. Knowing that the pursuing Spanish could not be far behind, Drake had his men built a few crude rafts from driftwood. On these, they were able to maneuver along the coast until they found their ships. They returned to England with a fortune, but it had come at a price. Drake's brother John, who had remained on one of the waiting ships during Drake's raid, was killed by Spanish fire; another brother, Joseph, was one of many privateers who succumbed to yellow fever during the expedition.

Circumnavigates the globe

By the time Drake returned to England in 1573, relations between England and Spain had improved. The queen was pleased that Drake had been able to seize so much treasure from England's major rival, but she could not publicly authorize more raids. So Drake sailed to Ireland in 1575 with Robert Devereux (Earl of Essex; 1566–1601) to put down a rebellion there against English rule. During his two years in Ireland, Drake made several important political and military connections, and these helped him to gain favor among the queen's most powerful advisers.

Early in 1577 Drake met with Queen Elizabeth about a new, and highly secret, venture. Although England and Spain were officially at peace, Spain continued, in secret, to support plots to overthrow the Protestant queen and place a Catholic monarch on the English throne. England was not prepared for outright war with Spain but wanted to weaken its enemy through other means. The queen and her advisers decided to send an English fleet around South America and into the Pacific. The official purpose of this mission was to seek trading rights in the region and to explore what lay south of the Strait of Magellan, the passage separating the southernmost point of mainland South American from the islands of Tierra del Fuego. But there was also another purpose, which the English government did not make public—to inflict as much damage on Spanish possessions as possible.

Drake was given command of this expedition, and he set out in December 1577 with five small ships and a crew of about two hundred men. The fleet reached Brazil in the spring of 1578. During the voyage, Thomas Doughty, captain of one of the vessels in the expedition, had quarreled with Drake, and Drake feared a mutiny, or an open rebellion against the ship's officers. Drake brought charges against Doughty and,

Did Drake reach Alaska?

Drake made claims that, during his voyage around the world, he sailed far north along the Pacific coast of North America. But his writings about this excursion are not clear, and historians have generally believed that the seafarer sailed only as far as northern California or the area around Seattle, Washington, and Vancouver, Canada. But in the 1950s, a gold prospector in southern Alaska found a heavy metal plate in a harbor in Chatham Strait, a sea passage through the numerous islands off the Alaskan coast near Juneau. The plate is engraved with a message stating that Francis Drake claimed possession of this land on behalf of the English queen, Elizabeth I. This evidence puzzled historians, who stated that it did not necessarily prove that Drake had been at that particular spot. They noted that Drake could have given the plate to native people living farther south, who later brought it to Alaska. But a Canadian historian, Samuel Bawlf, believes that Drake did sail all the way to Chatham Strait, which is about 600 miles (956.6 kilometers) north of Vancouver. In Bawlf's theory, the Englishman was looking for the Northwest Passage. This was the term people gave to a sea route that, they believed, would connect Europe and Asia through Arctic waters. Drake hoped to find this fabled route, but had to turn back, because of sea ice. Bawlf argues that, although Drake did not want England's enemies to know exactly where he had been, he revealed the geographic details of this voyage to European mapmakers. Bawlf's theory has sparked debate, and many historians continue to be skeptical that Drake ever sailed as far as Alaska. Archaeologists have continued to look for evidence that might prove that the Englishman was present at the site where the plate was found.

after a quick trial, Doughty was found guilty and beheaded. This was another episode that tarnished Drake's reputation. When Drake returned to England, Doughty's family attempted to have the seafarer charged with murder. Drake's friends in government, however, were able to block these efforts.

Continuing south, Drake entered the Strait of Magellan, a treacherous passage through numerous islands. After sixteen days in the strait, the fleet entered the Pacific. But massive storms sank one ship and separated another, the *Elizabeth*, from the rest. Believing that the *Golden Hind*, Drake's ship, had also sunk, the *Elizabeth* returned to England.

By this time Drake had only the *Golden Hind* left, with about eighty surviving crewmen. He sailed north along the coast of Chile, looking for plunder. The ports along the Pacific coasts were almost entirely unguarded, because Spain assumed that no rival ships would dare enter these waters. Drake pillaged towns all along the coast, raiding treasure ships as well. His biggest prize was the *Cacafuego*, which had left the port of Lima, Peru, with a load of gold, silver, and gems. It took six days for Drake's men to transfer this cargo to the *Golden Hind*.

Drake claimed to have sailed as far north as the present-day Vancouver, Canada, on this voyage, but modern historians dispute this claim. He may have reached San Francisco, California. Some historians believe he got only as far as San Diego, California.

Having filled his ship with all the treasure it could hold, Drake now had to find a safe route back to England. Fearing that the Spanish might set traps for him in the Strait of Magellan, he decided to risk sailing thousands of miles west across the Pacific. Although he had little knowledge of this ocean's currents and weather patterns,

Drake was confident he could make the voyage. Running desperately short of food and water after sixty-eight days in the Pacific, the sailors finally sighted land near Indonesia. Resupplying at various ports in Southeast Asia, Drake continued homeward around Africa. On September 26, 1580, two years after entering the Strait of Magellan, Drake sailed into Plymouth harbor. Only about half of the men who had set out with him on the *Golden Hind* had survived.

The financial success of the expedition was amazing. Investors in the voyage got double their money back. Drake reportedly received £10,000 worth of gold for himself, and £40,000 to share among his crew. The total plunder was equivalent to hundreds of millions in twenty-first-century dollars.

In appreciation the queen knighted Drake in 1581. (A knight is a man granted a rank of honor by the monarch for his personal merit or service to the country.) Later that year Drake was elected to Parliament, England's legislative body. He also served as mayor of Plymouth, in Devon county. In 1583 his wife of 14 years, Mary Newman, died. Two years later he married Elizabeth Sydenham, heir to a small family fortune.

Defends against the armada

Tensions between England and Spain escalated, and war broke out in 1585. The queen gave Drake command of a fleet of twenty-five ships and ordered him to attack Spanish possessions. After capturing Santiago, in the Cape Verde islands, he sailed to the Caribbean. There he sacked (captured and robbed) the Columbian city of Cartagena and the Florida town of St. Augustine, as well as San Domingo, the capital of Hispaniola (present-day Haiti and the Dominican Republic).

Back in Europe, Drake was next ordered to plan attacks on ports in Spain and Portugal. In Cadiz, in southwestern Spain, Drake destroyed or captured thirty-seven merchant ships. He also attacked the Portuguese city of Sagres and captured a large Portuguese trading ship in the Azores. Yet these actions failed to deter Spain's plan to launch a major naval invasion of England. Learning of Spain's intentions, the queen appointed Drake second in command of the English fleet. In 1588 Spain's armada, the mightiest navy in the world, sailed into the English Channel. England faced the very real possibility that the invasion would succeed, and that the English government would be toppled. But after a series of small skirmishes, the English were able to break Spain's formation, and the armada was forced to head northward toward

Ireland and Scotland. There it encountered a powerful storm; almost half the Spanish fleet was lost, and thousands of sailors died. England's defense had proved successful, but Drake could take little credit. At an early stage in the fighting, he ignored orders and captured a Spanish pay ship, quarreling with another English officer, Sir Martin Frobisher (1535–1594), about how the money should be divided up. Frobisher later accused Drake of withdrawing in the middle of an attack on another ship, calling him a coward and a traitor.

Still high in the queen's favor, Drake was sent to Spain in 1589 with Sir John Norris (1547–1597). With a fleet of about 180 ships they harassed Portuguese and Spanish targets but were defeated in their attempt to capture the Portuguese capital of Lisbon. The English lost several thousand men in battle and returned to England in humiliation.

Final privateering mission

Drake spent the next few years in Devon, where he was elected to Parliament again in 1593. When the queen offered him a privateering commission in 1595, however, he gladly accepted. Drake was leader of the expedition, with John Hawkins serving as second in command. They sailed for the Caribbean with twenty-seven ships and about twenty-five hundred men.

The privateers expected riches and glory, but they met with disaster. At Grand Canary Island in the Caribbean, Drake ordered his men ashore to obtain fresh supplies. But residents fired on them, killing four of the crew and capturing others. With information gained from the captives, the islanders were able to alert the Spanish authorities that the Englishmen planned to capture the Spanish treasure fleet in Puerto Rico. Spain dispatched a fleet of gunboats from Lisbon to destroy the English.

Reaching the Puerto Rican city of San Juan, the privateers made plans to attack. But Hawkins suddenly became ill and died aboard ship. Drake led the assault, but the battle went badly and, after losing about four hundred men, Drake withdrew back to sea. He convinced the men that there were "twenty places far more wealthy and easier to be gotten," as quoted by Peter Whitfield in *Sir Francis Drake*, and headed westward. He also sent a letter to Puerto Rico's governor, requesting that English prisoners taken in the battle be treated honorably.

Taking the expedition to Venezuela, Drake found little treasure there. Wanting to avoid battle with the Spanish in the well-protected city of Cartagena, he then headed for Panama. But bad weather and strong Spanish defenses forced him to change his plans yet again. In early January 1596

Drake changed course for Honduras and Nicaragua. But soon afterward he contracted dysentery, an intestinal inflammation that causes severe diarrhea and dehydration. Quickly becoming weaker and weaker, Drake dictated his final will. Early on the morning of January 28, he called his men to help him into his armor so that, according to Whitfield, "he might die like a soldier." An hour later, he was dead. His body was placed in a coffin of lead and buried at sea, to the accompaniment of the fleet's cannon fire and trumpets. The remaining ships returned to England, empty of any treasure.

Drake was the most famous mariner of his time. Despite several smears on his reputation, he was revered by the English for weakening Spain, enriching England with his plunder, and helping to tip the balance of European power in England's favor. His audacity in stealing Spanish treasure was legendary. And even though Drake provoked the rage of Spain, many Spanish admired him. As one Spanish captain, quoted by Whitfield, stated during the armada crisis that Drake was a man "whose felicity and valour were so great that Mars the god of war, and Neptune the god of the sea, seemed to wait upon all his attempts, and whose noble and generous carriage towards the vanquished had been oft experienced by his foes."

For More Information

BOOKS

Kelsey, Harry. *Sir Francis Drake: The Queen's Pirate.* New Haven, CT: Yale University Press, 1998.

Whitfield, Peter. *Sir Francis Drake.* New York: New York University Press, 2004, pp. 147–150.

PERIODICALS

Cummins, John. "'That Golden Knight' Drake and His Reputation." *History Today* (January 1996): 14.

Dudley, Wade G. "Pirate to Admiral: Sir Francis Drake: Sea Dog Francis Drake battled, looted and bought his way from scourge of Spain to Queen Elizabeth's favorite commander." *Military History* (June–July, 2009): 62+.

Schwarz, Frederic C. "1573; Drake Sees the Pacific." *American Heritage* (February–March 1998): 94.

WEB SITES

Chandonnet, Ann. "New Theory Links Sir Francis Drake with Alaska." *Juneau Empire.* www.juneauempire.com/stories/062401/Loc_drake.html (accessed on January 3, 2011).

"Sir Francis Drake." *National Maritime Museum, Royal Observatory, Greenwich.* www.nmm.ac.uk/server/show/conWebDoc.140 (accessed on January 3, 2011).

Eustace the Monk

BORN: c. 1170 • Courset, France

DIED: August 1217

French pirate

> "The Monk was a good warrior. He was very strong and fierce. He did much deviltry in the [English Channel] islands and other places."
>
> – Leah Shopkow, translator
> "EUSTACE THE MONK." TRANSLATION OF THE MEDIEVAL POEM *LI ROMANS DE WITASSE LE MOINE.*

In the early 1200s Eustace the Monk was a force to reckon with in the English Channel, the narrow body of water that separates England from France and the Netherlands. He was a skilled sailor, and he offered his pirating skills to whatever leader would pay him best. Early in his career, he served the king of England when that country was at war with France. He raided up and down the French coastline, pillaging English villages as well. Later he switched sides and assisted the French king. He was killed in a sea battle in which England defeated France.

Early life

Eustace was born in the French village of Courset, around the year 1170. His father, Baldwin Busquet, was a lord in Boulogne, and although Eustace was not the first-born son, who was usually the automatic heir, he apparently had some claim to inherit Busquet's estate. During his youth, Eustace went to the Mediterranean, where he learned sailing skills. When he returned to France, he entered St. Samer Abbey, near Calais, as a Benedictine monk.

Busquet died around 1190, allegedly killed by a political rival. Soon afterward, Eustace left the monastery and returned to Boulogne to deal with his dead father's affairs. Count Renaud de Dammartin (c. 1165–1227), a local noble, made Eustace his seneschal, a type of administrative officer. Eustace also became the count's bailiff, and as such was responsible for overseeing the manor.

Before long, however, Eustace quarreled with his employer, allegedly because the count accused him of mishandling his official responsibilities. Eustace left Boulogne in anger, after which the count seized Eustace's possessions and burned the fields that he had inherited after his father's death. In retaliation, Eustace burned down two grain mills belonging to the count. According to a description of the event in "Eustace the Monk," Leah Shopkow's translation of the medieval poem *Li Romans de Witasse Le Moine* (*The Romance of Eustace the Monk*), Eustace approached the city and found two mills nearby; they were unguarded, and the city was celebrating the count's son's wedding. Eustace sent the miller to the count with a message: "Say to him that Eustace the Monk is there to light [the Count's mills] up." The count's men were unable to catch Eustace, and the mills burned to the ground. After this, the count declared Eustace an outlaw.

A pirate for England

Eager to escape Count Renaud's men, Eustace went to sea. He then went to the court of King John (1167–1216) and offered his services to the English crown. The king welcomed him and gave him several galleys. (A galley is a long, low ship used for war and trading that was mainly powered by oarsmen, but might also use a sail.) With about thirty galleys, Eustace took control of the Strait of Dover, the narrowest point in the English Channel. Much of the sea trade between England and Europe passed through these waters, and Eustace seized many ships in this area. He also conducted raids up and down the northern coast of France, taking a fortune in plunder (goods stolen by force).

Among Eustace's most important prizes were the Channel Islands of Jersey, Guernsey, Alderney, and Sark. These islands lie in the western part of the channel, near the Atlantic Ocean. Situated closer to the French mainland than to England, the Channel Islands had a longstanding cultural connection to France but were officially claimed as English territory. Eustace recognized the islands' strategic importance and decided to put them under his control. But the islanders wanted nothing to do with the pirate and tried to fight him off. A major battle took place. The medieval poet of *The Romance of Eustace the Monk*, as translated by Shopkow, describes Eustace's assault on the islands:

> Then there began a great, harsh and long melée. Eustace held a great ax, with which he made great strokes in that place. He split many a helm [helmet] and broke the shoulder of many a warhorse.... He made himself the lord and master of the fleet.... That day many a corpse was made. Eustace threw them out of that place and assailed all the isles, so that there remained nothing to burn, neither in the castle nor in the manor.

Having seized the Channel Islands, Eustace established his pirate base on the island of Sark. (A pirate base is a place where pirates lived under their own rule and maintained their own defense system.) He enjoyed a successful career as a pirate in the channel. Not only did he attack merchant vessels crossing between England and the Continent, but he also raided towns along France's coast. This piracy was so troubling to the French that the seneschal of Normandy, a man named Cadoc, ordered three hundred soldiers to guard the region where the River Seine empties into the channel.

The Romance of Eustace the Monk tells of an episode when Eustace allegedly navigated upriver to the town of Pont-Audemar, where he saw Cadoc. The pirate had his beard shaved by a barber so that he would not be recognized. Then he struck up a conversation with Cadoc, offering to lead the seneschal to the pirate in return for Cadoc's splendid fur cape. Having received the cape, Eustace led Cadoc and thirty of his men toward a meadow and said that the pirate was hiding nearby. Galloping across the meadow, Cadoc and his forces rode into a large bog and got stuck there in the deep mud. As the men struggled to free themselves and their horses, Eustace approached Cadoc and laughed at him. He insisted that the men would never get out of the bog unless they followed his advice. He told them to stand on their horses' saddles, hold hands, and jump off. This, he said, would lighten the horses' load and help the animals pull free. The men climbed to their feet, and Cadoc jumped first. "He fell in the bog up to his rear end," wrote the poet, as translated by Shopkow, and "Eustace ... almost fainted from laughter." When the pirate mockingly revealed his true identity to Cadoc, the seneschal threatened to get his revenge. But Eustace, according to the poem, escaped down the river and "put himself into the waves' protection."

Back in the English Channel, Eustace collected payments from ports in the islands and along the coast. When Cadoc sent a fleet after him, the pirate captured five of these vessels and forced the fleet to retreat. Eustace later captured a large merchant vessel, seizing two hundred large silver coins.

Despite his pledge of loyalty to King John, Eustace also attacked villages along the English coast. Furious, the king outlawed the pirate. But this situation did not last long, because the king needed Eustace's services in the channel. He pardoned the pirate, and Eustace continued menacing ships in these waters.

Changes sides to support France

In 1209 King John, who had given Eustace property in London, named the pirate ambassador to Boulogne. But within a few years, Count Renaud began dealing personally with the king, thus reducing Eustace's political influence. In 1212 Count Renaud formed an alliance with England against King Philip II of France (1165–1223). After being defeated by Philip's forces at the battle of Bouvines in 1214, the count was sent to prison, where he committed suicide.

Eustace then decided to switch sides and support the French king. In 1215 when the English barons organized an uprising against King John, Eustace assisted them by running arms across the channel. As the barons gained increasing support for their rebellion, they asked the French prince, Louis (later crowned King Louis VII; 1187–1226) for support. In 1216 Louis invaded England, and Eustace was the sea captain who ferried him across the channel to English soil. When Louis's ships were lost in battle at the English port of Damme, however, Eustace was accused of betraying the French side. According to Shopkow's translation of *The Romance of Eustace the Monk*, "Eustace absconded [ran away], for there was no man bold enough to dare support him, and thus they let matters be."

In 1217 Eustace was bringing reinforcements across the channel to the pro-French rebel forces when he was attacked by a large English fleet at Dover. Although Eustace lost most of his ships in the fighting, he was able to escape with a small number of vessels. Soon afterward, however, English forces assaulted him again at Sandwich. Eustace and his men battled more than twenty ships. According to *The Romance of Eustace the Monk*, as translated by Shopkow, "Eustace fought hard with an oar he held. He broke arms and legs. He killed this one and threw another down; he attacked another, and struck down a second, and crushed the third's throat, but they attacked him on all sides." The English threw quicklime, a chemical compound, over the sides and the wind blew this dust into the French crew's faces, choking and blinding them. The English boarded

The English display the head of Eustace the Monk on a pole after the Battle of Sandwich.
MARY EVANS PICTURE LIBRARY/EVERETT COLLECTION.

Eustace's ship and took all of the noblemen as hostages. But the victors beheaded Eustace on the spot. After describing the pirate's death, *The Romance of Eustace the Monk* concludes, "No one can live for a long time who has bad intentions all his days."

Tall tales

Eustace did not enjoy a highly favorable reputation among the French or the English. People told many stories about him, most of them exaggerated or entirely fictional. These stories focused in particular on Eustace's trickery, cheating, and magic powers. It was widely believed, for example, that before entering the monastery, Eustace had traveled to Spain to study black magic in Toledo. *The Romance of Eustace the Monk*, as translated by Shopkow, states that Eustace "lived beneath the earth in a pit for all of one winter and one summer; there he spoke to the devil himself, who taught him the trickery and the art that deceives and gulls the world." Eustace allegedly learned one thousand spells, as well as one thousand tricks and another one thousand enchantments. "When Eustace had learned enough," according to the poem, "he took leave of the devil. The devil told him that he would live until he had done enough evil. He would fight kings and counts and he would be killed at sea."

In another episode recounted in the poem, Eustace went to a tavern where he and three friends ate a splendid dinner. Then said that they did not have the kind of coins accepted as money in that region, so they could not pay for their expensive meal. Eustace put a spell on the woman who owned the tavern. This caused her to tear off her skirt and break open a vat of wine. Everyone who entered the tavern was similarly bewitched, and soon there was a crowd of half-naked people at the tavern as the wine flowed out into the street. When the rest of the townsfolk realized what had happened, they chased Eustace and his companions, insisting that the young man pay for all the wasted wine. But, by magic, one of Eustace's friends made a river spring up between the townsfolk and the outlaws. And as the people retreated, the river followed them.

People also said that Eustace played similar tricks during the time that he lived in the monastery. He allegedly cast spells so that the monks ate when they were supposed to be fasting and fasted during the time for meals. He made them say the wrong words when they recited daily prayers. Although monks were supposed to take vows of poverty and follow a humble lifestyle, Eustace performed magic to supply himself with bountiful amounts of meat and wine. He ate, drank, and gambled as he pleased. According to these stories, Eustace left the monastery, because he caused so much trouble there. But historians believe that the real reason is that Eustace's father had died, and the young monk needed to deal with his father's estate.

Many stories about Eustace describe the ways he tricked Count Renaud. The pirate loved to wear disguises. In one story, he pretends to have leprosy, a dreaded disease that creates open sores on the skin. People in the Middle Ages (c. 500–c. 1500) would not go near lepers, or people who had leprosy, for fear of catching the disease, and lepers were required to carry rattles to warn others not to approach them. Eustace allegedly

Robin Hood

Stories about the English hero Robin Hood suggest that this figure lived around the same time as Eustace the Monk. But it is not clear that Robin Hood actually existed. Various legends say that his real name was Robyn Hode, Robert Hood, or Robin of Locksley, but historians have not been able to confirm that the hero of these tales was an actual person.

To modern readers, Robin Hood is depicted as a nobleman who has been cheated out of his inheritance. He retreats to Sherwood Forest, in Nottingham, and becomes an outlaw. He steals from the rich and gives to the poor in order to show the injustice of England's laws, which subject the people to high taxes and punish them if they are forced to steal food to survive. Although Robin Hood breaks England's law, he follows the higher law of morality. However, historians point out that the earliest Robin Hood stories do not mention these admirable virtues. They focus more on the pranks that Robin Hood pulled on his enemies. In fact, many of his tricks are very similar to those mentioned in stories about Eustace. Like the monk, Robin Hood liked to wear disguises in order to steal from his enemies. Some of the tales about Robin Hood are similar to those described in *The Romance of Eustace the Monk*. For example, both heroes ambush parties that are riding through the woods. They demand to know exactly how much money the riders are carrying. If the riders tell the truth, the outlaws let them go. And both heroes

A statue of Robin Hood. © ROBERT HARDING PICTURE LIBRARY LTD./ALAMY.

often use exactly the same disguise, as when they pretend to be potters to trick their enemies.

According to historian Mike Ibeji in his article, "Robin Hood and His Historical Context," the close similarities in the legends of Robin Hood and Eustace mean that the stories originated around the same time. They contributed to a popular mythology that celebrated outlaws for defying the tyrannical rule of England's King John.

waited for the count and his men on the road, dressed in a cloak and shaking a rattle. As the men rode by, the pirate tripped the last rider and stole his horse.

Another story says that Eustace once discovered that Count Renaud was in the city of Calais. The pirate baked waffles, pies, and crepes, and had them sent to the place where the count was staying, pretending that they were a present from a man who wanted to ask Count Renaud a favor. After finishing their dinner, Count Renaud's guests bit into the delicious-looking pies. But Eustace had stuffed the pastries with wax, and the men's teeth got stuck. In the last pie was a letter, which stated that Eustace was the one who had pulled this trick.

Most of the stories about Eustace's exploits have been exaggerated or invented. They depict the pirate as a comic figure, similar in some ways to the English folk hero, Robin Hood. But the actual Eustace played a significant role in the struggles for power between France and England in the early thirteenth century.

For More Information

BOOKS

Kelly, Thomas E., trans. "Eustache the Monk" in *Robin Hood and Other Outlaw Tales*. Stephen Knight and Thomas H. Ohlgren, eds. Kalamazoo, MI: Medieval Institute, 1997. Available online at www.lib.rochester.edu/camelot/teams/eustint.htm (accessed on January 3, 2011).

WEB SITES

Ibeji, Mike. "Robin Hood and His Historical Context." *BBC.* www.bbc.co.uk/history/british/middle_ages/robin_01.shtml (accessed on January 3, 2011).

"The Robin Hood Project." *University of Rochester.* www.lib.rochester.edu/camelot/rh/rhhome.htm (accessed on January 3, 2011).

Shopkow, Leah, trans. "Eustace the Monk." Translated from *Li Romans de Witasse le Moine: Roman du treiziéme siécle.* D.J. Conlon, ed. Chapel Hill, 1972. *Medieval Heroes Course Portfolio.* Indiana University, 2002. www.indiana.edu/~sotl/portfolios/shopkow/eustace.htm (accessed on January 3, 2011).

Henry Every

BORN: c. 1653 • Devon, England

DIED: c. 1699

English pirate

"[Every was] daring and good tempered, but insolent and uneasy at times, and always unforgiving if at any time imposed upon. His manner of living was imprinted in his face, and his profession might easily be told from it."

– A crew member testifying in 1697
QUOTED IN *THE PIRATES' PACT: THE SECRET ALLIANCES BETWEEN HISTORY'S MOST NOTORIOUS BUCCANEERS AND COLONIAL AMERICA* BY DOUGLAS R. BURGESS, JR.

Henry Every. PRIVATE COLLECTION/PETER NEWARK HISTORICAL PICTURES/THE BRIDGEMAN ART LIBRARY INTERNATIONAL.

Henry Every (also spelled Avery) conducted what is thought to be the single most successful pirate action in history when, in 1695, he captured the *Ganj-i-Sawai*. This vessel belonged to Aurangzeb (also known as Alamgir I; 1618–1707), the Mughal emperor. (The Mughal Empire ruled all of South Asia, including present-day Bangladesh, Bhutan, India, Nepal, and Pakistan.) It carried cargo worth the modern equivalent of four hundred million dollars, the most valuable prize ever captured in a pirate raid. The emperor's loss seriously damaged the English economy, because England relied heavily on trade with India. Some of Every's crew were eventually caught, tried, and executed, but Every himself evaded capture. He reportedly returned to England and likely spent the rest of his life in poverty.

Early life

Few facts are known about Henry Every's early life. He was born between 1653 and 1659, most likely in Devon, England. Some written accounts say that he came from the town of Portsmouth and that his father was a sea captain. It is possible that Every joined the Royal Navy as a youth or that he apprenticed himself to a merchant ship.

By 1693 Every was operating as a slave trader between Africa and the Caribbean. He had a commission from the English colonial governor of Bermuda to engage in this business. According to an agent of the Royal African Company, an English slaving company, Every was known as a deceiver who would trick Africans onto his ship and then carry them away into slavery.

Leads a mutiny

In May 1694 Every was serving as first mate on the *Charles II*, an English ship commanded by Charles Gibson. Gibson had received a privateering commission from the Spanish government to attack French interests in the Caribbean Sea. (A privateer is a private ship or ship owner commissioned by a state or government to attack the merchant ships of an enemy nation.)

When Spain failed to pay them, the crew of the *Charles II* become angry and Every led a mutiny, or an open rebellion against the ship's officers. At the port of La Coruna on Spain's Atlantic coast, where the ship had stopped for supplies en route to the Caribbean, the crew took over the ship and Gibson was put ashore. The ship was renamed the *Fancy* and Every was elected as the new captain.

Every set sail for the Cape Verde Islands, off the coast of West Africa, and began his brief career as a pirate. His plan was to sail around the African continent and into the Indian Ocean, where he could prey on merchant ships near the entrance to the Red Sea. At Cape Verde, the *Fancy* captured three small English trading vessels, but they did not yield much plunder, or goods stolen by force. Every then sent some men ashore to kidnap the Portuguese governor of the colony. They brought the governor back to the

Fancy, demanding a ransom for his return. (A ransom is a sum of money demanded for the release of someone being held captive.) They released the governor only after his friends and family were able to pay what the pirates had demanded. Every next took the ship to the coast of Guinea, in West Africa. There he went ashore to meet with the local chieftain to discuss trading some of the *Fancy*'s plunder for gold dust. But when the chieftain sent men aboard with the gold, Every chained them up and put them below decks with his cargo. He later gave several of these slaves to Portuguese colonial officials in exchange for their permission to sail freely in waters under their administration.

Joins a pirate fleet

In December 1694, Every passed the Cape of Good Hope, Africa's southernmost point, and entered the Indian Ocean. His destination was the island of Madagascar, which was located close to major trade routes between Asia, Africa, and the Red Sea and had become a haven for numerous pirates. (A pirate haven is a safe place for pirates to harbor and repair their ships, resupply, and organize raiding parties.) At Johanna Island, part of Madagascar territory, Every found a secluded beach where he could pull the *Fancy* out of the water for repairs. He also renovated the vessel to make it faster and more maneuverable.

While these repairs were being made, Every wrote a formal message that he sent to a local ruler, with instructions that it should be given to the first nonpirate English vessel that came along. The message declared that Every was captain of the *Fancy* and that he was out to seek his fortune. It also said, as quoted by Douglas R. Burgess, Jr. in *The Pirates' Pact: The Secret Alliances between History's Most Notorious Buccaneers and Colonial America*, "I have never as yet wronged any English or Dutch, ... nor ever intend whilst I am Commander." Every went on to state that, so long as an English ship identified itself with its flag, "I shall answer with the same and never molest you." Historians note that the statement was not quite true, because Every had already captured at least three English ships. The pirate may have written the message hoping that it would create the impression that he held a legitimate privateering commission, when, in fact, he was engaging in piracy.

Once the *Fancy* had been overhauled, Every began sailing near the sea lanes in search of plunder. On March 15, 1695, he was surprised by an East India Company ship that chased and almost caught him. The East India

East Indiamen

The East India Company was allowed to license its own ships, called East Indiamen. These were a special category of ship that differed from standard merchant vessels. The largest and most magnificent commercial ships of their era, East Indiamen were designed to carry both trade goods and passengers. And unlike most trade vessels of the 1600s and 1700s, East Indiamen were heavily armed to defend themselves against pirate attacks. In fact, many East Indiamen were deliberately built to resemble warships. Shapes resembling gunports—the openings through which cannons fired—were painted on the ships' sides, creating an optical illusion that exaggerated the number of guns that the East Indiamen carried. Because pirates were usually reluctant to attack military vessels, they were often scared away from engaging with East Indiamen, mistaking these ships for battleships. While most merchant vessels would either flee a pirate ship or surrender if attacked, East Indiamen were well-equipped to confront pirates if necessary.

Because East Indiamen were heavily armed, their decks needed bulky supports. This design made the ships strong and stable, but not particularly fast. After piracy declined in the Indian Ocean after about 1830, ship owners had less need to equip their commercial vessels with heavy guns, and smaller, faster ships began to replace East Indiamen.

Company (EIC) had been established in 1600 to promote increased trade between England and Asia. This trade had become a foundation of the English economy, and England had granted the EIC many special powers, including the power to govern the areas in India where it had built trading posts. The EIC also had the right to license its own ships, called East Indiamen, which carried guns to defend themselves against pirate attacks. Every was able to escape the East Indiaman, but in doing so left many of his crew stranded on Johanna Island.

Returning to Madagascar after shaking off the East Indiaman, Every was delighted to meet up with a whole fleet of vessels commanded by English pirates. They had arrived in the Indian Ocean with privateering commissions from various colonial governors of the North American colonies, but had decided to band together to prey illegally on trading vessels from India. Every decided to join them.

Six pirate ships sailed north toward the sea lane where they expected to find the Indian fleet, near the entrance to the Red Sea. On August 15, a lookout spotted a small vessel, and Every quickly seized it. The pirates expected to learn that this ship was the first one in the Indian convoy. But to their extreme disappointment, they were told by the captain of the captured vessel that the fleet of twenty-five Indian ships had already passed through the area during the night, and that his ship was the fleet's rear guard.

The pirate captains argued among themselves about what to do next. Some wanted to give up and look elsewhere for prey. Others argued that they should try to catch up to the Indian fleet. Putting the matter to a vote, the pirates decided to pursue the trade vessels. Within a day, they caught up with the slow-moving *Fateh Mohamed*, which they seized easily. It was carrying a fortune in silver, but Every resented having to share this treasure among all the crews in the pirate fleet.

Captures the *Ganj-i-Sawai*

Soon afterward, the pirates spied another ship near the coast of Surat, in northwestern India. Every thought it looked like an East India Company ship and hesitated to chase it for fear that its heavy cannons could easily sink the *Fancy*. This made the crew angry, and they began to grumble about overthrowing their captain. But when Every saw the other pirate vessels coming close enough to provide support in case of a fight, he prepared the *Fancy* for an attack. Drawing nearer to the targeted ship, Every was surprised to see it flying the flag of the Mughal emperor. He could also see that its crew was readying the guns.

The Mughal vessel carried sixty-two cannons, while the *Fancy* had only forty-six. Yet when the ships fired their first volley, Every had some good luck. A cannon on the deck of the Indian vessel exploded, causing a huge fire and killing several of its crew. While the Indians were frantically trying to put out the flames and tend to their wounded, Every brought the *Fancy* alongside the stricken ship, and ordered his men to climb aboard. After a brief but intense fight, the Indians surrendered.

Every discovered that he had captured the *Ganj-i-Sawai*, the greatest of the Mughal emperor's treasure ships. The vessel was carrying several members of the emperor's family back to India after their pilgrimage (journey to a sacred place) to the Arabian city of Mecca. Among the passengers were the emperor's daughter, her guardian, and numerous attendants and slaves. They carried large amounts of money, jewels, and other valuables with them. The pirates took about five hundred thousand pieces of gold and silver in addition to several pieces of jewelry and other items. Every's share of this loot, added to his plunder from the *Fateh Mohamed*, made him the richest pirate in the world.

But plundering the *Ganj-i-Sawai* was also Every's downfall. In addition to stealing everything of value on the ship, the pirates subjected the ship's passengers and crew to extreme brutality. They tortured the men into confessing where they had hidden their valuables, and then they threw the victims overboard. Many of the women were raped. Some passengers took their own lives before the pirates could lay hands on them. When some of the *Fancy*'s crew were later caught and brought to trial, they testified that they had participated in gang rapes so violent that women suffered mutilation and even death.

The capture of the *Ganj-i-Sawai* shocked and infuriated the Mughal emperor. He demanded that England bring the culprits to justice. He

Henry Every chasing the Mughal emperor's ship. ENGLISH SCHOOL/PRIVATE COLLECTION/PETER NEWARK HISTORICAL PICTURES/THE BRIDGEMAN ART LIBRARY.

closed several English trading ports in India and placed sixty-four East India Company representatives in jail, in effect holding them as hostages until the English government took action. The emperor made it clear that, if England did not stop such piracy, its business relationship with India would end.

England could not afford to lose its Indian trade. On August 10, 1696, the English government issued a warrant for Every's arrest, dead or alive. It states, as quoted by Burgess, "We do hereby command all His Majesty's Admirals, Captains, and other Officers at Sea, and all His Majesty's Governor Commanders of any forts, castles, or other places in His Majesties plantations, and all other officers and persons whatsoever, to seize and apprehend the said Henry Every." The proclamation also promised a reward of five hundred pounds, as well as a royal pardon, to any of Every's crew who surrendered and gave information as to the pirate captains' whereabouts. Every became the target of the first worldwide manhunt in recorded history.

Goes into hiding

Every's prize, the most valuable ever taken in a single attack, made the pirate an extremely wealthy man. But he could not enjoy his riches, for he knew that no government that had any ties whatsoever to England or to the Mughal emperor would harbor him. He could have retired in Madagascar, but his wealth would buy him few luxuries in the undeveloped land. His best hope, he decided, would be the Caribbean. He set course for New Providence, in the Bahamas. But several of the crew objected to this decision and asked to be put ashore in the Mauritius, a group of islands off Madagascar's east coast. Reaching the Atlantic, the captain faced an outright mutiny, but although only twenty of his crew remained loyal, he managed to keep control of the *Fancy*. He reached New Providence in March 1696.

Offering a substantial bribe which included the *Fancy* itself, Every was initially allowed to stay in New Providence. But conditions were not secure, and the pirates were afraid to go ashore to spend their loot. They remained aboard the *Fancy*, anchored in the harbor, until the ship was smashed against nearby rocks during a severe storm. The men escaped, but they had nowhere to go. The governor of Jamaica refused to give them refuge, and the governor of the Bahamas, fearing official retaliation for having at first protected Every, issued a warrant for his arrest and that of his crew. But he also immediately warned them of the danger, and they quietly escaped.

Most of the 113 pirates who were still with Every when he reached the Caribbean simply disappeared. But twelve were eventually captured; of these, six were executed for their crimes. Those who evaded capture fled to various locations, including Jamaica, North America, and England.

Every was never found. According to some reports, he changed his name to Benjamin Bridgeman and was able to live in disguise in England, in or near Bristol. Other stories say that Every was seen in Ireland. Wherever he went, he was unable to enjoy any of his stolen fortune. Spending such money would cause suspicion, and this was something he was desperate to avoid. The pirate who made the most profitable raid in history, according to many historians, probably lived the rest of his life like a pauper, unable to spend the riches he had acquired.

Authorities were able to build a case against six of the *Fancy* crew members, who were tried in court in two sessions in London, England, in 1696. In the first trial, all six men were acquitted. Knowing that this verdict would be deeply offensive to the Mughal emperor, the prosecutors brought new charges of piracy and held a second session. This time, the men were accused of mutiny and piracy against the *Charles II*. All were found guilty and hanged. The court made a careful record of all the testimony of this second trial, which included detailed accounts of how the pirates operated, what kinds of bribes they paid for safe harbors, and who had been willing to help them. With this information, which caused a sensation when it was made public, governments were able to conduct more efficient campaigns against piracy.

For More Information

BOOKS

Burgess, Douglas. R., Jr. *The Pirates' Pact: The Secret Alliances between History's Most Notorious Buccaneers and Colonial America.* New York: McGraw-Hill, 2009, pp. 133–34, 144.

Travers, Tim. *Pirates: A History.* Brimscombe Port Stroud, England: History Press, 2007.

WEB SITES

Vallar, Cindy. "Henry Every." *Pirates and Privateers: The History of Maritime Piracy,.* www.cindyvallar.com/every.html (accessed on January 3, 2011).

John Hawkins

BORN: 1532 • Plymouth, England

DIED: November 12, 1595 • Puerto Rico

English privateer, slave trader, admiral

"All the Hawkinses are born pirates. When I was in England they fitted out ships to plunder even in the sight of land."

– Spanish ambassador to England, 1586
QUOTED IN *SIR JOHN HAWKINS: QUEEN ELIZABETH'S SLAVE TRADER* BY HARRY KELSEY.

John Hawkins was one of the first English merchants to challenge Spain's control of the Americas. He made several voyages to the Caribbean, where he grew rich from legitimate trade and from treasure that he stole from Spanish ships. Although his activities brought considerable wealth back to England, they worsened political tensions between England and Spain, leading eventually to war.

In middle age Hawkins enjoyed a successful career as treasurer of England's navy. Under his administration, the English fleet became efficient and powerful enough to repel a major naval invasion from Spain, the mightiest navy in the world. Hawkins's activities contributed to a new dynamic of power between England and Spain in the 1500s.

John Hawkins. © NORTH WIND PICTURE ARCHIVES/ ALAMY.

Early life

John Hawkins was born into a prosperous family in Plymouth, England, in 1532. His mother was Joan Trelawney, and his father was William Hawkins, a local merchant and sea trader known for his quick temper. In 1527 William was arrested for severely beating a local man, who almost died from his injuries. On another occasion, William was accused of piracy and sent to prison, but he was soon released. An ambitious businessman, William made a trading voyage in 1530 from Plymouth to Africa and then to Brazil and back to England, becoming the first English sailor to follow this triangular trade route.

As a boy, John learned his father's trade and became proficient in matters of business and sailing. He also got into trouble drinking and fighting, and at age twenty, he killed a man in Plymouth. Local authorities determined that he had acted in self-defense, however, and he was not punished.

After his father's death around 1553, John and his older brother, William, inherited the family business. By now the brothers were skilled seamen and traders. They had also learned the arts of piracy and privateering. Piracy, the act of robbing ships at sea, was a common practice at the time but was illegal. But privateering—in which a private ship or ship owner is commissioned by a state or government to attack the merchant ships of an enemy nation—was considered legitimate. Governments issued licenses to privateers, allowing them to attack and plunder (rob of goods by force) any merchant vessel from an enemy nation. In return, privateers were required to turn a portion of their loot in to the government, but many kept as much for themselves as they could. Although privateering was supposed to occur only when countries were at war, few privateers bothered to observe this technicality.

Although many described Hawkins as a pirate, he considered himself a privateer. During an outbreak of war between England and France in the 1550s, the Hawkins brothers seized a French ship, which the French then retook. In 1555 after peace was established, Hawkins made a trip to the northwestern coast of France, where he got the ship back. On a voyage to the Canary Islands in 1560, where Hawkins traded textiles for sugar, he helped some English sailors hire a small boat that they then used to capture a Spanish merchant vessel. They sailed the stolen ship back to Plymouth, where the townsfolk believed that Hawkins had been behind the whole plan. In fact, many people in Plymouth suspected that Hawkins had willingly allowed his own crew to participate.

In 1559 Hawkins moved to London, where he began making important business connections while still managing the trade operation in Plymouth. During this time, he became father to a son, Richard, who, historians believe, was born out of wedlock but whom Hawkins considered his legitimate child.

Becomes a slave trader

Hawkins began planning a slave trade expedition and sought wealthy London investors who would agree to finance his first voyage. Africans had been trading in slaves long before European merchants began visiting the continent in the 1400s. But the colonization of the Americas profoundly changed the slave trade. Slave labor was in high demand in the Americas, where plantations were producing sugar, tobacco, and other products for European consumption. What had been a relatively small-scale activity before about 1500 suddenly grew into a major business. From about 1502 until the slave trade ended in the 1860s, an estimated eleven million Africans were transported to the Americas as slaves.

Spain and Portugal had begun trading slaves in 1502, but England had not yet become involved in this business. Nevertheless Hawkins had little trouble finding interested partners for his venture, and by 1562 he had the necessary financial support to begin. He set sail that year for west Africa. He took three ships, the largest of which, the *Salomon*, he captained. Because he knew that these small ships would be terribly crowded once they were loaded with hundreds of slaves, he brought only a minimal crew. Historians believe that his cousin, **Francis Drake** (1540–1596; see entry), was among them.

Reaching the coast of Sierra Leone, Hawkins planned to purchase slaves. But he was happy to come upon a fleet of Portuguese merchant ships. He seized six of these vessels, as well as their cargoes of spices, ivory, and about four hundred African slaves. Hawkins was delighted with this booty, because it provided him with an entire shipload of slaves for which he did not pay any money. (Booty is the goods stolen from ships or coastal villages during pirate raids or attacks on enemies in time of war.) He loaded the spices and other goods onto one of his ships and sent it back to England, and sailed for the Caribbean with the slaves. The Atlantic crossing was long and difficult, and the slaves, shackled in crowded rows below decks and deprived of fresh air and sanitation, suffered horribly. About half of them died on the voyage.

Slave Ships

It cost a lot of money to prepare a ship for a slave trading voyage, which also brought many risks. Ships could be damaged or wrecked in storms, or could lose their way and hit rocks or reefs. When such events occurred, merchants lost everything they had invested in the voyage. For this reason, they wanted to maximize the possible profits from each trip that their ships made. Slave traders did this by packing as many slaves as possible onto each ship so that there would be plenty of them to sell once the vessel reached the Americas.

Many slave ships had been originally built as cargo ships. Slave traders divided up the large cargo holds in these vessels, creating several sections where slaves were chained in rows. To use every inch of space, slaves were forced to lie on their backs or their sides. They could not sit up or stand, or even move. Slave ships were generally outfitted to carry about four hundred people, but sometimes carried as many as six hundred. This crowding caused terrible suffering. The slaves had no fresh air to breathe. They could not wash themselves, and they had no privacy. If they had to urinate, move their bowels, or vomit while they were chained in the holds, they were forced to do so where they lay. The slave holds became filthy with human waste.

Under these conditions, slaves often became sick. Some committed suicide by refusing to eat. On some voyages, as many as half of the slaves died. Historians estimate that only about half of the slaves that were brought to the Americas from Africa were able to serve as strong healthy workers. Conditions in the slave ships caused so much damage to their bodies that they never fully recovered.

Hawkins made a substantial amount of money from the trip. Since he had paid nothing for his cargo, he could afford to sell the surviving slaves at discount prices, and he found eager buyers in the Caribbean. But he was lucky. Spain and Portugal had been granted sole rights to the Americas in 1494, and since then Spain had controlled access to trade in the Caribbean. Any merchants wanting to send ships there had first to receive permission from the Spanish government. Hawkins, however, had not requested permission. It was a risk that soon backfired on him.

With his profits, Hawkins bought gold, silver, pearls, sugar, animal hides, and other materials to sell in England. There were so many goods that they could not fit on Hawkins's small ships, so he rented two empty Spanish vessels to carry the extra goods to Spain. He expected that once the merchandise arrived there, he could arrange to have it delivered to England. However, when these ships reached port, the Spanish government seized them. Officials said that Hawkins had not obtained legal permission to trade in the Americas, and they confiscated all the cargo. They refused to return any of it to Hawkins. Still, the goods that Hawkins had been able to send to England on his own vessels were enough to make him rich.

Continued success in the slave trade

Eager for even greater profits, Hawkins made a second slaving voyage in 1564. This time he had obtained financial support from several government officials, including the queen herself, Elizabeth I (1533–1603), who gave Hawkins the use of her ship, the *Jesus of Lubeck*. His cousin, Francis Drake, joined him. When the Spanish got wind of the planned voyage and told the queen that they suspected Hawkins of piracy, Elizabeth replied that Hawkins was an honest trader who had her full permission to make the voyage.

With the *Jesus of Lubeck* and three other vessels, Hawkins reached the coast of Sierra Leone. He sent raiding parties ashore to hunt for slaves, and bought slaves from Portuguese traders. Going ashore himself with about forty men to make another raid, Hawkins was attacked by the local people and barely managed to return to his ship. He gained ten new slaves, but seven crewmen were killed and almost thirty were wounded. To make matters worse, some of his sailors who were bathing near their ship were attacked by sharks. One was killed and another seriously wounded. The Portuguese later claimed that Hawkins stole sixty slaves from them on this trip, as well as gold, ivory, and other precious merchandise.

As before, the voyage across the Atlantic was rough. The sailors, and especially the slaves, suffered from cramped conditions and poor food. Yet Hawkins always made special arrangements for himself. He had a spacious cabin, and he brought along trunks full of fancy clothing, fine china, and the best food and wines. The ships reached the coast of Venezuela in the spring of 1565, with several slaves having perished during the voyage.

Hawkins had expected to sell his slaves quickly, but he discovered that the Spanish colonial governor had issued an order forbidding residents to trade with him. Hawkins spent several days trying to negotiate with the governor but was frustrated at the delay and resorted to threats. He eventually realized that, although residents were quite willing to buy his goods, they feared punishment if they did so. Hawkins decided to send armed men ashore in towns where he wanted to sell his goods. This gave local merchants a good excuse for trading with him. If the authorities asked questions, residents could say that Hawkins had forced them to do business with him. Hawkins returned to England with even more money than he had made on his first trip.

Disaster at San Juan de Ulúa

Hawkins's third, and final, slaving voyage was a disaster. With financial support from several highly placed officials in England, he set out for

John Hawkins defeated by the Spanish at the Battle of San Juan de Ulúa. © 2D ALAN KING/ALAMY.

Africa in 1567. He captured slaves along the West African coast, and, after bribing Spanish authorities in the Caribbean, he quickly sold most of his cargo. But then a devastating storm arose and forced him to anchor in San Juan de Ulúa (present-day Veracruz, Mexico). His ships had sustained heavy damage, and Hawkins hoped to sell his remaining slaves and then make the necessary repairs to his ships. But the next day, a large fleet from Spain sailed into the harbor. Hawkins was unable to convince them that his motives were peaceful, and the Spanish attacked. The English were outnumbered and outgunned, and Hawkins lost many of his crew as well as almost all of his goods. Only two of his ships, the *Judith* and the *Minion*, were able to get away. This episode sparked furious accusations between England and Spain, leading to a serious breakdown in relations between the rival countries.

Taking charge of the *Minion* and giving command of the *Judith* to Drake, Hawkins began the daunting journey back to England. His ships, already battered from the storm, had sustained further damage in the fighting. Much of his crew had been lost. And because the survivors had been forced to flee the coast before taking on new supplies, they had almost no food or fresh water. The desperate men ate whatever they could find, including rats and mice. They even gnawed on their leather belts. The ships became separated on the voyage, and the *Minion*'s crew begged Hawkins to set them ashore along a wild stretch of the Mexican coast. But when he asked for volunteers, no one came forward. Furious, the captain ordered 114 men ashore, promising that, if he survived, he would come back for them the next year.

It took more than three grueling months to reach England, and during this time, many of Hawkins's crew suffered from starvation and scurvy, a disease caused by the lack of vitamin C. By the time they reached the northwest coast of Spain, Hawkins doubted they had enough strength left to make it the rest of the way to Plymouth. According to one report, Hawkins came upon three Portuguese ships and immediately attacked them. He quickly overwhelmed the vessels, then he stole their supplies and sank the ships. A few miles farther up the coast, the *Minion* came to the town of Puerto Nuevo, where some fishermen helped guide the ship into port at Marín. Despite being desperate for provisions, Hawkins took care to guard his remaining treasure from the authorities. He invited a few officials aboard and managed to convince them that there was sickness on the ship. This story kept investigators away. Although his men were sick from disease and hunger and were wearing filthy rags, Hawkins, according to a description quoted by Harry Kelsey in *Sir John Hawkins: Queen Elizabeth's Slave Trader*, "was dressed in a coat trimmed with marten skins, with cuffs of black silk. He had a scarlet cloak, edged in silver and a doublet of the same material. His cape was silk, and he wore a great gold chain around his neck."

Crazed from hunger, many of Hawkins's men gorged themselves when they finally got food in Marín. As a result, several became ill and died. Their captain was so troubled at this additional loss of life that he tried to hide the deaths by having the bodies thrown into the sea during the night, with stones tied to their feet to make them sink. But a few bodies washed ashore anyway, and the shocked residents of the town spread the word about what happened. Meanwhile, William Hawkins heard about his brother's desperate plight and sent more provisions and men, as well as two ships, to help the *Minion* sail the remaining miles to Plymouth. Only a handful of the men who had set out with Hawkins returned with him.

Pleased as they were that Hawkins survived, his investors were angry that he had lost so many of his ships and men. They questioned how he had been able to bring unsold cargo, including some slaves, safely back to England, but had been unable to protect his crew from starvation and disease. They were also furious that he had abandoned so many of his crew in Mexico. Hawkins was called to London to defend himself to government authorities.

Government career

The sailors Hawkins abandoned in Mexico had meanwhile been captured by Spanish forces and were sent to Spain as hostages. Hawkins began working for their release, but his activities had seriously damaged diplomatic relations between England and Spain. To avoid worsening the situation, the queen's advisers asked Hawkins to use trickery. The pirate went to Spain, befriended King Philip II (1527–1598), and offered to become the king's spy. The king agreed. He released all the hostages and rewarded Hawkins by making him a grandee, the highest rank of Spanish nobility. Hawkins now had access to secret information, which he sent to England. In 1571 he informed the English government of a Spanish plot to assassinate the queen. England was able to arrest the English conspirators in this plot and prosecute them.

In 1567 Hawkins had married Katherine Gonson, daughter of the treasurer of the Royal Navy. In 1571, the same year he foiled the plot to assassinate the queen, Hawkins was elected to Parliament, England's legislative body. In 1577 Hawkins took over his father-in-law's position as treasurer of the Royal Navy. Hawkins took his naval responsibilities seriously, ordering many improvements to ship maintenance and design. Through his efforts, England's fleet became strong and nimble. In 1588, when Spain launched a major naval invasion, England's smaller and faster ships were able to outmaneuver the Spanish vessels, leading to the shocking defeat of the mighty Spanish armada (navy). For Hawkins's leadership during this attempted invasion, Queen Elizabeth made him a knight. (A knight is a man granted a rank of honor by the monarch for his personal merit or service to the country.)

His wife died in 1590, and a few years later Hawkins married Margaret Vaughan. In 1594 he received a royal charter to build a hospital for seamen at Chatham. Also that year, he was honored with election to the Honourable Society of the Middle Temple, where students were trained in law.

Last trip to the Americas

In 1595 Hawkins set out on his final voyage to the Caribbean. Drake had persuaded the queen to grant them a privateering license against Spanish ships and ports. She placed Drake first in command, with Hawkins second. They arrived in the West Indies in October. But before they could carry out any raids, Hawkins fell ill. Within a few days, it was clear that he would not survive. He dictated his will, stating in it that he hoped that any legitimate wrongs he had done to others should be compensated. He died on November 11, 1595, and was buried at sea.

Drake also died on this voyage, which brought no treasure back to England and further provoked Spain's anger. The survivors said that Hawkins shared much of the blame for the voyage's failure, being too stubborn to listen to others' ideas and slow to make decisions. But these men also gave Hawkins credit for bravery and for honoring his promises.

Hawkins's privateering adventures helped to destabilize Spanish control in the Americas. His commitment to the English navy contributed significantly to the growth of English power in the sixteenth century.

For More Information

BOOKS

Hazelwood, Nick. *The Queen's Slave Trader: John Hawkyns, Elizabeth I, and the Trafficking in Human Souls.* New York: Morrow, 2004.

Kelsey, Harry. *Sir John Hawkins: Queen Elizabeth's Slave Trader.* New Haven, CT: Yale University Press, 2003, pp. 96, 99, 178.

Konstam, Angus. *Piracy: The Complete History.* Briscombe Port Stroud, England: 2009.

Travers, Tim. *Pirates: A History.* Oxford, England: Osprey Publishing, 2008.

WEB SITES

"Admiral Sir John Hawkins." *Tudor Place.* www.tudorplace.com.ar/Bios/JohnHawkins.htm (accessed on January 3, 2011).

Rahmah ibn Jabir al-Jalahimah

BORN: c. 1760 • Qatar

DIED: 1826 • Qatar

Qatari pirate

"A certain Arab ... has been for more than twenty years the terror of the Gulf, and ... is the most successful and the most generally tolerated pirate, perhaps, that ever infested any sea."

– James Silk Buckingham, English author and traveler
TRAVELS IN ASSYRIA, MEDIA, AND PERSIA.

Rahmah ibn Jabir al-Jalahimah. THE NORTH WIND PICTURE ARCHIVES.

The pirate Rahmah ibn Jabir al-Jalahimah played an important role in the struggle for political power in the Persian Gulf in the early nineteenth century. In command of several fast vessels and thousands of men, he attacked shipping around the island of Bahrain in order to weaken the power of his adversaries, the al-Khalifa clan. Ibn Jabir al-Jalahimah chose his allies carefully, obtaining support from the powerful Wahhabis of Saudi Arabia and maintaining polite relations with the British, who had begun establishing colonial and commercial interests in the region in the 1760s. Having fought the al-Khalifas for many decades, Ibn Jabir al-Jalahimah died in a final confrontation with them in 1826, blowing up his own ship rather than allowing it to be captured.

Early life

Rahmah ibn Jabir al-Jalahimah, nephew of a local sheikh, or leader, of the al-Jalahimah clan, was born sometime around 1760. According to many accounts, his birthplace was Qatar, a peninsula that juts into the Persian Gulf from the northern coast of the Arabian Peninsula. Other accounts say that he was born in Graine, a port in Kuwait, at the eastern end of the gulf.

The al-Jalahimah clan was well established in Qatar. It was among several families that had united with the al-Khalifa clan to successfully repel an invasion of the nearby island of Bahrain by the Persians at the beginning of the 1800s. After the victory, however, the al-Khalifas claimed Bahrain as their sole territory. The al-Jalahimahs and other allies were expelled, depriving them of what they considered their rights to share in Bahrain's valuable trade economy. From then on, the al-Jalahimah clan was the sworn enemy of the al-Khalifa clan. As a leader of the al-Jalahimahs, Ibn Jabir al-Jalahimah spent his life fighting to regain the possessions he believed rightly belonged to his family.

Attacks Bahrain trade

As a young man, Ibn Jabir al-Jalahimah worked for a brief time as a horse trader. He used proceeds from this business to buy his first ship, and set out to damage the al-Khalifas' economic interests by attacking their sea trade. Ibn Jabir al-Jalahimah established his base of operations at Khor Hassan, at the northern tip of Qatar. This location had several advantages. The site overlooked the narrow body of water separating Bahrain, Ibn Jabir al-Jalahimah's main target, from the mainland. Vessels sailing to or from Bahrain had to pass close to Khor Hassan, making it easy for Ibn Jabir al-Jalahimah and his pirates to assault them and then make a quick escape. Khor Hassan also provided the pirate with a safe and convenient hideout. The spot was difficult to attack. A strong fort stood above its beach, and two coral reefs protected its harbor. There were only two navigable channels through these reefs, and Ibn Jabir al-Jalahimah and his men could prepare careful defenses against any vessels daring to maneuver through them. There was also a third channel a few miles west, but this could only be used during the spring tide. And the pirates could easily block it with rocks if necessary to defend their main position. If any enemies did manage to threaten Khor Hassan, Ibn Jabir al-Jalahimah could retreat to another base farther down the coast.

Ibn Jabir al-Jalahimah soon attracted numerous followers, and Khor Hassan became a center for opposition against the al-Khalifas. Ibn Jabir al-Jalahimah recognized the importance of forming useful political alliances to help him in his struggle against his enemy. He obtained support from the residents of Muscat in Oman, at the eastern part of the Persian Gulf. He also got backing from the Wahhabis, the conservative Islamic sect that had established the first Saudi state in Arabia in 1744.

For many years, Ibn Jabir al-Jalahimah and his fleet harassed trade vessels sailing to or from Bahrain. He soon earned a reputation as a daring and ruthless fighter. He owned five or six large ships and commanded about two thousand pirates, many of whom were slaves from Africa. With these pirates, Ibn Jabir al-Jalahimah attacked merchant vessels along the Arabian coast, seizing what plunder he wished.

The "Terror of the Gulf"

Ibn Jabir al-Jalahimah showed no mercy to his enemies. When the pirate chief captured a ship, he killed everyone aboard, even the sailors who surrendered. He was also extremely harsh with his own crew. On one occasion, when some of his sailors plotted a mutiny (an open rebellion against the ship's officers) Ibn Jabir al-Jalahimah reportedly put them into a large tank normally used to store water aboard ship. He then had the tank sealed shut and thrown into the sea. Such actions resulted in Ibn Jabir al-Jalahimah becoming widely feared as the "Terror of the Gulf."

Having participated in numerous battles, Ibn Jabir al-Jalahimah bore many deep scars. Knives, sabers, and bullets had wounded the pirate in about twenty different places, including his face, where he had lost an eye. His enemies and followers alike were often astonished that he had survived so many serious wounds.

Particularly gruesome was the damage to his right arm, which had been hit with grape shot, a cluster of small iron balls usually shot from a cannon. The wound had smashed Ibn Jabir al-Jalahimah's upper arm bone to splinters, turned the limb into a mass of bloody tissue, and knocked the pirate unconscious. For several days, he seemed near death. But eventually Ibn Jabir al-Jalahimah recovered. The bone fragments gradually worked their way out of the pirate's body, but the arm was useless. An English doctor, one of a group of medical officers who invited Ibn Jabir al-Jalahimah to let them examine the arm, once asked

Dhows

Since ancient times, sailors in the Persian Gulf, as well as east Africa and the Indian Ocean, have used a type of ship known as a dhow, a wooden vessel with one or more lateen sails. A lateen sail is a large triangular sail that is mounted to the mast at an angle, in a direction basically parallel to the ship's length. By contrast, many European ships in Rahmah ibn Jabir al-Jalahimah's time were square-rigged, meaning that they used large square sails, mounted perpendicular to the mast and in a direction basically parallel to the ship's width. Square-rigged ships were well-adapted to sailing on the open sea, where steady trade winds, always blowing in the same direction, could fill their enormous sails. Dhows, however, were well-adapted to conditions in the Indian Ocean and surrounding waters, where the wind directions were more changeable and mariners were often forced to sail into the wind.

Shipbuilders in the Persian Gulf and elsewhere developed many different kinds of dhows that were specialized according to their purpose. Smaller vessels ferried passengers and carried small cargos of fish or fruit from town to town along the coast. Larger ones were designed for deep-sea sailing. A type of dhow commonly used for ocean trading in the nineteenth century was the *baghlah*. Ibn Jabir al-Jalahimah owned several baghlahs, which could be as large as 130 feet (40 meters) in length and could weigh between 150 and 400 tons (136 and 363 metric tons). Like other pirates, Ibn Jabir al-Jalahimah adapted these ships for fighting, arming them with cannons and making room for large crews that could board enemy vessels and engage in hand-to-hand combat.

Made in the traditional manner until the late twentieth century, modern dhows often contain synthetic materials, such as fiberglass. In addition, most modern dhows carry outboard motors to supplement their sail power.

Dhows continue to play a role in piracy in and around the Persian Gulf in the twenty-first century. Modern pirates use motorized dhows as

the pirate if he could still use the injured limb to kill an enemy. The pirate, according to James Silk Buckingham, who wrote about his encounters with Ibn Jabir al-Jalahimah in his 1830 book, *Travels in Assyria, Media, and Persia*, drew his dagger, "and placing his left hand, which was sound, to support the elbow of the right, . . . he grasped the dagger firmly with his clenched fist, and drew it backward and forward, twirling it at the same time, and saying, that he desired nothing better than to have the cutting of as many throats as he could effectually open with this lame hand!"

Changes political alliances

Unlike many pirates in the Persian Gulf, who attacked European ships as well as rival Arab vessels, Ibn Jabir al-Jalahimah, realized that it would a floating base of operations. Large dhows feature modern technology, such as sonar and global positioning software. They carry supplies and small speedboats. When a band of pirates finds a suitable target, they launch the actual attack with the speedboats. If the pirates succeed in seizing any cargo, the dhows are used to transport it to a safe harbor.

Traditional dhows. YASSER AL-ZAYYAT/AFP/GETTY IMAGES.

serve his purposes to keep on friendly terms with the British, who had colonial interests in the region and were the dominant naval power there. In 1763 the British East India Company, a trade corporation, had established a trading post in the city of Bushehr, a port in Persia (present-day Iran). Originally formed to facilitate English trade with India and Southeast Asia, the company received permission from Britain to act as a colonial administrator in the regions where it operated. With Bushehr as its base, the East India Company strove to influence political and economic activities in the Persian Gulf in ways that would benefit Britain. Increased trade was one result, and by the early 1800s, British merchant ships were a frequent presence in the gulf.

Ibn Jabir al-Jalahimah made it a point not to challenge any of these British ships, and this earned him the colonial administration's respect. In fact, an official with the East India Company, as quoted by Habibur Rahman in *The Emergence of Qatar: The Turbulent Years, 1627–1916*, described the pirate as a man whose "conduct was scrupulously correct." But these good relations deteriorated after 1809. Ibn Jabir al-Jalahimah had given safe harbor at Khor Hassan to the Qawasim, a clan that had launched several attacks against British ships. Concerned about this threat to their trading activities, the colonial administration decided that Ibn Jabir al-Jalahimah must promise to stop aiding the Qawasim. If the pirate refused, the British would bomb Khor Hassan.

Ibn Jabir al-Jalahimah did not cooperate. But as it turned out, the proposed attack never happened. The British military officers assigned to the case disagreed on the practicality of the assault. And the colonial governor agreed with those who argued that bombing Khor Hassan would violate the principles of fairness that Britain hoped to uphold in the gulf. Instead of attacking, the British decided to send a letter to the Wahhabi leader of Qatar, asking him to force Ibn Jabir al-Jalahimah to withdraw his support for the Qawasim. Despite these efforts, the situation remained unresolved.

In 1814 the Wahhabi leader suddenly died. Soon afterward, a faction from Oman attacked Khor Hassan, driving Ibn Jabir al-Jalahimah out. The pirate established a new outpost at Dammam, on the Arabian coast just to the west of Bahrain. But the political climate was changing rapidly, and Ibn Jabir al-Jalahimah could no longer count on the support of his former allies. The new Wahhabi leader chose to unite with the al-Khalifas to try to undermine growing Omani control in Bahrain; this made him Ibn Jabir al-Jalahimah's enemy. In 1816 Ibn Jabir al-Jalahimah allied himself with the sultan of Muscat, Oman, who launched an invasion of Bahrain. This attack failed. It also provoked the Wahhabi ruler, who in 1816 bombed Ibn Jabir al-Jalahimah's fort at Dammam. The pirate was able to escape, taking his entire family, some five hundred people, to Bushehr.

Ibn Jabir al-Jalahimah received a warm welcome in Bushehr. The local sheik gave the pirate an entire neighborhood in which to reside and provided other material assistance. Ibn Jabir al-Jalahimah also visited the British administrator in the city, declaring that he would now help the British fight the Qawasim. In March 1817 the pirate attacked twelve Qawasimi ships, bringing four back to Bushehr and destroying the other eight. Later that year, Ibn Jabir al-Jalahimah went to Oman to try to persuade the sheik of Muscat to join him in another attempt to invade Bahrain. The sheik, however, declined.

Ibn Jabir al-Jalahimah then allied himself with Ibrahim Pasha (1789–1848), son of the ruling family in Egypt and another foe of the Wahhabis. With Pasha's support, Ibn Jabir al-Jalahimah was able to return to Dammam and rebuild his fortress there. From this position, he continued his assaults on Bahrain.

Frustrated at their inability to stop Ibn Jabir al-Jalahimah, in 1820 the al-Khalifas began paying the pirate an annual tribute of four thousand German crowns. (A tribute is payment from one ruler of a state to another, usually for protection or to acknowledge submission.) They hoped that this payment would convince Ibn Jabir al-Jalahimah to stop his attacks on Bahrain, but the piracy continued. In February 1824 the al-Khalifas signed a peace treaty with Ibn Jabir al-Jalahimah, negotiated with the help of Colonel Ephraim Gerrish Stannus (1784–1850), head of the British government at Bushehr.

Death and legacy

Even with a peace treaty in place, Ibn Jabir al-Jalahimah continued to harass Bahraini ships in the gulf. The al-Khalifas responded by imposing a blockade at Dammam. Ibn Jabir al-Jalahimah was able to slip through this blockade twice, but his luck did not hold. He fought his final battle off the coast of Dammam in 1826. Two al-Khalifa armies were approaching Ibn Jabir al-Jalahimah's fort by land. Their fleet, led by Ahmed bin Sulaiman, nephew of Bahrain's ruling sheik, waited outside the harbor. Ibn Jabir al-Jalahimah ordered his oldest son to defend the fortress from the land assault. With the rest of his crew, he sailed out to meet Bin Sulaiman.

The pirate soon realized that Bin Sulaiman's navy was far superior to his own and that he would not win this fight. He ordered his crew to draw close to the enemy and attack with all their might. Then, taking his eight-year-old son in his arms, he seized a lighted torch and ordered his crew to lead him below deck to where the gunpowder was stored. Although the men knew that their commander was going to blow up the ship, killing himself and everyone else aboard, they immediately obeyed. Ibn Jabir al-Jalahimah ignited the powder, causing a gigantic explosion. The ship was blown into tiny pieces, and Ibn Jabir al-Jalahimah and his son, as well as all his crew, died instantly.

In his final act, Ibn Jabir al-Jalahimah showed that he would rather die by his own hand than be captured or killed by his enemy. According to Samuel Hennell, who became British administrator of the gulf a few years later, and whose remarks are quoted by Rahman, the pirate's death "was felt as a blessing in every part of the Gulf."

But many in the region honored Ibn Jabir al-Jalahimah as a hero. According to Rahman, Ibn Jabir al-Jalahimah can be seen as "a brave and courageous maritime leader, who sought throughout his life not only to keep the al-Kahlifa away from the coast of Qatar but also to restrict their movements in the waters of the Gulf."

For More Information

BOOKS

Buckingham, James Silk. *Travels in Assyria, Media, and Persia.* 2nd ed. London, England: Henry Colburn and Richard Bentley, 1830. Reprint, Rye Brook, NY: Adamant Media, 2002, pp. 356, 358.

Rahman, Habibur. *The Emergence of Qatar: The Turbulent Years, 1627–1916.* London, England: Kegan Paul, 2006, p. 25.

WEB SITES

"Rahmah Ibn Jaber: The Scourge of the Pirate Coast." *Qatar Vistor,* www.qatarvisitor.com/index.php?cID=430&pID=1382 (accessed on January 3, 2011).

John Paul Jones

BORN: July 6, 1747 • Kirkbean, Scotland

DIED: July 18, 1792 • Paris, France

American naval captain

John Paul Jones. STOCK MONTAGE/ARCHIVE PHOTOS/GETTY IMAGES.

"I wish to have no connection with any ship that does not sail fast; for I intend to go in harm's way."

John Paul Jones played an important role in American history as one of the first officers of the U.S. Navy. During the American Revolution (1775–83; the American colonists' fight for independence from Great Britain), he led several attacks on British merchant ships and won significant battles against British naval forces. Jones also conducted numerous raids along the coasts of England and Scotland, burning property and allowing his crew to seize silver belonging to the Earl of Selkirk. The British denounced Jones as a pirate, yet the American revolutionaries hailed Jones as a hero determined to fight for freedom.

Early life

John Paul Jones was born John Paul in Kirkbean, Scotland, on July 6, 1747. He was the son of a landscape gardener, also named John Paul. The Paul family lived on the estate of a wealthy landowner, where the senior John Paul was a servant. The family was not poor but they lacked social status.

Jones grew up near the sea and from an early age dreamed of joining the British Royal Navy. A career as a naval officer could provide a chance to earn a good income and gain social standing. But it was not easy to become an officer. Jones decided at age thirteen to become an apprentice on a merchant ship for a term of seven years. This would give him the opportunity to learn seamanship as well as navigation (charting the course of a ship), and these skills would make him a good candidate for later employment in the navy.

Jones sailed on various trading voyages aboard the *Friendship*, a small merchant vessel that made frequent trips to the North American colonies. But the owner of the *Friendship* was forced to sell the ship before Jones's seven-year term was finished. This terminated the young man's contract, and Jones then signed on with a slave ship. Historians think that Jones may have disapproved of slave trading, because he resigned from this position before completing the term of his contract.

After quitting the slave ship, Jones found himself in Jamaica without a job or a way to get back to Great Britain. A merchant captain agreed to take the young man with him on his voyage to Scotland. But in the middle of the Atlantic Ocean, both the captain and the first mate suddenly became ill and died. The responsibility for getting the ship safely to Scotland fell to Jones, who was the only person onboard who knew how to navigate. The owners of the ship were so grateful for his success that they gave him command of the ship, the *John*, as a reward.

Maintains discipline

Jones ran his ship according to strict rules, and many of his crew resented this. When they complained or challenged his orders, he punished them. During his second voyage to the Caribbean as captain of the *John* in 1770, Jones clashed with the carpenter's mate, Mungo Maxwell. The mate had made insulting remarks, and Jones ordered him to be flogged.

Flogging, or whipping, was a common punishment on ships, where captains had to maintain strict discipline in order to avoid mutiny, or an open rebellion against the ship's officers. Life at sea could be extremely dangerous, and captains had to know that they could rely on every member of the crew to follow orders quickly and thoroughly. If a sailor challenged a captain's authority, this could undermine trust among the rest of the crew and cause them to disobey or ignore orders. And this could put a ship in peril. Still, flogging was a serious punishment, and many felt that Maxwell's offense had been too trivial to deserve it. When the *John* reached port in Tobago, Maxwell sued Jones for brutality in admiralty court. (An admiralty court is a court that administers laws and regulations pertaining to the sea.)

The admiralty court in Tobago physically examined Maxwell and ruled that his injuries were not severe enough to justify his claim. The judge also found that the punishment was appropriate, because of Maxwell's incompetence and disrespect. Angrily, Maxwell quit the *John* and made arrangements to return to Scotland on another ship. But on the voyage Maxwell died. When the *John* returned to Scotland some weeks later, Maxwell's family, who had powerful social connections, had Jones arrested and put in jail.

This incident caused the young captain lasting shame. He petitioned to be set free in order to collect evidence of his innocence, and permission was granted. Documentation from the Tobago court showed that Maxwell had not suffered any serious injury from the flogging. Other evidence showed that Maxwell had been in good health when he began his trip back to Scotland and that he died of some kind of fever. The Scottish court cleared Jones, but the incident remained a permanent stain on his reputation.

In 1771, the owners of the *John* sold the ship, and Jones found another commission as commander of the *Betsy*. Once again, he encountered difficulties managing his crew. In Tobago late in 1773, Jones hired some new sailors, including a man he came to call "the Ringleader." This man began complaining loudly that the captain had not paid the crew their wages. He threatened to steal the ship's launch (the small boat used to carry the crew to and from the main ship) and lunged at the captain with a big stick. Jones grabbed his sword. In the fight that followed, he killed the Ringleader.

Jones believed he had acted in self-defense and that he would be cleared by an admiralty court. Admiralty court, however, was not in session, and Jones feared that, if the matter were brought before a civil court, as sometimes happened, he would not receive a fair trial. He left the *Betsy* and went to Virginia, where his older brother lived in Fredericksburg. He stayed in Virginia for a few years. He also changed his name from John Paul to John Paul Jones. He never explained why he took this step, but historians believe that he may have wished to distance himself from the Ringleader controversy.

Freemasons

John Paul Jones was among the many key figures of the American Revolution who were members of a society known as the Freemasons. Masons, as they are known, observe secret rituals and confront deep questions about the meaning of life. They also pledge to help each other as brothers. Freemasonry has often been controversial, especially among people who considered it a challenge to established religion. But it was particularly popular in America in the 1700s. The first U.S. president, George Washington (1732–1799) was a mason, as was statesman and scientist Benjamin Franklin and patriots Paul Revere (1735–1818) and John Hancock (1737–1793). Membership in the Freemasons may have given Jones the kind of social contacts he wanted to improve his status in life.

One of the emphases of Freemasonry is charity. During the 1800s, American Freemasons established orphanages, homes for the elderly, and other institutions to provide for the needs of the poor. Although government later took over the responsibility of providing these services, the Masons have continued to support education and charitable causes. The Freemasons remain the world's largest fraternal, or brotherly, organization, numbering about five million members worldwide in the early 2000s. The majority—about three million—live in the United States.

Joins the Continental navy

Soon after the American Revolution began in 1775, Jones went to Philadelphia, Pennsylvania, to offer his services to the Continental navy. The navy had just been formed by the Continental Congress, the governing body of the United States during the revolutionary period, and Jones was eager to receive a commission, or an appointment as an officer in the military. On December 7, 1775, he became the first person in the Continental navy to be assigned the rank of first lieutenant, an honor he received while onboard the USS *Alfred*. His first mission was to sail to Nassau, in the Bahamas, and attack British merchant ships in the region. On this voyage Jones hoisted the first U.S. ensign, or flag, over a naval vessel.

Jones was next given command, in 1776, of the USS *Providence*, with which he attacked British shipping near Nova Scotia, Canada. On June 14, 1777, he was made captain of a newly built vessel, the USS *Ranger*. Jones was disappointed with this assignment, having hoped for command of a larger ship. He was ordered to go to France, which strongly sympathized with the American revolutionary cause. There, he was told, a better vessel that was under construction in the Netherlands would be given to him. In France Jones became good friends with American statesman Benjamin Franklin (1706–1790), who was serving there as a commissioner of the Continental Congress.

Raids the British coast

When the ship under construction in the Netherlands was sold to the French instead of to the Americans, Jones became impatient. With no clear orders from the U.S. Navy, he decided to set sail in the *Ranger* for the coast of Great Britain. He planned to burn the merchant fleet at anchor in the port of Whitehaven, near Scotland, and then kidnap the

Earl of Selkirk. He would keep the earl as a hostage to gain the release of American sailors who had been captured by the British.

The *Ranger*'s crew was unhappy with this plan. A few days after the ship left France, the crew rose up in a mutiny against their captain. One of the noncommissioned officers rushed at Jones, and the captain pointed a gun at the man's head to restore order. This was another episode that contributed to Jones's reputation as a difficult captain.

The *Ranger* reached Whitehaven on April 17, 1778. But bad weather forced Jones to cancel the raid on the town. The next day the *Ranger* skirmished with a small patrol ship, which eventually escaped. Realizing that the patrol vessel would report the incident, Jones took the *Ranger* westward to avoid any battleships that might be sent to chase him.

Soon afterward, the *Ranger* captured a fishing boat. From its crew, Jones learned that the HMS *Drake*, a small warship, was anchored near Carrickfergus, Ireland. Jones sailed there, planning to attack the *Drake* in broad daylight. But when the time came, his crew would not obey his orders to risk something so dangerous. The raid was postponed until late at night. The plan required the crew to bring the *Ranger* as close as possible to the British ship and then drop anchor so that they could throw grappling hooks onto the *Drake* and board it. But the anchor was dropped at the wrong time, and the *Ranger* ended up too far from its target. Jones decided that he needed to escape before the *Drake*'s crew realized what had happened. He ordered the anchor cable cut so that the *Ranger* could sail away quickly.

Jones then went back to Whitehaven. Reaching the harbor on April 23, he took a small landing party ashore just after midnight. He intended to capture the town's forts and disable their cannons and then set fire to the two hundred ships anchored in the harbor. He also planned to set additional fires on shore to frighten the townsfolk. But once again, Jones had bad luck. He was able to jam the cannons but could not light any fires, because he had run out of lantern oil for fuel. He sent some of his men to steal oil from a tavern, but when they got there, they wasted time getting drunk. Daylight was approaching by this time, and Jones realized he would not have time to torch the entire fleet. Finding a coal ship among those at anchor, Jones and his men managed to pour a barrel of tar onto its deck and set it ablaze.

Meantime, one of the sailors on the *Ranger*, who sympathized with the British, had slipped ashore to warn the residents of the attack. When they rushed to the harbor, they saw the coal ship in flames, with Jones

waving his pistol at them and ordering them back to their homes. The Americans had not destroyed much property, but the raid was still a huge spectacle that terrified the people of Whitehaven and outraged the British government. In Britain people began to describe Jones as a ruthless pirate.

The outrage increased after Jones sailed to Scotland and invaded the Earl of Selkirk's estate. The Americans were unable to capture the earl as planned, because he was not at home. But they did steal silverware and china from his house. Jones had not wanted to allow this, but his men were frustrated. They had not been able to seize any enemy ships, which were customarily sold for money that was divided among the crew, and this had made them angry. They demanded to take treasure from the earl's estate. Hoping to suppress mutinous feelings among the men, Jones allowed them to remove the silver. When it was later sold in France, Jones bought it and returned it to the earl after the war.

Commands the *Bonhomme Richard*

En route back to France, Jones sailed to Ireland and made another attempt to capture the *Drake*. After a fierce gun battle, he succeeded, giving the Continental navy one of its first significant victories. He then returned to France, hoping to replace the *Ranger* with a larger and better ship. But he had to wait many months before France, an important American ally, finally agreed to purchase an old ship for Jones in February 1779. He outfitted it with forty-two guns and renamed it the *Bonhomme Richard* to honor Franklin, whose book, *Poor Richard's Almanac* was known in France as *Les Maximes du Bonhomme Richard.*

Knowing that the *Bonhomme Richard* was not fast enough to do battle with British naval vessels, Jones set out to inflict more damage along the British coast. In September 1779, he reached the port of Leith, near the Scottish capital of Edinburgh. He planned to raid the city and then give the British an ultimatum: either they release their American prisoners or he would burn the city to the ground. He would give the city officials only one hour to accept his conditions.

Jones's plan failed, however, because of a heavy storm that hit Leith just as Jones began to send his landing parties ashore. The wind and rain were so heavy that the men could not land. Jones was forced to withdraw. He then turned south, where he would fight the most famous battle of his career.

Off Flamborough Head, in the North Sea near the Yorkshire coast, the *Bonhomme Richard* and its four companion vessels encountered the HMS *Serapis*, a fifty-gun frigate, and its smaller escort vessel, the *Countess of Scarborough*. A major battle began. The *Serapis* fired on the *Bonhomme Richard*, causing extensive damage. Jones realized he did not stand a chance against the British ship's superior cannons, so he ordered the *Bonhomme Richard* to get as close as possible to the *Serapis*. With cannon-balls slamming into its sides, causing extensive casualties, the *Bonhomme*

During a battle with the Serapis *in 1779, John Paul Jones allegedly responded to the enemy commander's call for surrender by shouting "I have not yet begun to fight!"* AMERICAN SCHOOL/PRIVATE COLLECTION/PETER NEWARK AMERICAN PICTURES/THE BRIDGEMAN ART LIBRARY.

Richard managed to touch the British ship. Then a sail from the *Serapis* fell onto the *Bonhomme Richard*'s deck, creating a bridge between the vessels. Jones ordered his men to fasten the two vessels together with grappling hooks. Then the battle continued with hand weapons. By this time both ships were on fire, and the *Bonhomme Richard* was close to sinking. But when the commander of the *Serapis* asked Jones if he was ready to surrender, the American captain allegedly replied, "I have not yet begun to fight!" Historians believe that these were probably not his actual words, but they have gone down in history as Jones's most famous quote.

The *Bonhomme Richard* did sink, but the Americans won the battle and forced the captain of the *Serapis* to surrender. Jones returned to France, where admirers of the American revolution hailed him as a hero. The French king honored Jones with the title of chevalier, or knight, and from then on Jones asked that this title be used when he was addressed. (A knight is a man granted a rank of honor by the monarch for his personal merit or service to the country.) The Continental Congress also honored Jones with a gold medal in recognition of his bravery and services to the American revolution.

Later life and legacy

In 1782 the Continental navy promised Jones command of another warship, but the position went to someone else. When the war between the American colonies and Britain ended in 1783, Jones did not receive another assignment from the Continental navy. The country was now at peace, and over the next two years the Continental navy was disbanded. In 1788 Jones agreed to command a naval force in service to the Empress Catherine II of Russia (1729–1796), and fought successfully for Russia against Ottoman-Turkish forces in the Black Sea. He returned to France in May 1790. He never married, although he had reportedly enjoyed many romances with women throughout his life. He lived quietly in Paris until his sudden death from a massive brain tumor in 1792.

Jones was honored not only for military successes, but also for his efforts in establishing a permanent American navy at the end of the Revolution. After disbanding the Continental navy, the United States struggled to find the resources to create a new maritime service. Jones fervently supported such a service, writing in a 1778 document quoted by Evan Thomas in *Jones: Sailor, Hero, Father of the American Navy*, "Our marine will rise as if by enchantment, and become, within the memory of persons now living, the wonder and envy of the world." Largely because of Jones's arguments, the new U.S. government passed the Naval Act of 1794, which authorized funding for a permanent navy.

In 1906 Jones's body was removed from France, where it had been unceremoniously buried, and taken to the United States. It was placed at the U.S. Naval Academy's Bancroft Hall, in Annapolis, Maryland, while a permanent tomb was constructed in the Academy's chapel. In 1913 Jones's remains were placed in a bronze and marble sarcophagus in the U.S. Naval Academy Chapel. On the marble floor in front of the sarcophagus are the words: "He Gave to Our Navy Its Earliest Traditions of Heroism and Victory."

For More Information

BOOKS

Thomas, Evan. *John Paul Jones: Sailor, Hero, Father of the American Navy.* New York: Simon and Schuster, 2004, pp. 4, 6.

WEB SITES

"Biographies in Naval History: Captain John Paul Jones." *Naval History & Heritage Command.* www.history.navy.mil/bios/jones_jp.htm (accessed on January 3, 2011).

John Paul Jones Cottage Museum. www.jpj.demon.co.uk (accessed on January 3, 2011).

"John Paul Jones." *U.S. Naval Academy.* www.usna.edu/PAO/facts/faqjpj.htm (accessed on January 3, 2011).

William Kidd

BORN: c. 1645 • Scotland

DIED: May 23, 1701 • London, England

Scottish pirate

William Kidd. PRIVATE COLLECTION/PETER NEWARK HISTORICAL PICTURES/THE BRIDGEMAN ART LIBRARY INTERNATIONAL.

"Because I would not turn Pirate, you Rogues, you would make me one."

Few pirates were more unfortunate than William Kidd. After a respectable early career as a privateer in the Caribbean, where he raided French ships on behalf of the English colonial government, he was hired to hunt pirates in the Indian Ocean. He had little success until he finally captured and plundered (robbed of goods by force) a trade vessel, the *Quedah Merchant,* thinking it was flying an enemy flag. It was not; the ship claimed English affiliation. But the damage had already been done, and Kidd was found guilty of piracy. He was hanged in London, and his decomposing body remained on display as a warning to other pirates. To the end, he protested that he was innocent.

One of the chief reasons for William Kidd's enduring fame is that he once buried his stolen treasure to keep it safe from other thieves, and near the end of his life, he suggested that other buried treasure remained undiscovered. The idea that pirates hid their plunder this way captured people's imaginations and became a common theme in pirate stories and legends. Even though there is no evidence that other pirates stashed their loot in secret places, as Kidd once did, people still like to imagine finding chests of gold and jewels hidden hundreds of years ago by a daring sea robber.

Becomes a privateer

William Kidd was born into a poor family in Scotland around 1645. His father, who was a seaman, died when Kidd was young, and the family had to rely on charity to survive. Kidd left home at an early age to become a sailor.

By 1689, at about age thirty, Kidd was a privateer in the Caribbean Sea. (A privateer is a private ship or ship owner commissioned by a state or government to attack the merchant ships of an enemy nation.) Like pirates, privateers plundered ships and seized their treasure. But while piracy was a crime, privateering was legal. Privateers were required to turn over a percentage of their plunder to the government, but they were allowed to keep the rest, which was divided among the crew. They did not receive a salary, so they were motivated to capture as much treasure as they could in order to make a good living.

In the mid–1600s, pirates and privateers from around the world were attracted to the Caribbean, because its waters were filled with merchant ships that carried gold, silver, and other treasures from the Americas to Europe. Spain and Portugal had dominated this trade since 1494, but since the early 1600s, rival countries had also established a presence in the region. When Kidd arrived in the Caribbean, he joined the crew of a French privateering ship based in Petit Goâve. This port was situated in the French colony on Hispaniola (present-day Haiti and the Dominican Republic).

With the French privateers, Kidd took part in an attack on the English colony of Saint Kitts. But because England and France were at war, Kidd's position aboard a French ship caused tensions among the crew. With seven other English sailors, Kidd led a mutiny (an open rebellion against the ship's officers) and took control of the French vessel. He sailed it to Nevis, another English possession, where the governor

Treasure Island

The novel *Treasure Island*, written by Robert Louis Stevenson (1850–1894) and published in 1883, is one of the most influential pirate stories in Western literature. As the title suggests, a major element of the plot is the search for pirates' buried treasure on a remote tropical island, and it is widely believed that an important inspiration for the novel was the story of William Kidd. In fact, one of the book's pirate characters refers to "Capt. Kidd's Anchorage" on a hand-drawn map of Treasure Island. The novel also mentions several other real-life pirates, including **Bartholomew Roberts** (1682–1722; see entry).

The story of *Treasure Island* has been adapted for the theater, film, and television. They include a Muppet version, an animated version set in outer space, a French German television adaptation, and a Japanese animated television series. There is also a computer game based on the story.

rewarded him by giving him command of the stolen ship. The vessel was renamed the *Blessed William* in honor of England's King William III (1650–1702).

Abandoned by his crew

As captain of the *Blessed William*, Kidd received a privateering license to attack French ships and property. He sacked (captured and plundered) the settlement on the French island of Mariegalante, which yielded a comfortable profit. After that, however, Kidd focused on assisting the English Royal Navy in its assaults on French battleships. But these attacks did not bring much profit, and the crew of the *Blessed William* grew frustrated. In February 1690, they mutinied. Kidd had gone ashore on the island of Antigua, and Robert Culliford, who had helped him seize the *Blessed William* from the French, took this opportunity to sail away with the ship and its crew, as well as the plunder from Mariegalante. Kidd was left stranded on the beach.

Charms the residents of New York

With the help of the English colonial governor, Kidd eventually obtained another ship, which he named the *Antigua*. Hearing that Culliford had headed toward the English colony of New York, Kidd set out to pursue him. New York was in the midst of political turmoil at this time. The acting governor, Jacob Leisler (1640–1691), was highly unpopular. He had given refuge to many pirates and refused to step down when the king's newly appointed governor arrived to replace him. England had sent troops to New York to force Leisler to resign, and Kidd provided assistance to the English by carrying guns and ammunition for them. For his loyalty to England, Kidd received a monetary reward and was hailed as a hero.

Kidd soon became an admired member of New York society. In 1691 he met the beautiful young Sarah Bradley Cox Oort, wife of business leader John Oort. A few months later Oort suddenly died, and within only a few days, Kidd and Sarah got married. People found these circumstances very suspicious but could not prove that Oort had been murdered. Despite this scandal, the marriage between Kidd and Sarah appears to have been a happy one. The couple had two daughters, Elizabeth and Sarah.

Kidd spent the next few years as captain of a merchant vessel trading between New York and the Caribbean. He also served as a privateer for the colonies of New York and Massachusetts. But these activities were not especially profitable. In 1695 he sailed to London, England, in hopes of obtaining a position as a ship commander for the Royal Navy. But the English government refused, insisting that he accept a privateering commission instead. This was not what Kidd had wanted. A naval command would have given him an excellent ship, a regular salary, and a highly trained and disciplined crew. As a privateer, however, he would have to find his own vessel and the money to outfit it, and recruit his own sailors. With some reluctance, he set out to do this.

Sets out on a privateer mission for England

Through his friend, New York official Robert Livingston (1654–1728), Kidd met Richard Coote (Earl of Bellamont; 1636–1701), who had recently been named governor of Massachusetts, New Hampshire, and New York. One of Coote's chief missions was to stamp out piracy and smuggling (illegally importing and exporting goods), and he agreed to hire Kidd to help him. Coote convinced four prominent English officials, including the treasurer of the navy, to invest in the project. They purchased a thirty-four gun vessel, the *Adventure Galley*, and in December 1695 obtained the legal paperwork allowing Kidd to sail as a privateer. They drew up a contract that specified how Kidd's plunder would be shared among them. It also stated that, if the venture failed, Kidd and Livingston had to repay all the costs to the investors. In January the king of England gave Kidd an additional authorization to hunt pirates. This commission explicitly stated that Kidd was forbidden to assault any ships or crew belonging to England or its allies.

As Kidd left England in February 1696, his crew failed to obey the custom of saluting a passing naval ship. When the naval vessel fired a shot to remind the privateers of this ritual, Kidd's sailors mocked the navy by climbing up the rigging, dropping their trousers, and showing their buttocks. In response to this insult, the naval commander stormed aboard the *Adventure Galley* and seized many of its crew, forcing them into service in the navy, which was a legal practice at the time. The few replacements that Kidd was able to find were mostly pirates or other criminals.

Kidd returned to New York, hoping to sign up more experienced and dependable sailors. But he was unsuccessful. He was forced to hire what the governor of the colony, quoted by Angus Konstam in *Piracy: The Complete History*, described as "men of desperate fortunes." The governor added the ominous prediction that "twill not be in Kidd's power to govern such a horde of men under no pay."

Required to complete his voyage within one year, Kidd set out across the Atlantic Ocean on September 6, 1696. He planned to sail around Africa and into the Indian Ocean, where both trade and piracy thrived. Kidd reached Madagascar, a large island off the coast of East Africa, in early 1697. Madagascar was known as a haven for pirates, but Kidd found no ships to raid. (A pirate haven is a safe place for pirates to harbor and repair their ships, resupply, and organize raiding parties.) To make matters worse, many of his crew became ill with cholera, a devastating intestinal infection. Some fifty sailors, about one-third of the crew, died. The surviving men became angry and frustrated. They had been aboard the *Adventure Galley* for many long months and had found no treasure.

Time was growing short, and the *Adventure Galley*'s crew was growing increasingly angry. When Kidd found a small Arab merchant ship, he seized its cargo; later, he battled with two Portuguese warships. But these encounters did not provide much plunder. Kidd's crew began complaining about the way Kidd was handling affairs. In October the *Adventure Galley* came upon a Dutch ship carrying a fortune in trade goods. The crew demanded that Kidd order an attack, but he refused. England and the Netherlands were allies, he said, and such an assault would be an act of piracy. The men began talking among themselves about mutiny. Overhearing his gunner, William Moore, complaining about letting the Dutch ship go, Kidd flew into a rage and threw an iron-rimmed bucket at the gunner, hitting him in the head. Moore's skull was fractured, and he died the next day.

Captures the *Quedah Merchant*

By now Kidd was growing desperate. He was six months overdue to return to his investors in London, and he had nothing to bring them. Finally spying a trading vessel on January 30, 1698, Kidd thought his luck had changed. It was the *Quedah Merchant*, on its voyage home to India after trading in Southeast Asia. When Kidd boarded the ship, its English captain produced French documents, so Kidd believed he had the right to raid the ship. He confiscated its rich cargo of silk, cotton, sugar, opium, and iron and sailed the *Quedah Merchant* to the nearest port. He sold most of the cargo for a huge sum, using the profits to pay his men. He kept the remaining plunder for himself.

Kidd had made a major mistake. An important Indian official owned much of the *Quedah Merchant*'s cargo, and he was furious that Kidd had stolen his merchandise. India's emperor brought a complaint to the English government, saying that if such piracy were not stopped, India would cease trade with England. Since this trade was a major part of England's economy, the English government quickly responded. It issued an arrest warrant for Kidd. It also specifically excluded Kidd from a general pardon issued that year for pirates who agreed to cease their illegal activities.

Buried treasure

Meanwhile, Kidd had sailed back to Madagascar to prepare for the homeward journey. There he found Culliford, the man who had stolen the *Blessed William* from him years earlier. Although Kidd had been hired to capture pirates, he made no effort to take Culliford into custody. The two men even had a friendly drink together. During this stop, many of Kidd's crew decided to leave the *Adventure Galley* and join Culliford.

By now the *Adventure Galley* had become badly rotted. Kidd decided to abandon it and headed home in the *Quedah Merchant*. But when he reached the Caribbean, he discovered that no colonial governor there would protect him. He left the *Quedah Merchant* in the Caribbean with some of his men and, with his treasure, took another ship to New York. There, he hoped to be able to straighten things out with Governor Coote. Before docking in New York harbor, he stopped at Gardiners Island, near the city, and buried his plunder. He arrived in New York on July 1, 1699, and after a brief visit with his family, he was arrested and put in jail.

Kidd wrote to Coote, explaining what had happened and revealing the hiding place on Gardiners Island. The governor was able to recover most of the buried treasure. But Kidd's actions had placed Coote in a difficult position. By investing in Kidd's voyage, it looked as though the governor was supporting piracy. And piracy was the very thing that he had been ordered to stop. He refused to help Kidd, who was sent to London to stand trial.

Trial and execution

Kidd remained in prison for almost a year before his first court appearance. There, he was surprised to learn that he had been charged with murder in the death of William Moore, the gunner from the *Adventure Galley*. Kidd

William Kidd burying his treasure on Gardiners Island.
© NORTH WIND PICTURE ARCHIVES/ALAMY.

defended himself by arguing that Moore had been planning mutiny. Nevertheless, the court found Kidd guilty.

The trial on piracy charges also went badly for the seafarer. He insisted that the captain of the *Quedah Merchant* had produced French papers, which identified the ship as a legitimate target for an English privateer. But Kidd could not produce these papers. He had given them to Coote, who had since died, and they could not be found. Without them to prove his case, Kidd was doomed. He was found guilty and sentenced to death.

On May 23, 1701, Kidd was taken to the gallows at Execution Dock in London, along the Thames River. He had sent a desperate message to an English legislator, saying that he had hidden a huge fortune somewhere and would reveal its location if his life were spared. But this plea was ignored. As the noose was placed around his neck, Kidd was so drunk he could hardly stand. When the support under his feet was taken away, the rope snapped and Kidd plunged, still alive, into the mud below. On the second try, however, the executioner succeeded. Kidd was hanged until he was dead. Then his body was coated with tar and hung from an iron cage. It remained there until only bones were left, as a gruesome message about the fate that awaited anyone found guilty of piracy.

Whether Kidd had really acted as a pirate, or only as a privateer, is a question that continues to be debated. The fact that the French papers, which had gone missing during Kidd's trial, were found years later suggests that the government withheld information that would have led to an acquittal. But others point to evidence that Kidd was willing to bend, or even break, the law to seize plunder. Even if he was truly a pirate, however, he was hardly among the cruelest. As Harold Thompson, quoted on the *Captain William Kidd* Web site, states, Kidd can probably be best described as "a man neither very good nor very bad, the fool of fortune and the tool of politicians, a pirate in spite of himself."

For More Information

BOOKS

Burgess, Douglas R., Jr. *The Pirates' Pact: The Secret Alliances between History's Most Notorious Buccaneers and Colonial America.* New York: McGraw-Hill, 2009.

Konstam, Angus. *Piracy: The Complete History.* Oxford, England: Osprey, 2008, p 260.

Stevenson, Robert Louis. *Treasure Island.* New York: Oxford University Press, 2007.

Zacks, Richard. *The Pirate Hunter: The True Story of Captain Kidd.* New York: Hyperion, 2003.

WEB SITES

Captain William Kidd. www.captainkidd.org (accessed on January 3, 2011).

Kuo Hsing Yeh

BORN: 1624 • Japan

DIED: 1662 • China

Chinese pirate

"Oh the Great river, dressed in mourning white, / swear to vanquish the Tartars; / The anger of my hundred thousand brave men / Shakes the land of Wu. / Wait and look! When resolutely we cross the Formidable Moat, / Who will still believe that China does not belong to the Ming?"

One of the most important military leaders in seventeenth-century China was the pirate Kuo Hsing Yeh, also known as Koxinga (also spelled Coxinga) and Zheng Chenggong. Commander of a huge fleet of merchant and pirate vessels, Kuo operated along the Chinese coast and surrounding waters. He controlled trade in this area and was the first Chinese pirate to raid the Dutch vessels that dominated shipping in this region.

Kuo used his wealth and power to aid the cause of the Ming emperor, whose rule was threatened by a violent rebellion. For twenty years the pirate fought to gain territory and support for the Ming dynasty. (A dynasty is a succession of rulers from the same family line.) Although the Ming dynasty was eventually defeated, Kuo succeeded in driving the Dutch out of the trade colony that they had established on the island

A statue of Kuo Hsing Yeh, also known as Koxinga, at a shrine in Taiwan.
© TIBOR BOGNAR/ALAMY.

of Formosa (present-day Taiwan). His achievements made him a hero to the Chinese people.

Early life

Kuo Hsing Yeh inherited his role as a pirate. Born in 1624, Kuo was the son of a Japanese mother, Tagawa Matsu, and a Chinese father, Ching-Chi-Ling (also written as Cheng Chih Lung or Zheng Zhilong; d. 1661). Ching-Chi-Ling was a powerful merchant and pirate from Fukien province, on the southern coast of China near the island of Formosa. He often did business in Japan, and it is widely believed that Kuo was born there in Nagasaki, where his mother's family lived.

Ching-Chi-Ling owned a huge fleet of merchant and pirate ships. His pirate ships sailed along the coast trading and plundering (robbing of goods by force) under his command. They raided vessels carrying valuable cargoes of silk, sandalwood, and spices and threatened townspeople and farmers with violence unless they paid for protection. China's central government at this time was not very strong, and the pirates generally operated without interference from officials. The local people feared these pirates and paid what Ching-Chi-Ling demanded in order to be spared from attacks.

Kuo remained with his mother in Japan until age seven, when he was sent to Fukien province, China, to be educated. The boy was intelligent and studious, completing school at age fifteen and then attending the Imperial Academy of Learning in Nanjing. But political troubles, and his father's role in them, would turn Kuo away from an academic career. Instead of becoming a scholar, he would take over his father's business.

The Manchu revolt

By the early 1640s, when Kuo was still in his teens, China faced a political crisis. The people had become increasingly frustrated with the government of the Ming dynasty, which had ruled China since 1368. The Manchus, a people native to Manchuria (a vast region in northeast China), organized a revolt. To help suppress this uprising, Emperor Chongzhen (1611–1644) appointed Ching-Chi-Ling as his official admiral of coastal waters, one of the highest positions in the emperor's administration. Ching-Chi-Ling received a royal salary to protect China's coastline, a job that also required him to suppress piracy.

In 1644 the Manchus captured China's capital, Beijing, and Emperor Chongzhen committed suicide. The Manchus then seized power, establishing the Qing dynasty. But supporters of the Ming dynasty continued to fight. For several years, Ching-Chi-Ling and his family remained loyal to the Ming dynasty, and Fukien province remained in Ming control. Grateful for this support, the Ming crown prince symbolically adopted Kuo, giving him the title Koxinga, which means "lord of the imperial surname." Kuo took this honor very seriously.

But in 1646 the Manchus captured and executed the crown prince. Ching-Chi-Ling faced intense pressure to shift his loyalty to the Manchus, and in 1649 he switched sides. Kuo strongly protested this decision by his father and swore that he would remain loyal to the Ming dynasty. By this time Kuo had taken over his father's business. With an enormous fleet of merchant and pirate junks, he waged war on the Manchus. (Junks are a Chinese form of sailboat.)

Kuo funded this war through piracy. As his father had done, he offered to protect merchants along the coast for a price, threatening anyone who refused. He also attacked merchant vessels belonging to the Dutch, who had established a trade colony on Formosa in 1624. At the height of his power, Kuo commanded three thousand junks and more than one hundred thousand men. He controlled nearly all of China's coastline from the Korean peninsula to Vietnam, an area that totaled about 9,010 miles (14,500 kilometers).

The Manchus had a strong army but a very weak navy and could not defeat Kuo in sea battles. Kuo was able to capture several Manchu cities along the coast. According to one story, the pirate warrior conquered the city of Zhangzou, but learned afterward that his mother had perished inside the city during the siege. (A siege is a military blockade that isolates a city while an attack is underway.) This made him responsible for her death. He atoned for this deed by going to the temple and burning his old clothes. But he would continue to fight against the Manchu. Kuo said, as quoted by Angus Konstam in *Piracy: The Complete History*, "In the past I was a good Confucian subject and a good son. Now I'm an orphan without an Emperor—I have no country and no home. I have sworn to fight the Manchu army to the end, but my father has surrendered and my only choice is to be a disloyal son. Please forgive me."

Chinese Junks

Many European sailors dismissed junks as primitive and inferior ships, but they were actually very well adapted to conditions along the coasts of China and Southeast Asia. The first junks were built during the Song dynasty (960–1270). Smaller vessels navigated rivers and ports, but during the Yuan dynasty (1271–1368) the Mongol emperors ordered a large treasure fleet to be built. These larger junks sailed as far as India and Indonesia to trade in spices, silk, gold, timber, and other precious materials.

The largest junks were more than 100 feet (31 meters) long and, unlike European vessels, did not have a keel, a strong beam that extends along the entire length of the bottom of a ship and supports its frame. Junks had three masts that supported four to six sails, some of which reached about 459 feet (140 meters) in length. The Italian explorer Marco Polo (1254–1324), who traveled to China in the late 1200s, described trading junks that contained sixty individual cabins for merchants and carried crews of up to three hundred men.

Junks were originally designed as trading ships, but they could easily be adapted for fighting. They could carry several cannons and hold ample supplies of gunpowder and ammunition. Below decks, junks were divided into many small compartments. Useful for organizing cargo, this design was also helpful for pirates, because it protected the junk from flooding if a section of the boat was damaged by enemy fire. Pirates also exploited junks' maneuverability and speed.

A major difference between Western pirate ships and junks was that the families of Chinese pirates lived with them aboard junks. Many Chinese families lived on river boats; it was normal for wives, children, and grandparents to work, eat, play, and sleep on the family's junk. It was no different for pirates. If a woman married a man who was part of a pirate fleet, she went to live

In 1656 the Manchus announced that any Chinese subject who traded with Kuo would be put to death. When this harsh policy failed to put Kuo out of business, the Manchus ordered China's coastal areas to be evacuated. Anyone living along the coast had to move 10 miles (16 kilometers) inland. This, the Manchus hoped, would deprive Kuo of his source of income. But this measure failed to wipe out piracy, because the sea raiders were able to operate in the rivers along which people continued to live.

Although he possessed a formidable fleet and thousands of soldiers, Kuo had little success against the Manchus on land. His navy was more powerful than theirs, but they had the advantage of a far superior army. In 1659, however, he decided to attack the Manchu capital, Nanjing, about 174 miles (280 kilometers) up the Yangtze River. It was Kuo's first major military failure. The Manchus trapped Kuo's fleet in the river and destroyed it. Kuo, however, escaped.

with him on his junk. Not only did wives cook, sew, and give birth aboard junks, but a few also helped in the fighting. In fact, one of China's most famous pirates was a woman, **Cheng I Sao** (1775–1844; see entry). For them, living and fighting at sea was a normal way of life.

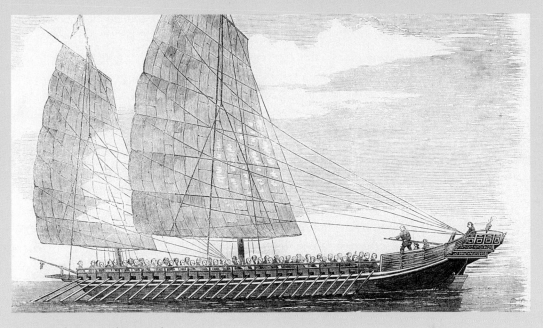

A nineteenth-century Chinese junk. © CORBIS.

Driving out the Dutch

In 1655 Kuo had sent a formal letter to the colonial governor of Formosa. It states that the Spanish who controlled trade in the Philippines, to the south, had mistreated his sailors and that, for this reason, all Chinese were forbidden to trade with the Philippines under penalty of death. The letter, as quoted in *How Taiwan Became Chinese: Dutch, Spanish, and Han Colonization in the Seventeenth Century* by Tonio Andrade, also states that the Dutch colonists "behave more like animals than Christians," and that they, too, would be punished if they continued to trade with the Philippines. When the Dutch governor refused to publish the letter, Kuo accused the Dutch of attacking some of his junks and stealing their cargo.

As tensions escalated, Kuo took a bold step. He decided to move his base of operations away from the mainland coast to Formosa. This would give him several important advantages. It would protect him and his fleet from the Manchus, who lacked the sea power necessary to reach him on Formosa. And by invading Formosa, where the Dutch were based, Kuo could expel his major business rivals, the Dutch traders, from the island. With four hundred pirate junks and a force of twenty-five thousand men, he launched his invasion, landing near the Dutch settlement of Oranjestad in April 1661.

Kuo placed the city under siege, while his forces attacked Fort Zeelandia. The Dutch had built this fortress to protect Oranjestad. For nine months, as Kuo's fleet waited in the harbor, no supplies could reach the city or the fort. Weakened by thirst and hunger, the Dutch finally surrendered on February 1, 1662. Kuo took control of the island, claiming it as Ming territory. This made Kuo the first Chinese to defeat a Western military power.

The pirate had achieved an amazing feat. He now had a strong military base. From Formosa he could continue his assaults against the Manchus on the mainland. His victory also showed Europe that its trade colonies in Asia were vulnerable unless the colonists cooperated with China's rulers. Without competition from Dutch merchants, Kuo also controlled a vast trade empire that could further increase his wealth. But Kuo did not live long enough to appreciate this success. He contracted malaria and died only a few months after the Dutch surrendered Formosa. He was thirty-seven years old.

Kuo's pirate empire passed to his oldest son, Zheng Jing (1642–1681). But Zheng Jing was not able to keep his father's imposing fleet together. It collapsed shortly after Kuo's death, splitting into smaller factions controlled by various pirate chiefs. Without a strong unified fleet to protect the island, Formosa eventually fell to the Manchus in 1683.

Heroic legacy

Kuo became a hero to the people of Formosa and to the people of mainland China. In some parts of China and Southeast Asia he was worshipped as a god, and several temples dedicated to Kuo were erected on Formosa. A shrine that Zheng Jing built to honor his father in 1663 still stands in the modern city of Tainan, Taiwan. Many legends have been told about the pirate hero. According to one myth, a mysterious fire appeared in the sky at his birth, which took place on an ocean beach during a storm. Kuo is also said to have performed several magical feats during his lifetime, including: changing a gigantic sea turtle into an island, making water appear by thrusting his sword into the sand, and conquering evil spirits.

In modern Asia Kuo is generally admired. In Taiwan and in the People's Republic of China he is considered a national hero for expelling the Dutch imperialists and establishing Chinese rule over Taiwan. The Japanese also honor him for his achievements and for his ethnic ties to Japan on his mother's side. The Chinese Nationalist Party, which opposed the Chinese Communist Party and established a government in Taiwan in 1912, revered Kuo for his opposition to the Qing dynasty on mainland China.

Kuo's story has inspired literary works and films. In 1715 the Japanese dramatist Chikamatsu (1653–1725) wrote a puppet play, *The Battles of Coxinga*, based on Kuo's exploits. It became Chikamatsu's most popular play. A movie about Kuo's life, *Zheng Chenggong*, was released in 2001, and National Geographic began shooting a documentary about the pirate hero's achievements in 2010. Kuo even appears as a character in the video game *Romance of the Three Kingdoms XI*.

For More Information

BOOKS

Andrad, Tony. *How Taiwan Became Chinese: Dutch, Spanish, and Han Colonization in the Seventeenth Century.* New York: Columbia University Press, 2008.

Konstam, Angus. *The History of Pirates.* Guilford, CT: Lyons Press, 2002.

———. *Piracy: The Complete History.* Oxford, England: Osprey, 2008, p. 294.

WEB SITES

Hadingham, Evan, "Ancient Chinese Explorers." *NOVA: Sultan's Lost Treasures.* www.pbs.org/wgbh/nova/sultan/explorers.html (accessed on January 3, 2011).

Jean Lafitte

BORN: c. 1776

DIED: c. 1823

French smuggler, pirate, spy

"I am the stray sheep wishing to return to the shepherd."

Jean Lafitte was an adventurer and entrepreneur whose thriving smuggling (illegally importing and exporting goods) business contributed to the economic development of New Orleans, Louisiana, in the early 1800s. He led a band of one thousand men who seized cargos from Spanish ships in the Gulf of Mexico and sold this contraband in New Orleans. Because he defied U.S. laws, he was denounced by the government as a pirate. But his reputation was rehabilitated when he helped to defend New Orleans against British attack in the War of 1812 (1812–15). Pardoned for his crimes as a reward for this service, Lafitte established a new smuggling base in Galveston, Texas. Forced out of Galveston in 1821, Lafitte disappeared. His exploits have inspired many stories and legends in southern Louisiana, where he has attained the status of a folk hero.

Jean Lafitte. PRIVATE COLLECTION/PETER NEWARK AMERICAN PICTURES/THE BRIDGEMAN ART LIBRARY INTERNATIONAL.

Early life

Jean Lafitte was born around 1776, most likely in France or in Haiti. But some sources say he came from Spain or from elsewhere in the Americas.

Jean Lafitte's blacksmith shop, where he sold smuggled goods.
© AKG-IMAGES/THE IMAGE WORKS.

Little is known about his origins or upbringing, but the fact that he was well-mannered, literate, and reportedly fluent in English, French, Italian, and Spanish suggests that he received a good education.

According to some stories, Lafitte claimed that he fought in Europe with the army of French general Napoléon Bonaparte (1769–1821). Others said that he was an aristocrat who had been forced to flee the French Revolution (1789–99; a revolution in France in which the monarchy was overthrown and a republic established) after his parents were executed. But Lafitte also reportedly claimed that he was a refugee from Spanish rule in the Caribbean Sea.

Sets up a smuggling ring

By the early 1800s, Lafitte and his brother, Pierre, were operating a huge smuggling ring in southern Louisiana. They disguised their business as a blacksmith shop that they opened around 1803 on the Rue de St. Phillippe in New Orleans. Residents of the region were eager to buy the Lafittes' goods, because necessities were often in scarce supply, and taxes and other regulations made trade complicated and expensive. By seizing goods from ships in the Caribbean, however, the Lafittes could promise their customers plenty of desirable merchandise, such as cloth, tools, spices, and dishes, at discount prices.

This profitable business benefited further when, in 1807, the United States banned trade with Great Britain and France because war had broken out in Europe. Legitimate merchants in New Orleans were soon faced with bare shelves and frustrated customers. The slave trade also suffered. New laws had made it illegal to bring slaves from Africa into Louisiana (and later, into the entire United States). Only American-born slaves could be bought and sold, and they were always in short supply. Seeing this shortage as a business opportunity, the Lafittes added slaves to the list of smuggled goods that they offered.

Establishes a base at Barataria

The region near New Orleans, with its miles of marshes, swamps, and sluggish waterways known as bayous, offered an excellent hiding place for smugglers and pirates. Dense vegetation, twisting riverways, and the presence of quicksand and sudden undertows made navigation treacherous. Anyone venturing into this watery maze ran a serious risk of getting lost or killed. Lafitte knew the area well. He and his men established themselves in an area called Barataria, south of New Orleans near the entrance to the Mississippi River. It consisted of three islands with numerous swamps and bayous and a well-protected deepwater harbor. From Barataria Bay, the outlaws hunted merchant vessels in the Gulf of Mexico. Any ship approaching or leaving New Orleans had to pass close to Barataria, and the outlaws seized goods worth a fortune.

Lafitte set up his headquarters on the island of Grande Terre, about 40 miles (64 kilometers) from New Orleans and created an elaborate transportation route by which his stolen goods could be smuggled into the city. He dug canals and widened existing river channels to make them large enough to accommodate the huge river barges that his men built from cypress trees. Several times each week, Lafitte's men sailed these barges into New Orleans, loaded with stolen merchandise to trade in the city.

Grande Terre became an outlaw haven, where renegades from many different countries found refuge. By 1812 Lafitte was in command of some fifty sailing ships and about one thousand followers, some of whom were runaway slaves or free black men. Many brought their wives or mistresses to live at Grande Terre. The settlement also had a fine restaurant, a gambling casino, and a brothel. The Baratarians enjoyed a high degree of freedom. They flew the flag of Columbia and did not consider themselves bound by the laws of the United States. Lafitte did, however, insist on a few basic rules. Any man who mistreated a woman was expelled from the island. The punishment for theft was a whipping, and the penalty for killing another Baratarian was death by hanging. Like many pirate captains, Lafitte also organized compensation for men who were disabled in action and provided benefits for the families of smugglers who were killed.

Lafitte's business provided a significant boost to the economy of New Orleans. Store owners flocked to the blacksmith shop to place orders for smuggled merchandise, which they then sold in their own stores. Lafitte held slave auctions at Barataria and also invited the general public to Grande Terre to browse his merchandise and make purchases. Even the most respectable citizens bought smuggled goods from Lafitte.

Indeed, Lafitte was often seen at parties and balls in New Orleans. He was an excellent dancer, and women considered him handsome and charming. He reportedly had several mistresses in the city and possibly one or more children out of wedlock.

Denounced as a pirate

What Lafitte did for a living, according to the U.S. government, was piracy. But Lafitte made it clear that he did not consider himself a criminal. He insisted that he was a lawful privateer. (A privateer is a private ship or ship owner commissioned by a state or government to attack the merchant ships of an enemy nation.) Lafitte, in fact, held a privateering license from the Colombian city of Cartagena, which had rebelled against Spain and authorized Lafitte to seize Spanish ships and cargoes. The United States, however, did not consider Lafitte's license valid, because it did not recognize Cartagena's status as a country. Furthermore, the United States suspected that Lafitte did not bother to obey the rules forbidding privateers from attacking friendly or neutral ships. The United States believed that Lafitte preyed on whatever ships he found and insisted that he was a pirate.

Lafitte evaded arrest several times, easily escaping into Barataria's labyrinth of swamps when government troops were sent in to hunt him. But in 1812, he and his brother, as well as several of their men, were captured by authorities and put in jail. After their bail was posted, however, the Lafittes escaped. Pierre was arrested again in 1814, but escaped from jail a month later.

The War of 1812

By 1814 the political and military situation in Louisiana had changed. War had broken out between the United States and Britain in 1812. This conflict, which became known as the War of 1812, had been provoked by disputes over naval trade restrictions and by the British practice, known as impressment, of forcing captured American sailors into service in the Royal Navy. At first the war had little effect in Louisiana. Most battles were fought far away, along the east coast of the United States or in the Atlantic Ocean. But in 1814, the British made plans to attack New Orleans and asked Lafitte for help.

Although this gave Lafitte the chance to hurt the U.S. government, which had persecuted him as an outlaw, he chose to warn the United States of Britain's plans. He also said that, if the U.S. government promised to pardon him and his men, he would help defend New Orleans from the British. "This point of Louisiana, which I occupy," he wrote to the governor of Louisiana in a letter, quoted by Joseph Geringer in the article "Jean Lafitte: Gentleman Pirate of New Orleans," "is of great importance in the present crisis. I tender my services to defend it; the only reward I ask is that a stop be put to the proscription against me and my adherents.... If you were thoroughly acquainted with the nature of my offenses, I should appear to you much less guilty and still worthy to discharge the duties of a good citizen."

In response, the governor sent the warship *Carolina*, three barges with men and ammunition, and six gunboats to Grande Terre. Thinking these forces had come as allies, Lafitte's men ran to the beach to welcome them. But then the troops opened fire. Lafitte was stunned. The invaders seized several of the vessels anchored in the harbor, destroyed the outlaws' settlement, and took a few prisoners, but most of the Baratarians, including Lafitte, escaped.

Instead of turning against the United States after this attack, Lafitte decided to approach General Andrew Jackson (1767–1845), who was in charge of the defense of New Orleans and who would later be elected U.S. president. At first Jackson was reluctant to trust the outlaw. But he needed Lafitte, who could supply men, guns, and ammunition, as well as valuable information about local geography. When the outlaw offered all of these to the general, Jackson gladly accepted.

Lafitte's assistance was central to the U.S. victory at the Battle of New Orleans, which took place a few miles south of the city on January 8, 1815.

Was Lafitte Jewish?

According to historian Edward Kritzler, Jean Lafitte descended from a Jewish family that was persecuted by the Spanish Inquisition (1478–1843; a government-authorized body that enforced obedience to Roman Catholic teachings). In his book *Jewish Pirates of the Caribbean: How a Generation of Swashbuckling Jews Carved out an Empire in the New World in Their Quest for Treasure, Religious Freedom—and Revenge,* Kritzler quotes from a note that Lafitte allegedly stuck in his family bible. The notes reads, "I owe all my ingenuity to … my Jewish-Spanish grandmother, who was a witness at the time of the Inquisition." Kritzler also quotes from a journal thought to be written by Lafitte, in which the pirate describes his maternal grandmother as a "Spanish-Israelite" and his maternal grandfather as an alchemist and "freethinking Jew" who starved to death in prison because he refused to cooperate with the Inquisition. According to this journal, Lafitte's motive in attacking Spanish ships was to get revenge for the injustices that the Inquisition had perpetrated against his family.

Many historians doubt the journal's authenticity, and some consider it a forgery. It was not discovered until the 1950s, and many scholars point out that its information seems so conveniently organized that it must be the work of a person who lived after Lafitte. The journal is kept at the Sam Houston Library in Huntsville, Texas. Historians continue to examine the journal to try to verify its origins.

Jackson led some four thousand men against more than twice as many invading British troops. In what is considered the most important land victory of the war, the Americans triumphed. The British lost some twenty-six hundred men, while only thirteen of Jackson's men were killed. Jackson became the hero of New Orleans but readily acknowledged the part that Lafitte and his men had played. He wrote to President James Madison (1751–1836), commending the Lafitte brothers for their bravery and loyalty. In a letter to Jean Lafitte, quoted by Geringer, the general promised the outlaw "my private friendship and high esteem," and said that he would press the federal government to drop charges against the pirate and his followers. President Madison acted on Jackson's request, officially pardoning the Lafittes and the Baratarians for any offenses against the United States. Many of the pardoned men then settled in or around New Orleans.

Establishes a smuggling business in Texas

Lafitte, however, grew bored with his law-abiding life in New Orleans. He requested that the government return the goods that it had confiscated from his warehouses at Grande Terre. But the authorities insisted that he had no legal right to merchandise that he had stolen. Neither did the government return the vessels they had seized from Lafitte. He was forced to buy eight of them back when they were put up for public auction.

Resenting this treatment, which he interpreted as disrespect from a nation that he had bravely served in battle, Lafitte left New Orleans in 1817. With Pierre and several of his closest Baratarian associates, he sailed to the Caribbean island of Hispaniola (present-day Haiti and the Dominican Republic). He hoped to get back into the smuggling business there, but the

Spanish government was not sympathetic to these pirates who had raided so many Spanish vessels. Lafitte then led the group to Galveston, which was then an uninhabited island off the coast of Texas. Technically the area was owned by Spain at the time, because Texas was part of Mexico and Mexico belonged to Spain. But revolutionaries in Mexico were struggling for independence, and this political upheaval suited Lafitte's plans. He made a proposal that the Mexicans accepted. He would be allowed to settle at Galveston, and in return he would plunder ships belonging to Spain, Mexico's enemy.

As he had done at Grande Terre, Lafitte established a thriving settlement with a luxurious house for himself and comfortable quarters for his men. He quickly organized a distribution network for his stolen goods, sending contraband, including slaves, to eager customers in Texas towns. One of his slave runners was James Bowie (1796–1846), who went on to become a leader in achieving independence for Texas.

Outlaws flocked to Galveston. Many were smugglers, but others were wanted for more serious crimes, including murder. These men were more difficult to control than the original group of Baratarians, and they provoked trouble with the Mexican and U.S. governments. Another problem was the local Karankawa Indians, who were hostile to the white men and often launched deadly raids on the settlement.

In 1818 a devastating hurricane struck Galveston. Hundreds of Lafitte's followers were killed, and the settlement was destroyed. Most of the outlaws' plunder was washed out to sea. The storm almost put an end to Lafitte's business. But he was able to rebuild.

Later life

In the early 1800s the United States was intent on forging good relations with Spain, its rival power in the Western Hemisphere. Because Lafitte's attacks on Spanish ships presented an obstacle to this goal, President Madison sent a naval officer to Galveston with orders to force Lafitte to leave the island. The outlaw made vague promises to depart, but did not leave. The officer returned in May 1821, bluntly telling Lafitte that if he did not leave immediately, he would be killed. That night, the outlaw burned the settlement to the ground. When the navy searched the island the next morning, they found only ashes. Lafitte and his remaining ships had disappeared.

No one knows what happened to Jean Lafitte next or how his life ended. Some say that he joined the army of Simon Bolívar (1783–1830), who was leading the fight in South America against Spanish rule. Others say he joined a band of pirates in the Caribbean. According to another story, he died of plague in Mexico, at age forty-seven. There are even reports that he married and settled with his wife in Illinois. Those who live in Barataria, however, say that the privateer lies buried in an unmarked grave in a bayou near the village of Lafitte, Louisiana.

In 1966 the state of Louisiana authorized a state park to be established in Barataria, named after Lafitte. In 1978 the state park was made part of a larger, national park, the Jean Lafitte National Historic Park and Preserve.

For More Information

BOOKS

Groom, Winston. *Patriotic Fire: Andrew Jackson and Jean Lafitte at the Battle of New Orleans.* New York: Random House, 2006.

Kritzler, Edward. *Jewish Pirates of the Caribbean: How a Generation of Swashbuckling Jews Carved out an Empire in the New World in Their Quest for Treasure, Religious Freedom—and Revenge.* New York: Random House, 2009, pp. 253–54.

WEB SITES

Geringer, Joseph. "Jean Lafitte: Gentleman Pirate of New Orleans." *truTV.* www.trutv.com/library/crime/gangsters_outlaws/cops_others/lafitte/1.html (accessed on January 3, 2011).

"Jean Lafitte: History and Mystery." *National Park Service.* www.nps.gov/jela/upload/Jean%20Lafitte%20pirate%20site%20bulletin.pdf (accessed on January 3, 2011).

François L'Olonnais

BORN: c. 1635 • Les Sables-d'Olonne, France

DIED: 1668 • Panama

French pirate

> "I shall never give quarter [show mercy] to any Spaniard whatsoever."

François L'Olonnais was known as one of the cruelest pirates in the Caribbean Sea. He treated the region's Spanish and native inhabitants with such savagery that many historians believe he was insane. He conducted many treasure raids against Spanish possessions and was killed while attempting a raid.

Early life

The man known as François L'Olonnais was born around 1635 in the town of Les Sables-d'Olonne, France. His birth name is believed to have been Jean-David Nau, but after he arrived in the Caribbean he was called by his nickname, L'Olonnais, which means "man from d'Olonne."

Few details about L'Olonnais's childhood are known. Because he came from an area with a large Protestant population, historians believe it likely that the family was Protestant, making them an often-persecuted minority in Catholic France. In his teens, probably around 1650, L'Olonnais was sent to the French colony of Martinique in the Caribbean as an indentured servant.

Indentured servitude was a type of business arrangement that enabled poor Europeans to come to the Americas to work. The terms of indenture were often harsh. The employer paid the price of the voyage; when the workers arrived at their destination, they were required to pay back the cost of the journey through their labor, staying with that employer for a specified number of years before they were legally released. Only when the contract was fulfilled was a worker allowed to leave that employer and look for a better position. In many cases indentured servants worked alongside slaves from Africa and were subjected to the same treatment. According to some historians, L'Olonnais may have been abused in some way during his service, causing him to lose his sanity.

Becomes a buccaneer

After three years of indentured servitude, L'Olonnais made his way to the island of Tortuga. The island lies off the northwest coast of Hispaniola (present-day Haiti and the Dominican Republic). By the mid–1600s, groups of French, English, and Dutch pirates had created a major base of operations on Tortuga. From here they could easily ambush Spanish treasure ships loaded with gold, silver, and other precious materials on their way back to Spain.

Spain had completely dominated this valuable trade since 1494, when the Treaty of Tordesillas gave sole control of the Americas to Spain and Portugal. With the treasure it took every year from the gold and silver mines of the Americas, Spain soon became the most wealthy and powerful country in Europe and the Western Hemisphere. Not wishing to share any of this valuable trade with rival countries, Spain had strictly regulated access to its ports in the Caribbean. Nevertheless, by the 1600s other European countries, particularly England, France, and the Netherlands, had begun to challenge Spain's dominance in the region, building colonies of their own or even, in a few cases, conquering Spanish territory.

France's major possessions in the Caribbean in the early 1600s were the island of Martinique, in the eastern Caribbean north of Venezuela, and the islands of Saint Kitts and Nevis, slightly north and west of Martinique. In 1625 French settlers from these colonies established an outpost on Tortuga. Many of them were buccaneers, a group of outcasts such as runaway indentured servants, pirates, and escaped African slaves. They lived mainly by hunting. Although the buccaneers generally shunned society and kept mostly to themselves, Spain could not tolerate their presence so close to Hispaniola, which it considered a Spanish possession. Spain began aggressive efforts to drive the buccaneers and the other settlers out. As a result, the buccaneers developed a hatred for the Spanish. They took to piracy and resolved to get their revenge on Spain. Tortuga became a pirate haven for the buccaneers. (A pirate haven is safe place for pirates to harbor and repair their ships, resupply, and organize raiding parties.)

Tortuga lies near the eastern tip of Cuba, and every year, the Spanish flota (treasure fleet), laden with gold, stopped at Cuba before sailing with its cargo across the Atlantic to Spain. These ships provided good prey for the buccaneers, who often launched sea raids with the permission of the French or English colonial authorities. During the seventeenth century, France and Spain were often at war. France worried that its Caribbean colonies, much smaller and more vulnerable than Spain's, might be invaded by the enemy. It became common practice to hire buccaneers to act as an unofficial navy, protecting the colonies by harassing the Spanish wherever they could be found. Buccaneers received no official pay but were allowed to keep a portion of any treasure they took.

On Tortuga, L'Olonnais joined the buccaneers and began sea raiding. By 1667 L'Olonnais had become the owner and captain of a small, ten-gun ship. The French colonial governor had called for buccaneers to plan attacks on Spain, so L'Olonnais gathered a crew of about twenty men and signed up. In the Mona Passage, which lies between the east coast of Hispaniola and the island of Puerto Rico, they fired on a large Spanish trading vessel, capturing the ship after a long fight. On another occasion, L'Olonnais and his men seized a ship carrying the payroll for Spanish troops in the Americas. L'Olonnais sent his booty back to Tortuga, selling any merchandise at a hefty profit and refitting the Spanish ships for his own use. (Booty is the goods stolen from ships or coastal villages during pirate raids or attacks on enemies in time of war.)

"The Flail of the Spaniards"

During his early years of buccaneering, L'Olonnais raided the town of Campeche, on the southern coast of Mexico near the Yucatán Peninsula. According to one account, some of his crew had been shipwrecked on the voyage from Tortuga, leaving the buccaneers without enough men to carry out an attack on the town. But L'Olonnais attacked anyway. The fight was fierce, and the buccaneers lost the battle. L'Olonnais barely escaped; he pretended to be dead, lying among the bloody corpses of his crew all day. When night finally fell, he and a handful of other survivors were able to sneak away in a couple of small wooden boats that they found. According to another account, however, there was no battle at Campeche. L'Olonnais was shipwrecked near the town in 1666 or 1667 with a small band of followers but was chased by Spanish soldiers until he finally made his escape.

Soon after his failure at Campeche, L'Olonnais sailed near Cay Largo, off the southern coast of Cuba. A patrol boat lay in the harbor, sent by the Spanish colonial authorities to protect local fishermen who had complained about pirates in the area. On the patrol boat was an executioner, with instructions to hang any pirates that were captured. During the night, the buccaneers boarded the Spanish vessel, slaughtered the soldiers onboard, and sent the single survivor back to shore with a message for Cuba's governor. The letter, quoted by Angus Konstam in *Piracy: The Complete History*, states: "I shall never henceforward give quarter [show mercy] to any Spaniard whatsoever; and I have great hopes I shall execute on your own person the very same punishment I have done upon them you sent against me. Thus I have retaliated the kindness you designed to me and my companions."

By the end of 1667 L'Olonnais had increased his force to eight ships and several hundred men. He was able to launch major attacks, and these were known to be so gruesome that the mere mention of his name created terror. Throughout the region he became known as the "flail of the Spaniards." Like many other pirates, L'Olonnais tortured his captives to force them to reveal the hiding places of their treasure. Such violence was not unusual at the time, but L'Olonnais's behavior was particularly cruel. According to an account quoted by Konstam, "it was the custom of L'Olonnais that, having tormented any persons and they not confessing, he would instantly cut them to pieces with his hanger (sword) and pull on their tongues." This account also states that the pirate's other tortures included "burning with matches and suchlike torments, to cut a man to pieces, first some flesh, then a hand, then an arm, a leg, sometimes tying a cord about his head and with a stick twisting it until his eyes shoot out, which is called 'woolding.'" L'Olonnais would also slice a victim to pieces with his sword and lick the blood off the sword.

In late 1667 or early 1668 L'Olonnais and his crew, numbering about seven hundred men, sailed to the coast of Venezuela to attack the city of Maracaibo, near the entrance to Lake Maracaibo. But the residents had fled, and the buccaneers found little treasure in the empty city. They moved on to Gibraltar, a city on the lake's opposite shore that was guarded by a strong fort. After a long battle, L'Olonnais entered the town. He demanded, and received, a ransom of ten thousand pieces of eight, or Spanish dollars, to spare the city from total destruction. Then he sailed back to Maracaibo, demanding another twenty thousand pieces of eight as ransom. With the booty from this expedition, L'Olonnais was welcomed back to Tortuga as a hero. He had seized treasure worth an estimated 260,000 pieces of eight.

Leads an assault on San Pedro

In 1668 according to some accounts, L'Olonnais planned a major attack on the eastern coast of Nicaragua. But bad weather forced him off course, and he landed near the small port of Puerto Cabellos (present-day Puerto Cortés) on the northern coast of Honduras. After capturing the town, as well as the Spanish trade ship in the harbor, he marched with three hundred of his men 30 miles (48 kilometers) inland to the region's capital, San Pedro Sula.

Along the way, L'Olonnais forced two captured soldiers to act as his guides. When the buccaneers marched into a Spanish ambush, L'Olonnais accused the soldiers of deliberately misleading them. Allegedly he sliced open the chest of one prisoner, ripped out the beating heart, and chewed on it before forcing it into the other man's face. This terrified prisoner immediately suggested a new course, which led the buccaneers safely to San Pedro. L'Olonnais and his men drove out the defending troops and then spent several days plundering (robbing of goods by force) the town before burning it to the ground. Once they had carried their loot back to their ships, L'Olonnais learned that a vessel carrying Spanish treasure was due in the area any day. He decided to wait there for it. When it finally arrived, three months late, the buccaneer and his crew attacked the ship only to find, after a furious battle, that it held no treasure at all. It had unloaded its precious cargo in another port nearby.

Downfall

Shortly after the attack on the treasure ship in Honduran waters, L'Olonnais lost the support of many of his men. Two captains under his command

François L'Olonnais was known for his cruelty. Here, after cutting out a man's heart during battle, he forces another man to eat it. © LEBRECHT MUSIC AND ARTS PHOTO LIBRARY/ALAMY.

refused to continue sailing with him, and when they returned to Tortuga, they took most of the ships in the pirate's fleet with them. L'Olonnais was left with only his own flagship and a crew of approximately four hundred buccaneers.

Sailing south from Honduras, L'Olonnais ran aground in southern Nicaragua, along a stretch known as the Mosquito Coast. The survivors made a camp on the shore and then divided into two groups. One group began building a smaller boat from the wreckage of their ship. The other, led by L'Olonnais, made its way along the San Juan River to the town of Solentiname. But the Spanish were ready and ambushed the invaders.

Cannibalism in the Caribbean

In his accounts of his voyages to the Americas, Italian explorer Christopher Columbus (c. 1451–1506) described the native Caribbean peoples as cannibals. His men found villages where human body parts had been hung up, as if to be cured like hams. From this evidence, and from other anecdotes, he reported that the Caribbean natives practiced cannibalism regularly and frequently, and that this practice must be a central part of their culture. Modern scholars, however, believe that Columbus's reports, and those of other early explorers in the region, were inaccurate.

Modern anthropologists explain that various ethnic groups lived in the Caribbean. Of these, some did in fact practice cannibalism—among these the Carib people. But cannibalism was not a frequent event nor was it a regular part of the natives' diet. Cannibalism was not practiced to provide regular food but was a ritual associated with war. Cannibals in the Caribbean ate the flesh of captives they took in battle. The practice,

according to modern evidence, had nothing to do with hunger. The victors consumed the flesh of their victims as a way to honor their courage as fighters or to eradicate them from the earth. Europeans did not understand this and described Caribbean peoples as savages who regularly consumed human flesh. This description, according to modern scholars, also served to make native peoples of the Americas appear morally inferior to the European invaders, allowing the Europeans to feel justified in enslaving or exterminating them.

The story of cannibals devouring L'Olonnais's body fits the theory of cannibalization as a ritual of war. The natives considered the pirate their enemy and killed him while defending their settlement from his attack. In this way, he was a casualty of legitimate battle. Consuming his body was a way for the natives to show symbolically that they had totally vanquished him and that he could never hold any power over them again.

The surviving buccaneers were barely able to escape back to their camp. By this time the small boat was finished, and L'Olonnais used it to sail farther south along the coast, hoping eventually to reach safety in the Gulf of Darien, which lies to the east of Panama. With little protection from the weather in this small boat, and without food or water, the men soon became exhausted. Going ashore to search for food along the coast of Panama, they discovered what they thought was a small native village that would be easy to attack. But the natives surrounded the buccaneers, killing most of them with poisoned arrows and hacking L'Olonnais to pieces. Only one man survived. According to one version of the survivor's story, the Indians killed L'Olonnais and then ate him. According to another version, the Indians burned the pieces of L'Olonnais's body and scattered all of his ashes. Hating the pirate for his cruelty toward them, they wanted to destroy any trace of his existence.

For More Information

BOOKS

Burg, B.R. "The Buccaneer Community." in *Bandits at Sea: A Pirates Reader*, edited by C.R. Penell. New York, NY: New York University Press, 2001, pp. 211–243.

Konstam, Angus. *Piracy: The Complete History.* Oxford, England: Osprey, 2008, pp. 122, 124–125.

Pennell, C.R., ed. *Bandits at Sea: A Pirates Reader.* New York: New York University Press, 2001.

Henry Morgan

BORN: 1635 • County Monmouth, Wales
DIED: August 25, 1688 • Port Royal, Jamaica

Welsh pirate, governor

"I left school too young to be a great proficient in [learning],

and have been much more used to the pike than the book."

In the 1600s Henry Morgan was one of the most feared and hated men in the Americas. He terrorized the Spanish in the Caribbean for some thirty years, stealing their treasure and destroying their towns and cities. Morgan amassed a huge fortune for himself and brought great riches to Jamaica as well.

Morgan's excessive violence outraged the Spanish, undermining diplomatic relations between Spain and England. Yet Morgan acted with the permission of the Jamaican government, and he considered himself a loyal subject of the English king.

Early life

Born in County Monmouth, Wales, in 1635, Henry Morgan came from a humble branch of a family that had some influence and social status in the area. His paternal uncles were professional soldiers, but there is no evidence that Morgan's father had a military career; historians assume

Henry Morgan. © INTERFOTO/
ALAMY.

165

that, because the area was primarily agricultural, he was probably a farmer. Morgan attended school as a boy but did not like studying.

In 1654 Morgan signed on with a Royal Naval force that sailed to the Caribbean. The Anglo-Spanish War (1654–60) had broken out, and the English government, led by Oliver Cromwell (1599–1658), sent forces to attack Spanish possessions in the Americas. Spain and Portugal had been granted sole control of the Americas by the Treaty of Tordesillas, signed in 1494. Since then, Spain had taken vast quantities of gold, silver, and other precious materials from the Americas every year and had strictly controlled other countries' access to this trade. Although England, the Netherlands, and France had made inroads in the area by the mid–1600s, Spain remained the region's dominant power. And the Americas were the source of Spain's wealth. By striking at Spanish targets there, England could greatly weaken its formidable enemy.

Arrives in the Caribbean

Morgan arrived at the island of Barbados, an English colony, on January 29, 1655. Among his force's first actions was the invasion of Santo Domingo, a Spanish city on Hispaniola (present-day Haiti and the Dominican Republic). The attack was a major failure, and the troops, suffering from disease, hunger, and inept leadership, fled. The English forces soon regrouped, however, and assaulted the island of Jamaica, also held by Spain. Poorly defended, the island was soon captured. With the capture of Jamaica, England now had a central Caribbean base for trade.

Now that they had Jamaica, the English faced the challenge of protecting it from any Spanish attempts to get it back. In 1656 England sent a naval force to Jamaica under the command of **Christopher Myngs** (1625–1666; see entry). Myngs realized that extreme tactics were necessary, since his force was greatly outnumbered by Spain's troops in the region. With authorization from Jamaica's colonial governor, he sought the help of seafaring fighters known as buccaneers. The buccaneers were men who had fled settlements or ships in the Caribbean and found refuge as hunters in the wilderness. Many had been prisoners, runaway servants, or escaped slaves. They lived by hunting and by trading with sailors and smugglers. However, the buccaneers eventually turned to piracy to survive.

Over the next five years, Myngs led several assaults against Spanish targets with the help of the buccaneers. By 1661 Morgan had joined them. Spain and England were now technically at peace, but the Jamaican government, distrusting the Spanish, continued to allow buccaneering raids. With Myngs's men, Morgan participated in at least two major raids: the assault on the Cuban fortress and city of Santiago in 1662 and the attack soon afterward on the port of San Francisco de Campeche, in southern Mexico. The spectacular success of these raids, which brought a fortune to the buccaneers and to the Jamaican economy, encouraged Morgan to continue buccaneering on his own.

A reputation for cruelty

Morgan gathered a crew of his own and, operating from Port Royal, Jamaica's capital, spent the next few years raiding Spanish settlements along the coast of southern Mexico and Nicaragua. The region's native Miskito people, who hated the Spanish, were happy to help the raiders, sharing their food and showing them paths through the jungle. The buccaneers attacked towns by surprise and grabbed whatever valuables they could find. If the inhabitants tried to resist, Morgan showed no mercy, torturing residents into saying where their treasure was hidden. He also took prisoners, demanding huge ransoms for their safe return. (A ransom is a sum of money demanded for the release of someone being held captive.)

The seventeenth century was a violent period; physical punishments, such as whipping and branding, were common, and executions by hanging or beheading were public events. Yet even by the standards of the day, Morgan's cruelty was considered shocking and excessive. He had men tied to racks by their wrists and ankles, stretching their bodies until their limbs were pulled out of joint. He placed lighted fuses between the fingers and toes of his victims. There are even accounts of him having his victims roasted alive or crucified. (Crucifixion is a slow and painful death by nailing the hands and feet to a cross.)

The Spanish colonists were terrified of Morgan. No fortress seemed safe from his assault. Morgan was so ruthless and successful that many people began to accuse him of being in league with the devil.

On a trip back to Jamaica in 1665, Morgan married a cousin, Mary Elizabeth. She was the daughter of Morgan's uncle, Colonel Edward Morgan, who in 1664 had been appointed deputy governor of the colony. Through this uncle, Morgan also met the new governor, Thomas Modyford (c. 1620–1679). By this time the pirate had amassed a sizable private fortune, but he was a young man and eager for more adventure.

Henry Morgan's forces attacking Puerto del Principe, Cuba, in 1668 © LEBRECHT.

He had no intention of retiring from seafaring and wanted to increase his wealth even further.

Attacking Cuba and Portobelo

Impressed with Morgan's achievements, Modyford gave approval for the pirate to continue harassing the Spanish. In 1668 Morgan assembled a buccaneer force of about seven hundred men near Cuba. Their target was the city of Puerto del Principe, which until then had never been raided.

Easily taking the city, the buccaneers were disappointed to find less treasure there than they had hoped. Concerned about possible unrest among his men, who wanted more loot, Morgan decided to attack the city of Portobelo, on the Caribbean coast of Panama.

This town, guarded by a strong fort, was the port where Spain's treasure ships were loaded with silver, gold, and pearls to be carried back to Europe. Numerous warships guarded its harbor, and the surrounding land was swampy and difficult to cross. It was one of the best-fortified towns in the Americas, and the buccaneers thought Morgan's plan to attack it was foolhardy. Yet he convinced them that they could succeed and that spectacular wealth would then be theirs.

Morgan sailed to Panama with twelve ships and 480 men. Anchoring at an inlet about 150 miles (241 kilometers) from Portobelo, he realized an assault by sea would be foolhardy. So he devised a plan to attack by land. Leaving his ships in the inlet with a few men, he marched with the remaining force through the jungle. They carried long wooden canoes, which they paddled along rivers whenever possible. After four days, the buccaneers had reached a point near the city. No one had seen them coming.

They attacked at night and easily captured the fortress of San Jeronimo, which guarded the city. Morgan then set explosives in the fortress and blew it up, causing terror among the city's inhabitants. The city's mayor urged his forces to gather inside the castle to defend the city. But Morgan used nuns and priests as human shields, ordering them to carry ladders toward the castle walls while his men walked behind them. The Spanish fired a few shots, wounding a couple of monks, and then stopped shooting. The pirates climbed the castle walls and overwhelmed the soldiers there. In the only act of mercy that Morgan was ever known to show, he offered the valiant mayor a chance to surrender. The mayor refused and died in a hail of buccaneer bullets.

Morgan and his men held Portobelo for thirty-one days. His buccaneers raped the women and tortured prisoners. Morgan wrote to the president of Panama, asking for an enormous ransom. Panama sent forces to rescue the city, but the buccaneers fought them off. The ransom was paid and the buccaneers returned to Jamaica with tremendous riches. Each man received money amounting to six times what an average worker in England could make in a year.

Soon Morgan was back at sea. He led a successful raid on Maracaibo, on the coast of Venezuela at the entrance to Lake Maracaibo, and then attacked the nearby city of Gibraltar, on the lake's opposite shore. The buccaneers found plenty of treasure in Gibraltar, but when they tried to make their escape they discovered that the Spanish, led by Don Alonso, had blocked the narrow passage out of the lake—the only route to the sea. Morgan ordered his men to pack one of their ships with gunpowder and flammable materials, and they sent this vessel, manned by only a few crewmen, toward the Spanish gunboats. The crew set the ship on fire and then escaped as both ships exploded. With Alonso's men distracted by the fire, buccaneers were able to reach the lake.

When they arrived at the town of Maracaibo, they were in a difficult position. Another of Alonso's fortresses stood across the water, and Morgan's fleet would be in range of its cannon fire if the pirates attempted to sail into the sea. The pirates waited at Maracaibo, uncertain of what to do. But the townsfolk, terrified that the pirates would ransack their city, paid Morgan a huge sum to spare the town. They also negotiated with Alonso to give the pirates safe passage out of the area. When these negotiations failed, Morgan was able to pull a trick on Alonso. He made it look as if his men were planning an attack on one side of the Spaniard's castle. When Alonso moved his cannons to that side, the buccaneers sailed safely out of the lake.

Destroys Panama City

Morgan's boldest and most notorious attack occurred in 1671, when he and his buccaneers sacked (captured and robbed) Panama City. Located on the Pacific coast of the Isthmus of Panama, the narrow body of land connecting North and South America, the city was one of the wealthiest in the entire world. Its residents had made fortunes on the gold, silver, and jewels that were brought to the city before being shipped to Europe. This treasure made Panama a tempting target for pirates, but the city's location made it almost impossible to attack. A sea assault was unthinkable; the only feasible route into the Pacific for English ships was to sail around South America, where the coastline was guarded by Spain. And the only way to reach Panama by land was to cross the isthmus, some 60 miles (97 kilometers) of jungle, swamps, and mountains. But Morgan had made a successful land attack at Portobelo, and he was determined to try it at Panama.

First Morgan gathered a force of about 2,000 buccaneers and captured the fortress of San Lorenzo, at the mouth of the Chagres River on the Caribbean coast of Panama. After a fierce fight, the buccaneers took the fort. Leaving his ships in the harbor with about five hundred men to keep watch over the fort, Morgan started up the river toward the

A captured Spaniard bows before Henry Morgan as Morgan's men sack the city of Panama. HULTON ARCHIVE/GETTY IMAGES.

Pacific. He and his men took several canoes and small wooden riverboats, hoping to get several miles inland before having to make the rest of the trek on foot. Morgan had calculated that it would take them two days to reach the coast, but it was the dry season and the river was too low to be of much use. The buccaneers had to slog through quicksand, dense jungle, and oppressive heat. To make matters worse, they had left most of their food behind, because it took up too much room on the boats. The men grew so hungry that they ate their leather belts and used pieces of rope to hold up their pants.

After nine grueling days, they finally reached a hill from which they could see Panama City. The men were weak from hunger. And word of Morgan's approach had reached the town, which had prepared a strong defense. There was little hope that a band of starving buccaneers could seize the city. But Morgan got lucky. His men discovered a pasture filled with cattle, which the Panamanians had forgotten about. The buccaneers slaughtered the cattle and had a feast, which fortified them for the coming attack.

The HMS *Oxford*

In 2001 divers off the coast of Haiti found the remains of the HMS *Oxford*, a frigate under Morgan's command that sank in the 1670s. Morgan and his crew of buccaneers had captured two French warships and were engaged in rowdy celebration while anchored near L'ile a Vache off Haiti's coast. The men had plundered (robbed of goods by force) the French ships and loaded the *Oxford* with loot. According to some reports, they had even stuffed treasure inside one of the frigate's cannons. Then they prepared a huge feast. Rum flowed freely, and the buccaneers roasted a pig on deck. But a spark from this fire ignited the ship's supply of gunpowder, causing a huge explosion that blew off the front third of the ship.

As the *Oxford* began to sink, the French vessels capsized on top of it, pushing it quickly down to the bottom of the sea. Morgan, who had been dining in his private cabin at the time, was thrown through his window by the force of the blast but survived. He escaped in another captured French ship, but 350 men were killed in the disaster. And all of the treasure they had loaded onto the *Oxford* was lost.

Morgan returned to the area later in an attempt to locate the wreck, but he never found it. In 2001 divers Rick Haupt and Bruce Leeming discovered the wreck in shallow but treacherous waters. "When I saw the whole reef littered with cannons and thousands of artefacts tumbling from the deep it was the most extraordinary sight in all my years of diving," said Haupt in a London *Times* article by Adam Sherwin. Haupt also recalled, "Black clouds of powder spiraled off one of the cannons when I scratched it with my knee."

Outside the city, Spanish soldiers battled the buccaneers, but the defense was useless. After a two-hour fight, Morgan's men had killed about five hundred soldiers, sustaining only a few casualties of their own. The buccaneers then swarmed into the city. Before they fled, surviving soldiers set fire to the buildings and most of the city burned down. The buccaneers spent four weeks ransacking every corner of the town before making their way back across the isthmus and then to Port Royal. The city of Panama lay in complete ruins.

Morgan presented an official report of his activities, claiming to have taken treasure worth about thirty thousand English pounds—the equivalent of about ninety million dollars today. But it is likely that the real amount was more than twenty times more and that Morgan kept much of the unreported treasure for himself after giving a share to Governor Modyford. Jamaica hailed Morgan as a hero. But when word of the attack reached England, King Charles II (1630–1685) was furious. For several years he had struggled to improve relations between England and Spain, and he had promised to clamp down on piracy in the Caribbean.

But Morgan's raids had continued, and Spain had grown increasingly impatient with Charles's ineffectiveness. After the attack on Panama, the outraged Spanish ambassador threatened a return to outright war unless Morgan and Governor Modyford were punished.

The king immediately had Modyford arrested, replacing him with a new governor. Morgan was also brought to London in 1672. Morgan defended himself to the king by declaring that he had acted on the belief that the government of Panama had been secretly gathering a fleet to invade Jamaica.

Returns to Jamaica

Morgan was rewarded with a knighthood in 1674. (A knight is a man granted a rank of honor by the monarch for his personal merit or service to the country.) But his days of buccaneering were over. He returned to Jamaica in 1675. Now his mission was to stop piracy, not practice it. He had been appointed the colony's new lieutenant governor.

Although Morgan did not get along with Lord Vaughan, Jamaica's new governor, he fulfilled his administrative responsibilities. He closed Port Royal to ships suspected of piracy and boasted in a letter to the king that any pirates brought before him received swift and severe justice. On one occasion, he invited the crew of a pirate vessel to dine at his mansion and got them so drunk that they could not return to their ship. The next morning, as they staggered out of Morgan's house, they were arrested and brought before a judge, who turned out to be Morgan himself. Morgan sentenced them to death, and they were all hanged that same day.

But Morgan sometimes found it convenient to treat the buccaneers more leniently. He often dismissed charges against them, and sometimes sold them secret official information, such as the location of patrol boats or Spanish treasure ships. In a letter to a friend in 1683, he said that he refused to execute a group of convicted pirates because "I much abhorring bloodshed and being greatly dissatisfied that in my short government so many necessities have lain upon me of punishing criminals with death," as quoted in *The Pirates' Pact: The Secret Alliances between History's Most Notorious Buccaneers and Colonial America* by Douglas R. Burgess Jr.

Morgan enjoyed the wealth and prestige of his new position. He lived in a stately mansion and wore the finest clothes and jewels. But by 1683 he was in poor health. After years of heavy drinking, he now suffered from liver disease, gout, and other problems. He also faced growing hostility from the new governor, Sir Thomas Lynch, who considered Morgan an untrustworthy man. In October 1683 Governor Lynch convinced the Jamaican legislature to expel Morgan from public office. Morgan died on August 25, 1688, and was buried the next day with state honors. Four years later, an earthquake destroyed Port Royal, and Morgan's coffin was washed into the sea.

For More Information

BOOKS

Burgess, Douglas R., Jr. *The Pirates' Pact: The Secret Alliances between History's Most Notorious Buccaneers and Colonial America.* New York: McGraw Hill, 2009, p. 73.

Konstam, Angus. *Scourge of the Seas: Buccaneers, Pirates and Privateers.* Oxford, England: Osprey Press, 2007.

Marrin, Albert. *Terror of the Spanish Main: Sir Henry Morgan and His Buccaneers.* New York: Dutton, 1999.

Pennell, C.R., ed. *Bandits at Sea: A Pirates Reader.* New York: New York University Press, 2001.

Travers, Tim. *Pirates: A History.* Briscombe Port Stroud, England: The History Press, 2009.

PERIODICALS

Sherwin, Adam. "Divers Close in on Pirate King's Treasure." *Times* (London) (May 3, 2004).

Murat Reis

BORN: c. 1570 • Haarlem, North Holland, Netherlands

DIED: c. 1641 • Morocco

Dutch pirate, president, governor

"This last night, a little before day, came two Turk men of war … and they have carried away of our townspeople, men, women and children, one hundred and eleven, and two more are slain; the ships are at present going westward."

– Joseph Carter, mayor of Baltimore, Ireland
QUOTED IN *THE STOLEN VILLAGE: A THRILLING ACCOUNT OF THE 17TH-CENTURY RAID ON IRELAND BY THE BARBARY PIRATES* BY DES EKIN.

Murat Reis was one of the most successful pirates of the Barbary Coast, the region of North Africa stretching from Morocco along the Mediterranean to Libya. He enjoyed a long and profitable career in the early 1600s, raiding ships and ports in the western Mediterranean Sea and in the Atlantic Ocean. With a band of fellow pirates known as the Sallee Rovers, he established the independent city-state of Salé (also spelled Sallee), Morocco, and was elected as its first head of state.

Later in his career Murat was captured by the Knights of Malta, a Christian military order. He was kept in their dungeons for five years, where he suffered mistreatment and torture before managing to escape during a major Barbary attack. He was hailed as a hero upon his return to Morocco, and was made governor of the town of Qualidia. He is remembered as daring seafarer and brave fighter who served the interests of the Ottoman Empire.

Murat Reis is sometimes referred to as Murat Reis the Younger, to distinguish him from an earlier Turkish sea commander, Murat Reis the Elder (d. 1609).

Early life

The man who became known as Murat Reis was born around 1570 in Haarlem, the Netherlands. His birth name was Jan Janszoon van Haarlem, and he came from a prosperous family. He married young and had a daughter, Lysbeth. Around 1600, he began operating as a Dutch privateer. (A privateer is a private ship or ship owner commissioned by a state or government to attack the merchant ships of an enemy nation.) With the Netherlands and Spain at war at this time, Janszoon began targeting Spanish shipping, primarily in the North Sea off the Netherlands coast.

Janszoon soon became frustrated by the limited opportunities for privateering in the waters near Haarlem. He sailed southward toward the Barbary Coast, where, in violation of his privateering license, he began attacking ships of all nationalities. He flew the Dutch flag when he assaulted Spanish ships, which gave him legal protection as an authorized Dutch privateer. But if he wanted to target other vessels, he flew the flags of different Barbary countries, in effect posing as a corsair, or a pirate of the Barbary coast.

Joins the Barbary corsairs

In 1618 Janszoon was captured by Barbary corsairs and taken to the North African port of Algiers. There, he converted to Islam. Some historians believe that the pirate was forced to accept his new religion; others say there is no evidence to prove this claim. Having become a Muslim, he decided to join the Barbary corsairs, who, with the encouragement of the Ottoman sultan, actively harassed European ships in the Mediterranean. He also took a Turkish name, Murat Reis. ("Reis," also spelled "Rais," means "captain" or "chief" and was used as part of many corsair leader's names.) He never returned to Christianity.

One of the corsairs' chief targets was their centuries-old enemy, Spain. In the 600s and early 700s, Muslim Arab armies had swept across North Africa, conquering the region and converting the inhabitants to Islam. In 711 North African armies invaded Spain, and by 718 most of Spain and Portugal had been incorporated into this new Muslim empire. By about 1030, however, the Christian kings who had been displaced began fighting to regain their lost territory. After several centuries, Spain succeeded in expelling the Muslims from the Iberian Peninsula in 1492. Believing themselves displaced from territory that was rightfully theirs, Muslim fighters took to the sea to make pirate raids against Spain. For more than three hundred years, the states of the Barbary Coast continued to wage war against Spain and other Christian countries in the Mediterranean.

While he was in North Africa, Murat encountered several fellow Dutchmen who had joined the corsairs. Among these were Dutch seafarer Ivan Dirkie de Veenboer (d.1620), who had also converted to Islam and was known as Sulayman Reis; and Simon de Danser (also known as Siemen Danziger or Zymen Danseker; c. 1579–c. 1611). Murat sailed with Sulayman until that pirate's death in 1620.

By 1620 Algiers had negotiated peace agreements with several countries in Europe. This meant that Algiers could no longer permit privateering, and could not legally allow corsairs to bring their plunder (goods stolen by force) into the city. Murat, who had been operating out of Algiers and commanded several ships, was forced to find another base of operations. He and his crew moved to the Atlantic coast of Morocco, establishing a pirate community at the small port of Salé. It proved to be a good location from which to launch raids. With about eighteen small ships, the pirates attacked numerous merchant vessels, stealing cargoes worth a fortune. Within a few years, Salé became quite prosperous.

The pirates at Salé, which was technically under the control of the sultan of Morocco, elected Murat as their first president and grand admiral. In 1627 the pirates rebelled against Moroccan rule and declared Salé an independent city-state. The sultan sent troops to retake the city, but this military action failed and the sultan was forced to acknowledge Salé's independence, as well as Murat's position as president.

In 1622 Murat sailed to Veere, in the Netherlands, for repairs to his fleet. He had previously been raiding ships in the English Channel and the North Sea, and he flew the Moroccan flag and identified himself to the Dutch authorities as an admiral of the Moroccan government. This status protected him from Dutch laws against piracy. Even so, the Dutch government urged him to abandon the corsairs and even brought his Haarlem family to Veere to increase the pressure on him to agree. Murat, however, had no interest in returning to Europe. By this time, the pirate admiral had married again, and established a family with his second wife, who was a Muslim. He returned to them in Salé, bringing with him several enthusiastic Dutch sailors who had joined his crew in Veere.

Ventures to Iceland and Ireland

By the late 1620s, the responsibility of ruling Salé had become burdensome to the pirate admiral. He appointed an assistant, a fellow Dutch seaman, to take care of Salé's administration in his absence, and in late 1627 moved with his family back to Algiers. From Algiers Murat continued to expand his seafaring exploits, increasing his wealth and power. In 1631 he embarked on the most ambitious journey ever taken by a Barbary pirate. He hired a Danish slave, who had come to Algiers as a corsair captive, to guide his fleet to Iceland.

Sailing to Iceland was an astonishing undertaking at the time. Iceland lies at least 2,350 miles (3,782 kilometers) from Morocco, and the corsairs had to navigate through the treacherous waters of the North Atlantic to reach their destination. Unlike the more sheltered Mediterranean, the Atlantic has frequent storms with unpredictable winds, and the coastlines of the landmasses in this area, which include Ireland, Scotland, and their off-coast islands, are filled with rocky promontories where navigation, or charting the course of a ship, is often extremely difficult. Nevertheless, Murat was determined to take the risk. He led his fleet out of the Mediterranean and headed north. Reaching the Faroe Islands, north of Scotland, the pirates attacked a few fishing vessels and then turned west, raiding Iceland's capital city of Reykjavik. Finding little treasure there except salt fish and some animal hides, the invaders kidnapped several Icelanders to sell in North Africa as slaves.

On the way back to the Barbary Coast, Murat seized several ships, including at least one Dutch vessel, and took additional slaves. Still, the voyage had not yielded the treasures that the pirates had hoped for. Questioning one of the captives, Murat was told that the town of Baltimore, on the southwest coast of Ireland, would be a good target for a raid. The captive, John Hackett, was an Irish Catholic who had a grudge against the English Protestant residents of Baltimore and their supporters, and steered the pirates toward that town in order to protect his own home. Murat launched his assault on Baltimore on June 20, 1631, and ransacked the town, taking 103 prisoners, many of them women and children, to be sold into slavery.

Although many stories about the Barbary corsairs say that the pirates abused their captives, the Icelandic prisoners were treated well. Aboard ship, they were given decent food and shelter. The women and children were not shackled. And although the male prisoners were kept in chains

Famous Descendants of Murat Reis

Unlike many pirates of his era, Murat Reis lived a long life and had many children who survived into adulthood. He had at least one child, daughter Lysbeth, with his Dutch first wife. But as a Muslim convert, Murat was allowed to have as many as four wives. He and his second wife, a Muslim woman from Cartagena, Spain, had four sons. Murat also had a third wife, who most likely bore him children as well. Having acquired spectacular wealth in his long career as a pirate, Murat was able to provide his children with fortunes that, in many cases, contributed to their own successful careers. The family's wealth and prominence were also likely reasons why they kept careful records about births and marriages through the generations. The pirate's descendants through his first and second marriages include many notable figures, among them several members of the British and Hungarian aristocracy.

Anthony Jansen van Sallee, the third son born to Murat and his second wife, married a Dutch woman and immigrated with her to North America. His wealth enabled him to buy several acres of land on the island of Manhattan, and he and his wife became some of the first settlers there in 1638. A legal disagreement, however, led to Van Sallee's expulsion from the settlement, after which he bought land in Gravesend, Brooklyn. Among the American descendants of Murat are railroad and shipping entrepreneur

Actor Humphrey Bogart is a descendant of Murat Reis.
© PHOTOS 12/ALAMY.

Cornelius Vanderbilt (1794–1877), acclaimed actor Humphrey Bogart (1899–1957), and journalist Anderson Cooper (1967–). The pirate is also allegedly an ancestor, on her father's side, of Jacqueline Kennedy Onassis (1929–1994), the wife of U.S. president John F. Kennedy (1917–1963).

while the pirate vessels were within sight of land, to prevent any escape attempts, the kidnapped men were unshackled once the fleet reached the open sea. A few of the Icelandic captives were eventually able to return to their homes.

The Irish captives, though, were not so lucky, and the raid on Baltimore remained a traumatic event for residents of the British Isles. According to Des Ekin in *The Stolen Village: A Thrilling Account of the 17th-Century Raid on Ireland by the Barbary Pirates*, the attack was "the most devastating invasion ever carried out by the forces of the Islamist jihad [holy war] on Britain or Ireland," and was "recognized at the time as an unprecedented act of aggression by the Islamist empire." Although European governments and wealthy families of captives were sometimes able to secure the release of victims kidnapped by the Barbary corsairs, the English government did not take effective action to obtain the Baltimore captives' freedom. Their fate has never been discovered.

Imprisoned on Malta

Returning to the Mediterranean, Murat intensified his attacks on Christian targets there. He launched raids on Sicily, Corsica, Sardinia, and the islands of Majorca and Minorca. By now the pirate was regarded as one of Europe's most dangerous enemies. He established a close personal alliance with the ruler of Tunis, a port on the central coast of North Africa. This gave the pirate another safe base where he could sell his plunder and from which he could make forays into the central and eastern regions of the Mediterranean. In addition to raiding ships and ports in southern Italy, Murat became active in the Ionian Sea, which separates Italy from the western coast of Greece. With a fleet consisting of Dutch, North African, Arab, and Turkish pirates, as well as specialized military fighters known as *janissaries*, Murat did battle with the Venetian fleet near the islands of Crete and Cyprus.

Near the coast of Tunis in 1635, Murat was captured in a surprise raid by the Knights of Malta. Previously known as the Knights Hospitallers, this Christian order was founded around 1023 in Jerusalem to provide care for wounded crusaders. As the Crusades continued the Knights became a powerful military force. (The Crusades were a series of military campaigns to take control of the Holy Land [roughly the present-day territory of Israel, the Palestine territories, and parts of Jordan and Lebanon] from the Muslims.) After Muslim armies won control of the Kingdom of Jerusalem in 1291, the Knights were expelled, and they established a new base on the island of Rhodes. Frequently doing battle with Barbary corsairs, the Knights were eventually expelled from Rhodes in 1522. In 1530 King Charles I of Spain (1500–1558) gave them territories that included Malta, a group of Mediterranean islands south of Sicily and close to the port of Tunis. From Malta the Knights were within easy reach of some of the busiest pirate ports in North Africa.

Having seized Murat, the Knights kept the pirate in a well-guarded dungeon for five years. He was reportedly tortured, and his long captivity damaged his health. In 1640 the ruler of Tunis organized a major attack on Malta to free Murat and other Muslim sailors who were being held there. With difficulty, the pirate admiral was able to escape. He soon returned to Morocco.

Considered a hero, Murat was appointed governor of Oualidia, on the Atlantic coast of Morocco near Safi. In this position, the pirate enjoyed wealth and luxuries, as well as the esteem of the region's inhabitants. In 1640 his Dutch daughter, Lysbeth, arrived in Oualidia to visit her father, staying for almost a year.

Few details are known about Murat's final years. It is likely that he retired from piracy and from government, living quietly until his death, at about age seventy, in around 1641.

For More Information

BOOKS

Ekin, Des. *The Stolen Village: A Thrilling Account of the 17th-Century Raid on Ireland by the Barbary Pirates.* Fall River Press, 2008. Originally published as *The Stolen Village: Baltimore and the Barbary Pirates.* Dublin, Ireland: O'Brien Press, 2006, pp. 11–12, 120.

Wilson, Peter Lamborn. *Pirate Utopias: Moorish Corsairs and European Renegades.* 2nd ed. Rye Brook, NY: Autonomedia, 2003.

PERIODICALS

Shah, Tahir. "Morocco's Buried Pirate Republic." *Financial Times* (July 3, 2010). Available online at www.ft.com/cms/s/2/1ac50542-8563-11df-aa2e-00144feabdc0.html (accessed on January 3, 2011).

WEB SITES

"Jan Janszoon van Haarlem, aka Murad Reis." *Roll Family Windmill.* http://homepages.rootsweb.ancestry.com/~windmill/html/murad%20reis.html (accessed on January 3, 2011).

Christopher Myngs

BORN: 1625 • Norfolk, England

DIED: 1666

English naval officer, pirate

"Unhinged and out of tune."

– Colonial governor of Jamaica, describing Myngs
  QUOTED IN *SCOURGE OF THE SEAS: BUCCANEERS, PIRATES AND PRIVATEERS* BY ANGUS
  KONSTAM.

In command of an English naval force, Christopher Myngs (also spelled Mings) was sent to the Caribbean Sea to defend the English colony of Jamaica against threats from Spain. He accomplished this by using pirate tactics, conducting unprovoked raids on Spanish ports and stripping them of any riches. His actions damaged relations between England and Spain, but greatly increased Jamaica's wealth and whetted the colonial government's appetite for more Spanish gold. Myngs's successful use of piracy inspired later colonial governors to encourage the practice, weakening Spain's dominance in the region.

Christopher Myngs.
© NATIONAL MARITIME
MUSEUM, LONDON/THE IMAGE
WORKS. REPRODUCED BY
PERMISSION.

Joins the English navy

Little is known about Myngs's early life except that he was born in Norfolk, England, in 1625, and he joined the English navy at a young age. According to some accounts, Myngs started as a cabin boy and worked his way up the ranks to become an admiral. By the 1650s he had achieved the rank of captain, with command of the *Elisabeth*.

During the First Anglo-Dutch War (1652–54; a naval conflict between England and the Netherlands over trade disputes) Myngs captured a Dutch convoy sailing with two warships. His successes during this war brought Myngs high favor with the English government, and he was recommended for promotion.

In 1655 Myngs was given command of the *Marston Moor*. The crew aboard this fifty-two-gun frigate was on the verge of mutiny (an open rebellion against the ship's officers), and Myngs instituted strict discipline to put down the brewing revolt. In January 1656 Myngs was sent to Jamaica as deputy to the commander in charge of the island's defense.

Attacking the Spanish in the Caribbean

England, eager to increase its levels of trade in the Caribbean, had seized Jamaica from Spain in 1655. Spain had completely dominated the region since 1494, when the Treaty of Tordesillas divided all of the Americas between Spain and Portugal. Spain had built numerous trade colonies in Mexico, Central America, South America, and the Caribbean, and the tons of gold and silver that it took from the Americas had made it the richest and most powerful country in Europe. Spain did not welcome other European ships that ventured into these waters. The wealth of the Americas was a treasure that Spain considered its own, and it did not want to share.

Yet since the late 1500s other European countries had ignored the treaty and sent ships to the area. At times Spanish colonial authorities allowed these vessels to trade in Caribbean ports. The ships brought many household goods that colonial residents were eager to buy and that cost far less than similar goods from Spain. Although Spain had deemed this kind of business illegal, colonial officials often ignored it, allowing it to continue. English ships also brought African slaves, for which there was also a large demand. But trade in this region was always risky. Local governors often demanded bribes from the European captains before allowing them to unload their cargoes. And because political conflicts between Spain and England, France, and the Netherlands were acute, the rival countries were often at war, making their ships vulnerable to attack.

The conquest of Jamaica gave England a strong base from which to operate in the Caribbean. But the island was surrounded by Spanish possessions, and the English faced the challenge of defending their new colony from invasion. Myngs, a confident and decisive military leader, proved a good choice for this command. He was "tall, florid, with a determined nose and intelligent eyes," according to Douglas R. Burgess Jr. in *The Pirates' Pact: The Secret Alliance between History's Most Notorious Buccaneers and Colonial America*, and he was a "competent leader of men." Myngs decided to go on the offensive, striking at Spanish ports throughout the Caribbean to destroy their ability to mount attacks on Jamaica.

To supplement his troops, Myngs enlisted the help of seafaring fighters known as buccaneers. These men had once been hunters who had left the coastal settlements to live largely on their own, curing meat and trading with passing ships and smugglers. Many of them were desperate characters: ex-convicts, escaped slaves, servants who had run away from their masters, or sailors who had deserted from the navy. Persecuted by the Spanish and lured by the promise of riches carried by Spanish treasure ships that often passed near the island of Tortuga, where they were based, the buccaneers had become pirates by the 1650s. With their seafaring skills, knowledge of the region's coastal waters, and fighting experience, the buccaneers became an important component of England's Caribbean defense.

Falls into disgrace

After successfully fighting off a minor Spanish assault on Jamaica in 1658, Myngs led his men on several raids along the northern coast of South America. During this time, he developed a reputation for cruelty. His men raped and pillaged, torturing inhabitants into giving up their valuables and then massacring and burning down entire villages and towns. In 1659 Myngs captured the Venezuelan port of Coro, where ships in the harbor were loaded with silver

Rum

One of the pirates' favorite products from the Caribbean was rum, an alcoholic drink distilled from the fermented byproducts of molasses. Molasses is itself a byproduct that results from the processing of sugarcane into sugar. African slaves working on sugarcane plantations in the 1600s first discovered how to ferment molasses, and the creation of distilled rum soon followed.

Rum became a highly popular drink, and demand for molasses skyrocketed throughout the 1600s and 1700s. This demand led to a huge increase in sugarcane plantations in the Caribbean and to a corresponding increase in the slave trade that supplied workers for the cane fields. Traders bought slaves in Africa and transported them to the Caribbean, where they were sold. There the traders picked up cargoes of sugar or molasses to take back to Europe, where it could be made into rum. The profits from this rum gave traders money to go back to Africa to buy another cargo of slaves and repeat this cycle of trading. This pattern became known as the triangular slave trade, because the route from Africa to the Caribbean to Europe and back to Africa is roughly the shape of a triangle.

The Caribbean buccaneers often traded in rum, which they could either drink or sell for a good price. The English navy also developed a fondness for rum and included the drink as part of each sailor's daily rations. Rum manufacture became an important industry in North America; New England grew into a major center for rum distilling, because of the superior technical skills of those who worked in the industry.

valued at more than a quarter of a million English pounds. Instead of delivering this treasure to the governor of Jamaica, however, Myngs divided most of it with his crew and the buccaneers before giving the governor a share. Spain was outraged by Myngs's behavior, calling him nothing more than a common criminal and a mass murderer. The governor of Jamaica was also furious and sent a letter to the English government saying that the captain was, as quoted by author Angus Konstam in *Scourge of the Seas: Buccaneers, Pirates and Privateers*, "unhinged and out of tune" and accusing him of embezzlement, or the theft of money or property entrusted to one's care but owned by someone else.

Parliament ordered Myngs back to England to stand trial on embezzlement charges before the High Court of Admiralty. But when Myngs arrived in London in the spring of 1660, the country was preoccupied with political change. The death of Oliver Cromwell (1599–1658), who had run the country since overthrowing and executing King Charles I (1600–1649) in 1649, had resulted in a crisis that reinstated the monarchy. Charles's son, Charles II (1630–1685), who had been living in exile, returned to England in 1660 and assumed the throne. In the tensions surrounding the English Restoration, as these events came to be known, the charge against Myngs was dropped.

Myngs had risen to his command with Cromwell's support. But the captain was able to convince the new king of his political loyalty. With Charles II's approval, the captain returned to Jamaica in 1662 as commander of the forty-gun royal warship the *Centurion*.

Attacking Cuba and Mexico

England and Spain had signed a peace treaty in 1660, and Lord Windsor, the new governor of Jamaica, paid off and dismissed the soldiers that Cromwell had sent to defend the islands. Many of these men joined the buccaneers. Myngs was happy to enlist them for his next plan—an assault on Cuba. England and Spain were not officially at war, but the English government wanted to weaken Spain's dominance in the Caribbean and had ordered Myngs to take actions that would accomplish this. Though he served the political and economic interests of England, Myngs now operated as a pirate.

He drew up careful plans for the invasion, which would target the port of Santiago de Cuba. This town was protected by a major fortress, the Castillo del Morro. Myngs organized a force of twelve ships and fifteen hundred men, comprising what Burgess describes as "nothing less than a pirate armada."

As this fleet sailed toward the city in 1662, many of the troops in the fort abandoned their posts in fear. Outside the harbor, Myngs ordered his forces to blast the Castillo's walls with cannon fire. After three solid hours of bombardment, the walls cracked. Finally, with a dramatic roar, the fortress crashed to the ground. The remaining Spanish soldiers hastily fled, and Myngs's men were able to land with little resistance. Later that day Myngs entered the town, where his men were already busy grabbing riches. This is considered the first time that a military commander had used buccaneers and buccaneering tactics to conduct a major raid on enemy territory, and it brought significant wealth back to Jamaica. As Konstam points out in *Scourge of the Seas*, "it set the scene for scores of similar amphibious operations over the next thirty years."

Next Myngs set his sights on Mexico. He sailed for the coast of Campeche, a region in southern Mexico near the Yucatán Peninsula. But the Spanish here had been warned in advance, and they had made preparations to defend the port of San Francisco de Campeche. A large military force was garrisoned at the town, and its fort had massive walls that were much thicker than those of the Castillo del Morro. Cannon fire from outside the harbor would not be strong enough to destroy these fortifications, and Myngs' forces had to fight hard to take the city.

The battle for San Francisco de Campeche lasted an entire day. Myngs's men, including naval forces as well as English, French, and Dutch buccaneers, attacked at dawn and encountered strong resistance from Spanish troops. Despite heavy casualties, the buccaneers fought on. By the end of the day they had forced the exhausted Spanish to surrender. Only about half of the invading force had survived, but their reward was enormous. They took fourteen treasure ships and 150,000 Spanish dollar coins known as pieces of eight.

When Myngs returned to Port Royal in Jamaica, Governor Windsor called an official prize court into session. This court ruled on whether a ship had been seized legally, and also determined how to divide up any booty. (Booty is the goods stolen from ships or coastal villages during pirate raids or attacks on enemies in time of war.) The gold and silver were given to the various captains and crews who had participated in the battle, and about one-tenth of the entire treasure went to the admiralty. Sir Charles Lyttleton, Governor Windsor's lieutenant, made seventy-two English pounds from the proceeds of just one small naval vessel. Two hundred English pounds went to the government treasury. According to Burgess in *The Pirates' Pact*, this was one of the most successful buccaneering raids of the era, and it made both Governor Windsor and Myngs extremely wealthy. As Burgess puts it, "in one week's time Mings and his sponsor, Governor Windsor, had enriched themselves and Jamaica more than any two men in the colony's brief history."

The king's wrath

Myngs's success delighted Governor Windsor, who quickly gave the captain permission to plan another raid against Campeche in the fall of 1662. But the king was not so pleased. Spain had complained bitterly about Myngs's raids, calling him a thief and a murderer. Spain denounced Myngs'actions as blatant piracy, and urged the English king to forbid the colonial government from authorizing such activities. While Cromwell's government had actively tried to provoke Spain in the Caribbean, resulting in the Anglo-Spanish War (1655–60), Charles had no wish to rekindle hostilities. The king did not share Cromwell's intense opposition to Spain, which had been based in large part on the Protestant Cromwell's animosity toward Catholic Spain. But Charles, who had spent most of his childhood and youth on the European continent where he had been exposed to Catholicism, had a more tolerant attitude toward religion. At the same time, he faced the challenge of holding his new government together. Although he had many supporters, there was still a considerable faction who favored the antimonarchist ideas of Cromwell. Charles could not risk alienating them further by plunging England into another war with Spain.

The king promised the Spanish ambassador that he would act to suppress piracy against Spanish targets. Yet his instructions to Governor Windsor took months to arrive by ship from London to Jamaica. In the meantime, Myngs had made another successful raid on Campeche. This time the city was totally unprepared, and the buccaneers captured another fortune in Spanish gold.

When King Charles heard of this, he was furious. It seemed that the governor had brazenly disobeyed his orders. The king sent Thomas Modyford (c. 1620–1679) to replace Governor Windsor. Modyford's instructions made it clear that under no circumstances should he authorize any more pirate raids.

Later life

Myngs had been seriously wounded by a cannonball during his last attack on Campeche, and he had sailed back to London to recover from his

A painting of the Four Days Battle. Christopher Myngs was made a knight for his service in this battle. WILLEM VAN DE VELDE, THE YOUNGER/THE BRIDGEMAN ART LIBRARY/GETTY IMAGES.

injuries. By the time the captain was ready to resume his activities at sea, Modyford was in charge of Jamaica's government, and piracy had been officially forbidden. Myngs did not return to the Caribbean, but he remained in the Royal Navy. He was promoted to vice admiral in 1665.

Myngs's career as a naval commander ended much as it had begun—in battle against the Dutch. Another trade dispute between England and the Netherlands broke out in 1665, resulting in the Second Anglo-Dutch War (1665–67). Myngs participated in an engagement in this war that became known as the Four Days Battle, which raged from June 1 to June 4, 1666. For his service in this battle he was made a knight. (A knight is a man granted a rank of honor by the monarch for his personal merit or service to the country.) Two months later, in another sea battle, he was killed by a Dutch cannonball.

Although Myngs's ruthlessness against the Spanish had prompted King Charles II to forbid further acts of piracy in the Caribbean, Jamaica's governors felt that they had no choice but to use the buccaneers to defend the island. The colonial governors continued to issue permission for buccaneering raids, and these were so successful that plunder (goods stolen by force) became the basis of Jamaica's economy. By the late 1660s, the buccaneers operating in the Caribbean were following Myngs's example of ruthlessness and brutality against the Spanish. **Henry Morgan** (1635–1688; see entry), one of the men who sailed on some of Myngs's raids, went on to become one of the most notorious buccaneers in Jamaica's history.

For More Information

BOOKS

Burgess, Douglas R., Jr. *The Pirates Pact: The Secret Alliance between History's Most Notorious Buccaneers and Colonial America.* New York: McGraw Hill, 2009, pp. 49–50.

Konstam, Angus. *Piracy: The Complete History.* Oxford, England: Osprey, 2008.

————. *Scourge of the Seas: Buccaneers, Pirates and Privateers.* Oxford, England: Osprey, 2007, p. 50.

Grace O'Malley

BORN: c. 1530 • County Mayo, Ireland

DIED: 1603 • County Mayo, Ireland

Irish pirate

"A terror to all merchantmen that sailed the Atlantic."

– Sir Henry Sidney, lord deputy of Ireland
QUOTED IN *BANDITS AT SEA: A PIRATES READER*, EDITED BY C.R. PENNELL.

Hailed by the Irish as the "Sea Queen of Connemara," Grace O'Malley was the sixteenth-century leader of a large pirate clan that operated along Ireland's western coast. Her ships patrolled the harbors between Galway and Clew Bay, forcing any merchant ships that wanted to do business in the area to first pay a commission. If the traders refused, the pirates seized their cargoes. When the English began imposing stricter control over Ireland during the reign of Queen Elizabeth I (1533–1603; ruled 1558–1603), government authorities decided that O'Malley's pirating activities posed an unacceptable threat to trade, and they took official steps to stop her. Intent on protecting her livelihood and her family, O'Malley sailed to London and met with the queen. The audience proved successful, and the pirate leader was able to return to Ireland with permission from the crown to raid any ships belonging to England's enemies.

Early life

Grace O'Malley, also known as Gráinne Ní Mhálle, was born around 1530 in County Mayo, Ireland, where her father, Owen "Black Oak" O'Malley, was chieftain of a powerful clan that made its living at sea. Based in Clew Bay, on County Mayo's rocky west coast, the O'Malley clan kept exclusive fishing and trading rights to these waters, requiring others who wished to fish there to purchase expensive licenses. Similar demands were imposed on

191

The O'Malley castle in County Mayo, Ireland. © WILLIAM SUTTON/DANITA DELIMONT, AGENT/DANITA DELIMONT/ ALAMY.

trading vessels, which were required to give the clan a percentage of their expected profits before being allowed into enter O'Malley ports. The clan also made raids along the coast, capturing merchant ships and fighting with rival clans.

To protect themselves from enemy clans and from government authorities, which imposed the death sentence on pirates, the O'Malleys built fortresses at strategic positions along the coast and on Clare Island, which sits at the entrance to Clew Bay. Grace, Owen's only daughter and his favorite child, grew up in her father's castles and often went sailing with him. Although she did not receive much schooling, Grace learned how to read and write. She also learned how to manage a boat—a complex skill in Ireland's rocky and often stormy waters.

Details about Grace's life have often been romanticized. One story tells how the feisty girl cut off her hair in defiance after her father said he could no longer permit her to accompany him on his boat, because she was a girl and her hair would get tangled in the ship's ropes. Legend also says that Grace was a fearless fighter who saved her father's life when Owen's vessel was attacked by an English warship. Jumping onto the back of an English sailor who had boarded Owen's boat and drawn a knife, Grace allegedly screamed a warning to her father, which alerted him to the danger and allowed him to fight the English off.

Marries into the O'Flaherty clan

At age sixteen, O'Malley married Donal O'Flaherty, son of the chieftain of a neighboring clan. This family was based in Connemara, and O'Malley moved there to Bunowen Castle. She bore O'Flaherty two sons, Owen and Murrough, and a daughter, Margaret. Donal proved to be a violent and careless man who picked fights with rival clans and was not able to lead the O'Flahertys effectively. Many of his kinfolk, who endured enemy raids and hunger under Donal, grew to hate him. With her husband thus undermining the strength of the O'Flaherty clan, O'Malley began exercising her own leadership. She organized O'Flaherty sailors, ordering them to patrol the waters near Galway and to demand money for safe passage from any merchant ships in the area.

When Donal was killed in a battle at Cock's Castle, a fortress he had stolen from another clan, O'Malley took over the castle's defense. She held off the enemy so effectively that English soldiers were called in to help. In response she ordered her men to strip the castle of lead, melt it down, and pour it over the walls onto the enemy below. Bold as this move was, it was not enough to save the castle. O'Malley was eventually forced to surrender the fortress to its original owners, because of a legal technicality that prevented her from inheriting her late husband's property.

Women Ashore

While Grace O'Malley's status as a pirate commander was a relatively rare achievement for a woman, piracy directly affected the lives of Irish women in many other ways. Irish pirates usually operated along coastal waters near their homes and often had wives or mistresses who lived ashore. English pirates, too, regularly visited Irish ports, and local women often found lovers or husbands among them. These women, who enjoyed the money that the men spent on them during their frequent visits, gave the pirates much valuable assistance. They helped arrange food and supplies, and provided useful information. In at least one case, a pirate wife was able to warn her husband about the arrival of an English patrol ship in the area, allowing him to plan a safe escape. Some pirate wives operated legitimate businesses, such as lodging houses. Others helped to hide stolen goods from the authorities and traded these goods. They also ran safe houses for pirates who were on the run from the law.

Prostitutes also inhabited coastal towns, hoping to earn money from pirates when they came into port. According to Henry Mainwaring (1587–1653), a former pirate of the 1600s quoted in C.R. Pennell's book *Bandits at Sea: A Pirates Reader*, one of the main reasons that so many pirates flocked to Ireland was "the good store of English, Scottish, and Irish wenches which resort unto them." But the piracy business did not necessarily provide women on shore with a large or stable income. And when pirate wives were widowed—a frequent occurrence—they often received little support. In most cases, women participated in the pirate economy because it was the only choice available to them.

O'Malley returned to O'Malley territory, settling on Clare Island. Several men from the O'Flaherty clan chose to give their allegiance to her and accompanied her to Clew Bay. When her father died, O'Malley assumed control of his fleet, amassing a force of about two hundred pirates. With these fighters, O'Malley began organizing raids on the French, Spanish, and Portuguese merchant vessels that traded in the area.

A fearless leader

O'Malley soon gained a reputation for fearless leadership. Her fleet attacked enemy castles up and down the coast of County Mayo and forced local fishing villages to pay protection money. When O'Malley considered herself badly treated, she was known to take ruthless revenge. In one instance, O'Malley captured Doona Castle, allegedly to punish its owners, the MacMahon clan, for having killed her lover, Hugh de Lacy. According to another story, O'Malley was refused hospitality one night at Howth Castle, where she had gone to seek shelter while her crew was anchored for supplies at nearby Dublin. Furious, she kidnapped the grandson of Lord Howth and took the boy back to Clare Island. Lord Howth immediately offered a high ransom for the boy's return, but the pirate leader refused. (A ransom is a sum of money demanded for the release of someone being held captive.) Her only condition, she told Howth, was that his castle must never again turn any traveler away.

Piracy made O'Malley a wealthy and powerful leader. She owned many castles and more than one thousand head of cattle. In 1566 she married Richard "Iron Dick" Bourke and through his powerful clan connections obtained control of Rockfleet Castle and the waters in the northern areas of Clew Bay. According to popular stories, O'Malley proposed to Bourke, telling him that she wanted both him and his castle. Within a year, the marriage ended in divorce. Nevertheless, O'Malley and Bourke remained business partners until Bourke's death seventeen years later, when O'Malley legally inherited one-third of his property. The marriage produced a son, Tibbot-ne-Long, which means "Toby of the Ships." Legend says that O'Malley gave birth to this child at sea and that her ship was attacked by Algerian pirates the very next day. Seeing that her crew was struggling to repel this attack, O'Malley rushed up to the deck, screaming and only half dressed. She fired her musket at the invading pirates, who were so shocked by the sight of this wild-looking woman that they fled in fear.

Defies the English

With Irish piracy taking an increasing economic toll on trade, in the 1570s the English government began serious attempts to suppress it. Ireland had been under English control since the thirteenth century, but England had not made consistent efforts to establish a strong government presence there. Over time the English lords sent to rule the island had intermarried with local nobility, adapting to a culture in which rival clans continued to wield political and social power. Although England's King Henry VII (1457–1509) had issued new policies to subdue these clans and strengthen the power of Ireland's English governors, it was not until the reign of his granddaughter, Elizabeth I, that a strong, consistent policy against Irish power was established. Determined to force the Irish to accept English governance and laws, Elizabeth offered the chieftains a bargain. If they submitted to the authority of the English crown, they would be allowed to keep their rights to their ancestral lands and given titles. But the chieftains would not be entirely free. They would have to submit to English law and pay rent and taxes to live on their own lands.

Many of the chieftains hated this policy and refused to accept it. Others decided to submit to the agreement, although many of them had no intention of actually abiding by its terms. O'Malley was among those who claimed to be willing to accept English authority. In 1577 she appeared before the English administrator in Galway, Lord Deputy Henry Sidney (1529–1586) and told him that she and her fleet were at his service. Soon afterward, though, she betrayed this promise by attacking the property of the Earl of Desmond, a chieftain who had decided to cooperate with the English. But on this occasion O'Malley failed. Desmond captured her and turned her over to the English, who sentenced her to prison.

After eighteen months in prison, O'Malley was released. Soon after she returned to County Mayo, Rockfleet Castle was attacked by the English. It was clear to O'Malley that further resistance would only endanger her life. With Bourke, she approached the English again in 1581 and promised allegiance. She and Bourke were subsequently rewarded with titles.

But the situation changed for the worse in 1584, when a new English governor, Sir Richard Bingham (1528–1599), was sent to northwestern Ireland. He detested the fact that clan leaders promised loyalty to the crown but then continued to act with defiance against English law. With a large number of troops at his disposal, Bingham made it his mission to defeat the power of the chieftains, and in particular, Grace O'Malley.

Bingham tried to deprive O'Malley of any of Bourke's property, even though Grace had a legal right to a share in what Bourke had owned. He also declared that she had fomented rebellion among the clans against the English. Considering her an enemy of England, he executed two of her stepsons. He may also have authorized the murder of her oldest son, Owen O'Flaherty. Bingham threw O'Malley into prison again and ordered her hanged. He seized O'Malley's youngest son, Tibbot, as a hostage to ensure that his mother's fighters would not try to help her escape. According to one account, she was standing on the gallows ready to die when her daughter's husband came forward to offer himself as a hostage in her place. Bingham agreed to this, and Grace was freed. Her son-in-law was later released.

Sails to London

Returning to her base at Clew Bay, O'Malley resumed her raids along the coast. Furious, Bingham slaughtered her cattle and burned her crops. When this failed to stop her piracy, Bingham sent a military force to Clew Bay in 1592 to capture O'Malley's ships. This action deprived O'Malley of her livelihood. She evaded capture by retreating north, where she gained some support from chieftains in Ulster.

But O'Malley longed to return to her seafaring life. Realizing that Bingham would never allow her this freedom, she decided to plead her case before the queen. She sent a letter to Elizabeth in 1593, explaining that she had no way to support herself without the use of her ships and promising to serve the queen if Elizabeth would order the fleet returned. "In tender consideration ... and in regard to her great age," wrote O'Malley, as quoted by Anne Wallace Sharp in *Daring Pirate Women*, "she most humbly beseeches your majesty ... to grant her some

Grace O'Malley meets Queen Elizabeth I and petitions for the right to return to sea raiding.
HIP/ART RESOURCE, NY.

reasonable maintenance for the little time she has to live." The Irish-woman also asked Elizabeth to grant her "free liberty during her life to invade with sword and fire all your highness' enemies." Intrigued by this letter, the queen replied with a series of questions. O'Malley carefully answered each one in writing and also requested a personal meeting with

Elizabeth. Apparently pleased with what O'Malley had written, the queen granted her an official audience.

The voyage to meet the queen in London was probably the longest distance that O'Malley had ever sailed. Having always stayed close to the Irish coast, the pirate queen had to navigate through dangerous sea passages to reach England. Not only were these waters often stormy, but they were also frequented by enemy pirates, and O'Malley, now in her sixties, risked attack and capture at their hands. Nevertheless, the pirate queen reached London safely, sailing up the Thames to meet the English ruler.

The English found O'Malley's behavior shocking. It was unheard of for a commoner to think she had the right to speak with the queen, and Elizabeth's advisers did not know if they could trust the Irishwoman. But the queen was favorably impressed. There is no record of the conversation between the women, and the only fact that is known about their meeting is that Elizabeth and Grace spoke in Latin. Although Elizabeth had shown little sympathy for other Irish chieftains who had come before her, she listened to O'Malley and was apparently convinced that the pirate leader posed no threat to England. O'Malley left the meeting with all of her requests granted.

The queen ordered Bingham to return O'Malley's ships and to release her son. The queen also gave O'Malley permission to attack merchant ships from Spain and France, countries that were then England's chief enemies. O'Malley was soon back in business as a pirate, much to Bingham's frustration. She built three new ships, each large enough to hold a crew of three hundred men, and took them raiding along County Mayo waters. When Bingham attempted to suppress these attacks, O'Malley sailed to London again to explain the situation to Queen Elizabeth's advisers. She returned to Ireland with their official support.

Final years

With legal permission to raid ships belonging to England's enemies, O'Malley remained a pirate until her death at age seventy-three. Bingham had fled to England in 1595 after his own supporters had risen against him. Without his interference, O'Malley operated freely in O'Malley territory. According to a report in 1601 from an English captain who captured one of O'Malley's boats, the pirate queen was still leading her fleet as she entered her seventies.

O'Malley died in Rockfleet Castle in 1603. Realizing that the political situation in Ireland was changing, O'Malley's son, Tibbot-ne-Long, chose to fight for the English in the Battle of Kinsale in 1601. This proved to be the chieftains' final defeat. For his service, Tibbot was rewarded with a knighthood and title to an extensive estate.

Unlike some pirates of other eras, O'Malley's plundering (robbing of goods by force) was largely confined to the coastal areas near her family territory. She did not sail thousands of miles to capture enemy ships laden with vast treasures or take prisoners for a fortune in ransom. But her exploits strengthened the power of her clan and made her a legendary figure in Ireland. She is remembered as a woman who insisted on playing a leading role in affairs concerning her clan and her country.

For More Information

BOOKS

Chambers, Anne. *Granuaile: Ireland's Pirate Queen.* Dublin, Ireland: Wolfhound Press, 1979; reprinted 2003.

Konstam, Angus. *Piracy: The Complete History.* Oxford, England: Osprey, 2008.

Pennell, C.R., ed. *Bandits at Sea: A Pirates Reader.* New York: New York University Press, 2001, p. 286.

Sharp, Anne Wallace. *Daring Pirate Women.* Minneapolis, MN: Lerner, 2002, pp. 39–40.

Sjoholm, Barbara. *The Pirate Queen: In Search of Grace O'Malley and Other Legendary Women of the Sea.* Emerville, GA: Seal Press, 2004.

PERIODICALS

St. Claire, Joe. "The Pirate Queen." *Modern English Digest.* (2007): 16.

WEB SITES

Staley, Judy. "Grace O'Malley." *Adventurers.* www.rootsweb.com/~nwa/grace.html (accessed on January 3, 2011).

Bartholomew Roberts

BORN: May 17, 1682 • Newydd Bach,
Pembrokeshire, Wales

DIED: February 10, 1722 • Gabon

Welsh pirate

Bartholomew Roberts. ©
LEBRECHT MUSIC AND ARTS
PHOTO LIBRARY/ALMAY.

"In an honest service, there is thin commons [little food], low wages, and hard labour; in this [piracy], plenty and satiety, pleasure and ease, liberty and power."

Although he entered piracy against his will, Bartholomew Roberts, also known as Black Bart, became one of the most successful pirates in the Atlantic Ocean in the early 1700s. During a career that lasted only about four years, Roberts captured more than four hundred ships and an enormous fortune in plunder, or goods stolen by force. Prowling the coasts of West Africa and the Americas, he attacked ships of all nations, even daring to engage in battle with heavily armed warships. His activities were such a serious threat to Britain's sea trade that Roberts became one the British Empire's most-wanted criminals.

Early life

Bartholomew Roberts came to piracy at a relatively late age. Born on May 17, 1682, in the village of Newydd Bach, Wales, the pirate was originally

Impressment

The practice of forcing captured sailors to serve aboard other vessels was a common one in the eighteenth and early nineteenth centuries. The practice even had a name, impressment.

The British Royal Navy considered impressment to be legal, and employed the practice as a way to get needed manpower for its fleet. Because conditions in the navy were extremely inhumane, sailors were often reluctant to join. Seafarers preferred signing on with merchant vessels, where their pay and treatment were much fairer. When naval recruitment was particularly low, or additional sailors were needed because of war, the Royal Navy took men by impressment. It sometimes sent groups of sailors, known as "press gangs," ashore to find suitable candidates and force them into service. It also acquired American sailors by impressment. This practice was a major factor in tensions between Great Britain and the United States that led to the War of 1812

(1812–15). But most sailors pressed into the Royal Navy were taken from merchant vessels.

Although pirate captains insisted that they never used force to persuade captured sailors to join them, this was not always true. Roberts himself said that he had accepted piracy with reluctance, and a considerable number of Roberts's pirates who stood trial after his death pleaded innocent, stating that they had been forced to join his crew against their will. There are even reports that some pirate captains in the Caribbean threatened to have sailors flogged to death if they refused to join the outlaws. Such threats may have been used more often if the pirate vessel had suffered casualties and needed to replace large numbers of sailors. Even so, many seamen willingly joined the pirates when given the choice. Piracy offered them freedoms that were not available elsewhere, and for many men it was worth the risk to accept the offer to become part of a pirate crew.

A press gang forces men into service in the navy. © MARY EVANS/CASTLE HOWARD/THE IMAGE WORKS.

named John Robert and was the son of a prosperous farmer. But Roberts had no desire to inherit his father's property, and left the farm at an early age to go to sea.

It is likely that Roberts served several years in the British navy before becoming a merchant seaman. He gained excellent seafaring skills and was known as a handsome and confident man who could take control in difficult situations. In 1718 at the age of thirty-seven, Roberts was serving as second mate aboard an English slaving ship, the *Princess of London*, which was en route to the west coast of Africa to pick up a cargo of slaves to be sold in the Americans.

Just as the *Princess of London* reached the coast of Guinea in early 1719, it was attacked by the *Royal Rover*, a vessel under the command of Welsh pirate Howell Davis (c. 1690–1719). Seizing plunder from the slave ship, Davis invited some of its sailors to join his crew. Believing that he had no choice, Roberts reluctantly agreed.

Once he became a pirate, John Robert changed his name to Bartholomew Roberts, perhaps in order to protect his family back in England. He quickly proved willing to use cunning and violence against his targets, earning the respect of his fellow sailors. His shipmates soon began calling him "Black Bart" or "Black Barty," in reference to his striking dark hair.

Elected captain

Soon after Roberts signed on with the *Royal Rover*, Davis was killed in a skirmish on the island of Principe, a Portuguese colony off the west coast of Africa. As was customary with pirates, the crew voted democratically to elect a new captain. Recognizing Roberts's superior leadership skills, the men selected him as their new commander.

Roberts's first action as captain was to avenge Davis's death. He returned to Principe, shelled the town, and then sent his men ashore to ransack it before burning it to the ground. He then set sail for the coast of Brazil. In September 1719 the pirates came upon a fleet of forty-two Portuguese merchant vessels loaded with gold and other treasure in the northern Brazilian port of Bahia. Two seventy-gun warships guarded the vessels, which were preparing to transport the treasure to Lisbon, Portugal's capital. There seemed to be no way that the crew of the *Royal Rover* could survive an assault against this formidable fleet. But Roberts was determined not to let this opportunity escape him. Disguising the *Royal Rover* as a trading ship, he approached one of the smaller Portuguese vessels, seized its captain, and forced him to identify the merchant ship with the richest cargo. Sailing straight for this ship, the *Sagrada Familia*, Roberts forced his hostage to hail its captain and invite him aboard the disguised pirate vessel. But when the pirates drew close enough to the *Sagrada Familia*, they swarmed aboard and overwhelmed its crew. Roberts and his men stole sugar, hides, tobacco, gold coins, and jewelry, including a golden cross studded with diamonds that had been intended as a gift for the king of Portugal. The Portuguese warships rushed forward, attempting to cut off the *Royal Rover*'s escape, but the pirates were able to evade them and, with the *Sagrada Familia* in tow, reached the safety of the open sea. They had stolen treasure worth the modern equivalent of about twenty-three million dollars. From that day onward, Roberts wore the diamond cross around his neck.

Roberts loved other finery as well. He dressed in luxurious fabrics and carried a small sword and two pistols tied around his waist with silken cords. He kept a band of musicians aboard his ship and ordered them to play during battles. Unlike most other pirates, he did not drink alcohol or gamble, and he disapproved of his crew doing these things. He encouraged his men to drink tea and to say regular prayers. The men did not always follow Roberts's example, but they respected him because his attacks were so extraordinarily successful.

Creates a pirate code

Shortly after capturing the *Sagrada Familia*, Roberts experienced his first major challenge as a captain. Having decided to raid a nearby supply ship for basic necessities, he set out with forty men in a small sailing vessel, the *Fortune*. He left the *Royal Rover* and the *Sagrada Familia* in the care of an officer named Walter Kennedy. Kennedy had hoped to be elected captain after Davis's death and resented the fact that Roberts got the position instead. As soon as Roberts set out in the *Fortune*, Kennedy convinced the remaining men to mutiny, or engage in an open rebellion against the ship's officers. They sailed off with both ships, which were still laden with all the treasure the pirates had stolen. When Roberts returned, the *Royal Rover* and the *Sagrada Familia* were nowhere to be found. The pirate never got the treasure back.

Furious, Roberts drew up a list of rules, or articles, to prevent any further challenges to his authority. These articles, which other pirate captains adapted for use on their own ships, explained how duties and plunder should be shared, how important matters should be voted on, and how offenses should be punished. Roberts's articles also banned gambling on his ships.

With the battered *Fortune*, Roberts headed north into the Caribbean Sea. Although he had only forty men and ten cannons, the pirate assaulted so many ships that the British colonial government sent three battleships after him. The battleships fired on Roberts and his men, but the pirate was able to escape.

Attacks ships along the North Atlantic coast

Wishing to avoid further military attacks, Roberts turned northward along the coast of North America. In late June 1720, he reached Newfoundland, in eastern Canada. There the pirates attacked the town of Trepassey, the center of the region's rich fishing industry. Ordering his musicians to blow their trumpets and pound their drums, Roberts sailed into the harbor and ordered the town ransacked. Terrified, the crew aboard the *Bideford*, assigned to guard the harbor, fled. An account quoted by Angus Konstam in *Piracy: The Complete History* states, "It is impossible particularly to recount the destruction and havoc they made here, burning and sinking all the shipping, except a Bristol galley, and destroying the fisheries, … without remorse or compunction." The pirates captured twenty-two ships.

Roberts took the Bristol galley as his new flagship, renaming it *Good Fortune*. For the remainder of July, he attacked other vessels at will, capturing or destroying at least forty ships and hundreds of smaller boats. Roberts's trip to Newfoundland was one of the most successful pirate voyages in history.

Hangs the governor of Martinique

Heading back to the Caribbean, Roberts captured ship after ship, causing fear wherever he went. His pirates became so bold that they no longer retreated to safety after attacking, believing that no ship sent to fight them could succeed. When Roberts learned that the colonial governors of Barbados and Martinique had offered a reward for his capture, he responded by creating a defiant new banner for his flagship: an image of himself on a black background, with sword raised, standing on the skulls of his enemies. Lettering on the bottom made it clear that the two skulls represented the governors who had offended him. Around this time he renamed his ship once again, calling it the *Royal Fortune*.

As he continued his rampage in the Caribbean, Roberts was delighted to come upon a man-of-war (the largest and most heavily armed warship) on which the Martinique governor was a passenger. Easily capturing the vessel, Roberts promptly ordered the governor hanged from its mast. Then he seized the vessel as his new flagship, naming it, as he did all subsequent captured flagships, the *Royal Fortune*.

Finding it increasingly difficult to sell his plunder in the Americas, where the British Piracy Act of 1721 made it a criminal offense to do business with pirates, Roberts sailed to West Africa, where he had a better chance of finding buyers for his stolen goods. During the voyage, the pirate assaulted whatever ships he encountered. Stories were told about his cruel treatment of those he defeated. Not satisfied to steal whatever treasure a ship carried, Roberts allegedly tortured passengers and crew, killing many.

Final voyage

In January 1722 Roberts and his crew were in West Africa, sailing near the coast of Benin. On January 12, they seized eleven slave ships in the harbor of Benin's major trading port, Whydah (present-day Ouidah). The pirate demanded a ransom of 8 pounds (3.6 kilograms) of gold dust for each ship. Ten of the captains paid, but one refused. Furious that this man defied him, Roberts ordered his crew to cover the ship's deck with tar. Then they set it on fire. Ignoring the fact that eighty slaves were shackled in pairs inside the burning ship, Roberts took his ransom money and sailed away. Still in their chains, many of the Africans burned to death. Those who were able to jump overboard either drowned or were eaten by sharks.

By now the British government was ready to take stronger action against the pirate. It sent two Royal Navy warships, the HMS *Weymouth* and the HMS *Swallow*, to patrol the coast of West Africa. Reaching the town of Cape Coast, in Ghana, their commander was told that residents had seen pirate ships in the area. Aboard the *Weymouth*, most of the crew were suffering from tropical diseases, such as malaria and yellow fever. They were too weak to fight or even manage their ship. Leaving the *Weymouth* behind, Chaloner Ogle (1681–1750), commander of the fifty-gun *Swallow*, set out to find the pirates. He reached Whydah on January 15. The remains of the burned slave ship still smoldered in the harbor. Roberts had sailed away only three days earlier.

Learning that Roberts had stolen a French ship at Whydah, Ogle reasoned that the pirates would have to anchor in a safe place in order to make repairs and convert the vessel for piracy. He guessed that the outlaws had taken shelter at the Bight of Benin, a deep harbor nearby. Reaching the Bight on February 5, he spied three of Roberts's ships at anchor at Cape Lopez, off the coast of Gabon.

The *Swallow* drew near to Roberts's ships but then had to change course in order to avoid a sandbar. Ogle was not able to get a shot at his targets. Seeing the *Swallow* approach and then turn away, the pirate captain mistook it for a merchant vessel that was desperate to avoid a pirate attack. Roberts sent one of his ships, under the command of a Captain Skrym, after this apparent prize.

When he saw the pirate ship moving toward him, Ogle figured out what had happened. He saw his chance to lure the pirates into a trap. He ordered his crew to slow the *Swallow* down so that Skrym's ship could catch up. When the pirates were within range, Ogle suddenly swung the *Swallow* around and blasted the pirates with cannons. The pirates were completely unprepared, expecting the *Swallow* to be unarmed. But they fought for more than an hour before finally surrendering to the naval captain. Twenty-six pirates were killed and Skrym lost a leg.

Death and legacy

Ogle ordered repairs to the captured pirate ship and then sent it to Principe. With the *Swallow*, he returned to Cape Lopez to look for Roberts. He found the pirate's ships just where he had last seen them. Roberts himself was entertaining a group of merchants onboard the *Royal Fortune*, while his men were having a drunken party.

Ogle attacked at dawn on February 10, 1722. The *Swallow* approached the pirate ships in heavy rain, displaying a French flag. Unsure about the identity of this ship, the pirates waited. As the *Swallow* got closer, Ogle took down the French flag and hoisted the British flag. The Royal Navy had found Roberts.

Hungover after a night of heavy drinking, the pirates struggled to prepare a defense. Roberts ordered them to ready their guns and take their battle stations. Then, realizing that he would have to pass Ogle's ship in order to reach safety, Roberts began to steer the *Royal Fortune* toward the *Swallow*. But the pirate's luck had run out. As the pirate ship passed close to the naval vessel, Ogle ordered his men to open fire. Roberts was hit with grapeshot (a cluster of small iron balls shot from a cannon) and died instantly.

Bartholomew Roberts was killed in a battle against the Royal Naval warship Swallow. MARY EVANS PICTURE LIBRARY/EVERETT COLLECTION.

The pirate captain had always told his crew that, if he were killed, they must never let his enemies have his body. Government authorities often put the corpses of executed pirates on display as a public warning, and Roberts did not want to suffer this fate. Obeying his orders, his men threw his body overboard, still clad in its lavish clothes and jewels.

The battle between the *Swallow* and the *Royal Fortune* lasted for three hours before the pirates gave up. Ogle also captured two other ships belonging to Roberts. The naval commander recovered 300 tons (272 metric tons) of gold dust from the pirate vessels.

The surviving pirates were imprisoned near Whydah. The more than seventy Africans among them were sold as slaves, and the remaining pirates stood trial. Thirty-seven men were sentenced to indentured servitude, a form of involuntary unpaid labor, in the West Indies. Another seventy-four were acquitted, having convinced the court that they had been forced to join Roberts's crew. The rest of the pirates received the death sentence. They were hanged together on the Whydah waterfront.

Ogle returned to England a hero and was knighted for his service. (A knight is a man granted a rank of honor by the monarch for his personal merit or service to the country.) Roberts's defeat marked the end of a golden age of piracy that had made pirates the robber kings of the Atlantic since 1690.

For More Information

BOOKS

Hamilton, Sue. *Bartholomew Roberts.* Edina, MN: ABDO, 2007.

Konstam, Angus. *Piracy: The Complete History.* Oxford, England: Osprey, 2008, p. 238.

————. *Scourge of the Seas: Buccaneers, Pirates and Privateers.* Oxford, England: Osprey, 2007.

Rediker, Marcus. *Villains of all Nations: Atlantic Pirates in the Golden Age.* Boston, MA: Beacon Press, 2004.

WEB SITES

"Bartholomew Roberts." *Pirate Shipwrecks.* http://pirateshipwrecks.com/bartholomew_black_bart_roberts (accessed on January 3, 2011).

Woodes Rogers

BORN: c. 1679 • England

DIED: July 15, 1732 • Nassau, Bahamas

English privateer, governor

A statue of Woodes Rogers.
© M. TIMOTHY O'KEEFE/
ALAMY.

"We have a good governor, but a harsh one."

– Thomas Morris, a pirate executed by Rogers
QUOTED IN *THE REPUBLIC OF PIRATES: BEING THE TRUE AND SURPRISING STORY OF THE CARIBBEAN PIRATES AND THE MAN WHO BROUGHT THEM DOWN* BY COLIN WOODWARD.

Woodes Rogers, the first governor of the British colony of the Bahamas, played a major role in eradicating piracy from the Caribbean in the early 1700s. As a merchant with extensive seafaring experience, Rogers understood the threat that piracy posed to commerce. He also knew what motivated pirates. Rather than simply fighting them, he urged them to accept a general amnesty. This was a pardon for pirates who were willing to surrender themselves and abandon their criminal activities. Although this amnesty did not put a complete stop to piracy, it significantly decreased it. Rogers's motto was, "Piracy expelled, commerce restored," according to Nick Britten in an article for the (London) *Telegraph*. The phrase remained the motto of the Bahamas until the country declared independence in 1973.

Inherits merchant business

Woodes Rogers came from a wealthy family with good social connections. Born around 1679, he spent his early childhood in Poole, a port in southern England, and later moved to Bristol with his family. His father, also named Woodes Rogers, was a merchant and owned shares in several ships. When he was eighteen years old, the younger Rogers became an apprentice to a Bristol sea captain. During his seven years of training, he acquired maritime skills that served him well when, in 1706, he inherited his father's business after the elder Rogers's death.

In 1705 Rogers married Sarah Whetstone, daughter of Rear Admiral Sir William Whetstone (d. 1711). This match advanced Rogers's social standing, giving him citizenship rights in the city of Bristol. The couple had three children.

Circumnavigates the world

Rogers faced several challenges when he took over his father's business in 1706. War had broken out among rival European powers in 1701, pitting England against France and Spain. Several of the ships in which Rogers owned shares were granted privateering licenses. Privateering was a legal form of piracy. It authorized sea captains to raid and plunder (rob of goods by force) ships belonging to enemy countries, allowing them to keep a share of the profits after turning over a percentage to the government. Privateering was a common practice in Rogers's era, and could make a seafarer wealthy. But it could also be financially devastating for the ships that were the victims of privateers. When the *Whetstone Galley*, one of the ships that Rogers owned shares in, was captured by French privateers, the young merchant lost his entire investment in the voyage. This was only the first of several financial damages inflicted on him by the French. To recover from these losses, Rogers agreed to lead a privateering expedition against the Spanish in the Pacific Ocean.

The expedition, proposed by former pirate and seafarer **William Dampier** (1651–1715; see entry), embarked from Bristol on August 1, 1708. It consisted of two ships, the *Duke* and the *Duchess*. Rogers served as commander of the expedition and as captain of the *Duke*. Making the treacherous voyage around South America into the Pacific Ocean, the expedition, guided by Dampier, sailed to the remote Juan Fernández islands off southern Chile to get fresh supplies. There, the group noticed a fire onshore. Suspecting that this was evidence that a Spanish ship might

The Duke, *Woodes Rogers's privateer ship.* MARY EVANS PICTURE LIBRARY/EVERETT COLLECTION.

be nearby, Rogers sent some of his crew to the island to investigate. What they found was a castaway, Scottish sailor Alexander Selkirk (1676–1721). The sailor had been left on the island four years earlier. He had quarreled with his captain and had asked to be put ashore. He had expected another ship to come along within a short time and rescue him, but when this did not happen, he was forced to use his wits to survive. Completely on his own for four years and four months, Selkirk learned to catch wild animals, forage for food, and make clothing out of goatskins.

Rogers rescued Selkirk and made him a mate on the *Duke.* The castaway proved so valuable that Rogers later made him captain of a smaller vessel captured in the Pacific. Selkirk's story inspired the 1719 novel *Robinson Crusoe* by English writer Daniel Defoe (c. 1659–1731).

Rogers captured several Spanish prizes in the Pacific, most notably the treasure ship *Nuestra Señora de la Incarnación Disenganio,* which the privateers attacked off the coast of Mexico. Rogers was shot in the face during this battle, and when the expedition later reached Indonesia, he had surgery at the Dutch port of Batavia to remove a musket ball from the roof of his mouth. From southeast Asia the expedition continued westward, sailing around Africa and into the Atlantic Ocean.

After more than three years at sea, the expedition returned to England on October 14, 1711. Rogers was hailed as a hero for having circumnavigated, or sailed around, the globe, and for damaging Spanish shipping. But he was not able to enjoy the wealth he had obtained as a privateer. The British East India Company (EIC), a corporation with a monopoly (exclusive control) on British trade in Asia, objected to Rogers's dealings with the Dutch in Indonesia, to whom he had sold some of his plunder. The EIC did not want any competition in the area, and sued Rogers for a percentage of his takings. The EIC won, leaving him with a disappointingly small profit to show for three years of hardship.

In 1712 Rogers published an account of his voyage titled *A Cruising Voyage Round the World*. The book contains fascinating stories of adventure, as well as practical information about navigation (charting the routes of ships) and the possible benefits of establishing British colonies in the South Pacific. It became a best seller.

Madagascar

Profits from his book were not enough to help Rogers out of his deepening financial problems. Two hundred members of his crew filed suit against him, claiming that he had not paid them their proper share of the privateering profits. Rogers was forced to sell his house in Bristol and declare bankruptcy. Shortly afterward, his wife gave birth to their fourth child, who did not survive infancy. After the birth, Rogers and his wife separated.

To make some money, Rogers organized an expedition against pirates operating off Madagascar, a large island in the Indian Ocean off the coast of Africa. With the permission of the British East India Company, he set out in 1713 on a slaving voyage to Madagascar. While there, he collected detailed information about the pirates operating in the region and convinced several of them to seek a pardon from Britain. Having sold his slaves at a good profit in the Dutch colonies in Indonesia, Rogers returned to England in 1715. He hoped to win support for the establishment of a British colony on Madagascar, but the British East India Company objected to this idea and nothing came of it.

Appointed governor of Bahamas

Through his social and political connections, Rogers was able to get approval from King George I (1660–1727) to form a company to manage the Bahamas, a major British colony in the Caribbean. Lacking an effective government, the Bahamas had become the region's primary pirate haven, and Rogers believed he could bring this lawlessness under control. (A pirate haven is a safe place for pirates to harbor and repair their ships, resupply, and organize raiding parties.) The king approved of Rogers's plan, under which the new governor would not be paid a salary but would receive a percentage of the Bahamas's profits, generated primarily from agriculture.

On January 6, 1718, the king appointed Rogers the captain general and governor in chief of the Bahamas. The day before, Great Britain had announced a pardon for all pirates who agreed to surrender by September 5 of that year. Rogers made it a central point of his governorship to encourage pirates to accept the terms of this pardon.

Rogers arrived in the Bahamas on July 22, 1718. His force consisted of seven vessels, including three Royal Navy ships with full crews, as well as soldiers and colonists. On reaching Nassau, the capital of the colony and the largest town on the island of New Providence, the expedition immediately encountered pirate Charles Vane (c. 1680–1721), whose ship was now trapped in the harbor by Rogers's fleet. Vane tried to negotiate an escape but failed. He then set fire to a French vessel he had captured, using it to distract the naval contingent and slip away.

The new governor ordered New Providence's fortresses to be repaired and strengthened, and set about building a functional government. Despite his failure with Vane, Rogers had a high degree of success in persuading the other pirates of New Providence to take the king's pardon. But when Vane resurfaced with a written threat that he and his associate, the notorious pirate known as **Blackbeard** (c. 1680–1718; see entry), would defeat Rogers and take control of the island, Rogers shifted to harsher tactics. In September he heard that Vane was at Green Turtle Cay, an island about 120 miles (193 kilometers) north of Nassau. Rogers also learned that some of the pardoned pirates from New Providence, violating the terms of their amnesty, had decided to join Vane.

Rogers sent ex-pirate Benjamin Hornigold (d. 1719) to Green Turtle Cay to get more information on Vane's activities and, if possible, to capture or kill him. But when several weeks passed without any word from Hornigold, Rogers feared that he, too, had returned to crime and that the pirates were planning an attack. The governor declared martial law and ordered all residents of the island to prepare to defend their territory. (Martial law is military rule imposed on a civilian population in time crisis.) Hornigold eventually returned. He had not captured or killed Vane, but he did return with a pirate ship and several captives.

Executes pirates

Meanwhile Rogers was also dealing with threats from Spain, and had sent one of his naval vessels to Cuba on a mission of diplomacy. Its crew, however, mutinied before the ship arrived in Havana and had taken to piracy. (A mutiny is an open rebellion against a ship's officers.) Rogers sent Hornigold after these renegades. He brought ten of them back to Nassau, where they stood trial on December 9, 1718.

Nine of the men were convicted and sentenced to death; the tenth was acquitted. Three days after the trial, Rogers ordered eight of the convicts hanged, having granted one man a reprieve. The execution had the effect that Rogers had hoped for, shocking the island's residents and demonstrating that the government would not tolerate contempt for the law.

Despite the facts that about one hundred of his men had died of disease and that he had lost one naval ship to the pirates and two others to a new assignment in New York, Rogers continued to work at organizing the Bahamian economy and defense. He spent his own money to buy supplies needed in case of a Spanish attack, and he continued to shore up New Providence's fortifications. In May 1719 a Spanish fleet set out to invade Nassau but then turned away when an opportunity arose to fight the French, now an ally of Britain and an enemy of Spain, in Florida. In 1720, however, Spain did attack the Bahamas at Paradise Island, near the entrance to Nassau's harbor. Well prepared, Rogers's troops succeeded in repelling the invaders.

When peace was declared later that year, Rogers was able to focus on domestic issues. But his economic problems continued to escalate. He had borrowed money to pay for defense materials and received no compensation for this. Nor could he find a way to buy further supplies for New Providence. Suffering from health problems, he traveled to South Carolina, spending six weeks in Charleston in hopes of regaining his strength. While there, he encountered a rival, Captain John Hildesley of the HMS *Flamborough*. The men had become caught up in a personal dispute in New Providence, and when they met again in Charleston, they fought a duel to

Debtors' Prison

Until the 1800s, it was common practice in Great Britain to imprison people who could not pay their debts. They remained in prison until their families were able to come up with the money that was owed. To make matters worse, inmates were required to pay for their food and shelter in the prison. If they lacked the money for these fees, the amount was added to their original debt. Unable to work because they were behind bars, imprisoned debtors often sank further and further into financial ruin. If family or friends were unable to help them settle their debts, they could languish in prison for several years and even die there.

Among the most notable debtors' prisons in England was Marshalsea Prison in London. It was a privately operated institution, run for profit, and established an elaborate system of privileges that inmates could purchase for various fees. Prisoners who had the money could, for example, purchase alcohol and goods at an affiliated shop. The luckiest prisoners were those who could afford to pay for permission to leave the prison during the day, which gave them the opportunity to earn some money toward paying their creditors. But many were not so lucky, and lacked even the money to buy food. An investigation by the British parliament in 1729 found that, in a period of three months, some three hundred inmates at Marshalsea had starved to death. Another institution, London's Fleet Prison, also held a large number of inmates who were debtors. The Fleet, which like all debtors' prisons required prisoners to finance their own upkeeps, built an iron grille in its wall to enable inmates to beg money from people passing on the street.

Conditions in debtors' prisons caused outrage in Britain and provoked calls for prison reform. Imprisonment for debt was finally abolished in Britain in 1869.

resolve the matter. Having suffered a wound in the duel and frustrated by Britain's lack of support for New Providence, Rogers sailed to London in March 1721. There, he hoped to make the case for increased financial and legal resources to govern the colony.

Sent to debtors' prison

Arriving in England in June, Rogers learned that his Bahamas company had been dissolved and that a new governor had been appointed for the colony. Unable to repay what he had borrowed in Nassau, he was thrown into debtors' prison. Eventually, however, his creditors relented and agreed to cancel his debts. Rogers was released but was seriously discouraged by his financial woes.

Sometime in 1722 or in early 1723, a man working on a book about pirate history approached Rogers and asked for his help. Having sailed as a privateer and hunted pirates in the Caribbean, Rogers supplied this author with a wealth of details. The book, *A General History of the Robberies and Murders of the Most Notorious Pirates*, written by Captain Charles Johnson, was published in 1724. It captured the public's imagination with its exciting images of buried treasure, swashbuckling battles, and romanticized pirates with wooden legs and eye patches. The book became the standard source of information on pirates and inspired many works of literature, including Robert Louis Stevenson's novel *Treasure Island*, published in 1883; and J.M. Barrie's play *Peter Pan*, first performed in 1904. Modern historians, however, consider many of the book's details to be embellished or romanticized. Nevertheless, they believe that most of the basic facts in Johnson's book are accurate.

Johnson's book, a best seller in Britain and in the Americas, restored Rogers's reputation. Hailed as a hero, he was able to win a government pension and in 1728 was appointed to a second term as governor of the Bahamas.

Although piracy and defense did not plague the Bahamas during Rogers's second term there, the governor struggled to win support for local taxes and other issues. He died in Nassau in 1732. A street in the city is named in his honor, and a plaque in Bristol commemorates him as a "Great Seaman, Circumnavigator, [and] Colonial Governor."

For More Information

BOOKS

Rothman, David, and Norval Morris, eds. *The Oxford History of the Prison: The Practice of Punishment in Western Society.* England: Oxford University Press, 1995.

Woodard, Colin. *The Republic of Pirates: Being the True and Surprising Story of the Caribbean Pirates and the Man Who Brought Them Down.* Boston, MA: Houghton Mifflin Harcourt, 2008.

PERIODICALS

Britten, Nick. "Diaries of Swashbuckling Hero Who Rescued Robinson Crusoe Unearthed." *The Telegraph* (London) (January 5, 2009). Available online at www.telegraph.co.uk/news/newstopics/howaboutthat/4125577/Diaries-of-swashbuckling-hero-who-rescued-Robinson-Crusoe-unearthed.html (accessed on January 3, 2011).

Manco, Jean. "The Real Rescue of Crusoe." *Bristol Magazine* (August 2008). Available online at www.buildinghistory.org/bristol/woodesrogers.shtml (accessed on January 3, 2011).

John Ward

BORN: c. 1553 • Feversham, Kent, England

DIED: 1623 • Tunis, Tunisia

English pirate

> "Tell those ... who have been the occasion [cause] that I am banished out of my country, that before I have done with them I will make them sue for my pardon!"

Among the most notorious of the North African pirates known as the Barbary corsairs was Englishman John Ward. Having served in the Royal Navy, Ward was attracted to the freedom and wealth that the life of piracy offered. He established himself as a corsair who raided ships carrying valuable cargoes to and from Venice, Italy. Ward soon made a fortune and settled into a life of luxury in the North African city-state of Tunis. He dressed as an Ottoman Turk, adopted Ottoman customs, and took a Turkish name, Yusef Reis. He is remembered as a daring figure whose adventures have inspired romantic images of piracy. His activities have historic importance as well, because they focused England's attention on the need to establish a strong naval presence in the Mediterranean Sea in the early sixteenth century.

Forced into the navy

John Ward, who was also called Jack, was born in the village of Feversham, England, around 1553. Little else is known about his childhood, except that his family was poor and uneducated, and was employed in fishing. As a young man Ward made his way to the seaport of Plymouth, where he likely found work on fishing or trade vessels. According to Andrew Barker, an English merchant captain who was captured by Ward in 1609 and whose testimony is quoted by Leslie Hotson in *Atlantic*

Monthly, Ward spent most of his time in the local alehouse. Barker also noted that men who had sailed with Ward in his younger days considered him a "mad rascall" who loved to drink, swear, and gamble.

During hostilities between England and Spain in the late 1500s, Ward was pressed into service in the English Royal Navy. This means that he was seized by the navy from a civilian vessel, or picked up onshore, and forced to join the crew of an understaffed military ship. He spent time in the Caribbean Sea and by 1603 was serving on the naval ship *Lion's Whelp*. Dissatisfied with military life, which offered poor wages, strict rules, and harsh punishments, he decided to desert. He persuaded some crewmates to join him in an escape from the *Lion's Whelp*. With three captured vessels, they made their way into the Mediterranean and to the port of Tunis in Tunisia.

Attacks Venetian shipping

Desertion from the navy made Ward a criminal. After arriving in the Mediterranean, he made his legal status worse by becoming a pirate and preying on the Venetian trade vessels that frequented its shipping lanes. He raided ship after ship, stealing tons of rich cargo that he then sold in Ottoman ports. Because he gave Ottoman traders a generous discount, selling his goods for a fraction of what they were really worth, the Ottomans became Ward's friends and supporters. In 1606 the pirate brought cargo worth two hundred thousand dollars to the bey, or local ruler, of Tunis, asking for only forty thousand dollars in exchange. After this, the bey gave Ward safe haven in the city.

Within three years, Ward's piracy had brought him a huge fortune. His wealth increased even more spectacularly when, in 1607, he captured one of Venice's greatest merchant vessels, the *Reneira e Soderina*. It was carrying about 1,400 tons (1,270 metric tons) of cargo, all of which Ward seized. Now he had so much money that he could retire in luxury. Ward was now in his fifties, and he had grown homesick for his native country. But his desertion, his piracy against European interests, and his alliance with the Barbary corsairs made him a traitor to England and to Christian European countries, and he feared arrest and perhaps execution if he dared return. Yet he did not want to spend his old age in exile. He petitioned England's king, James I (1566–1625), for permission to return to England with the king's pardon.

At first Ward asked to be allowed back with all the fortune he had taken in the Mediterranean. But King James made it clear that he would

John Ward petitioned King James I (pictured) to pardon his crimes and allow him to return to England, but the king refused. © THE ART GALLERY COLLECTION/ALAMY.

never permit these conditions. The pirate then sent a messenger to London to present an offer to the Venetian ambassador there. If the Venetian authorities would not object to the king pardoning Ward, the pirate would return whatever treasures he still possessed to the Venetian merchants whose ships he had raided. Ward hoped that this would convince the king to allow him to back into England.

While waiting for an answer, Ward overhauled the *Reneira e Soderina* to make her into a pirate vessel. He streamlined the ship's decks and added sixty cannons. He also sent a lot of money to England to bribe officials who could put in a good word for him with the king. But in late 1607, James formally banished Ward from England. He also promised Venice, a Christian city-state with whom England wanted to maintain good relations, that he would never issue a pardon for the pirate who had done so much damage to its commercial interests without Venice's consent.

By this time, Ward had a fleet of eight swift ships, and in February 1608 he resumed his attacks on Venetian ships. Venice responded by increasing the number of warships that were assigned to escort its merchant fleet. This did not stop Ward. In March 1608 the English ambassador, quoted by Hotson, wrote, "The hatred of [Ward] increaseth, and full as fast, the feare of him."

Escapes a shipwreck

In 1608 Ward lost the *Reneira e Soderina*. His fleet was off the coast of Crete, an island in the eastern Mediterranean to the southeast of the Greek mainland, when a storm struck. During the storm, Ward got into a small boat and left the ship, without any explanation. Shortly after this, the *Reneira e Soderina* sank. A crew of four hundred Ottoman and English sailors was aboard. All of them went down with the ship except for four men who escaped in a makeshift raft. When word reached Europe of the shipwreck, people hoped that Ward had also drowned. But the pirate survived, steering his small boat toward another vessel in his fleet and then sailing to safety in Tunis.

The Tunisians were not happy to see Ward. They, too, had heard about the wreck and were sad and angry at the huge loss of life. The fact that Ward had abandoned the ship troubled them, and they suspected that Ward had planned for the Ottoman crew to die. When Ward came ashore, the Tunisians were ready to lynch him. But the pirate somehow managed to persuade the Ottoman government of his innocence and good will. According to Hotson, Ward drew on his "personal courage and an unsurpassed ability to 'swear through a nine-inch plank'" to convince the Ottomans that he remained their friend.

Angers King James

Venice, meanwhile, was pressuring King James to take more decisive action against piracy. The Venetians wanted the king to allow English merchant ships to carry guns for protection, but the king was firmly opposed to this idea. He worried that, if trade vessels were armed, their captains would be tempted to become privateers. (A privateer is a private ship or ship owner commissioned by a state or government to attack the merchant ships of an enemy nation.) Although privateering had been a common practice among English sailors throughout the 1500s, James was firmly opposed to it. One of his first missions after taking the English throne in 1603 had been to negotiate peace between England and Spain, which had been at war, on and off, since 1585. During these years, English privateers had done considerable damage to Spanish shipping. Spain had lodged several bitter complaints, denouncing English privateers as pirates and criminals. As part of the peace agreement with Spain, James had promised to do everything in his power to stop theft on the high seas. Instead of agreeing to let merchant ships carry guns, he proclaimed stricter laws against piracy. He also issued an order requiring all English ships to, as quoted by Hotson, "pursue and engage the pirate Ward as the man who above all others has inflicted heavy damage on Christians."

Ironically James's rigid stance against privateering led to more piracy, not less. In the years immediately before his reign, privateering in the seas along England's southern coast was big business. At least eighty-five privateering ships operated there, and their plunder (goods stolen by force) accounted for 10 to 15 percent of English imports. The king's banning of privateering suddenly put hundreds, and perhaps thousands, of sailors out of work. Unable to operate legally as privateers and lacking the skills and experience for other work, they became pirates. As one captain stated, quoted by Tinniswood, "[the king] hath lessened by this general peace the flourishing employment that we seafaring men do bleed for at sea." And since they were no longer bound by the limits of privateering, these men attacked ships of any nation. Many of them, including Ward, established themselves in the Mediterranean, where ships from Venice and other European countries provided tempting targets. The more honorable of these English pirates made a point of attacking only ships belonging to Spain or its allies. Less scrupulous ones robbed everyone except the English. And the worst scoundrels declared any ship fair game.

Converts to Islam

Despite the king's obvious anger toward him, Ward tried once more to win a pardon. He offered a bribe of £40,000—a tremendous fortune—if the king would relent. But once again, James refused. Realizing that he would never again set foot in England unless he surrendered as a criminal, Ward petitioned the city-state of Florence, Italy, for permission to live there without being prosecuted for piracy. He offered a bribe of 150,000 gold crowns. But this request was also turned down.

It was clear that no Christian country would accept Ward. He responded by rejecting his European culture and adopting the ways of the Ottomans. He dressed in long robes and a turban, built an enormous palace for himself, and converted to Islam. When news of the pirate's conversion reached England, it caused "the great indignation of the whole nation," according to a report by the Venetian ambassador quoted by Tinniswood. Ministers preached sermons condemning Ward, and ballads and theater pieces presented him as a demonic figure who had sold his soul to the devil in return for wealth.

An English sailor who saw Ward in 1608 described the pirate captain, as quoted by Peter Earle in *The Pirate Wars*, as "very short with little hair, and that quite white, bald in front; swarthy face and beard. Speaks little and almost always swearing. Drunk from morn till night. . . . A fool and an idiot out of his trade." At his palace Ward was waited on by numerous servants. Among these, according to a 1615 account by Scottish traveler and author William Lithgow (1582–1645), quoted by Hotson, were "some fifteen circumcised [Christian] English Runagates [renegades], whose lives and countenances were both alike, even as desperate as disdainfull."

England, meanwhile, continued to put pressure on Ward to cease his piracy. It sent an English sailor, Captain Pepwell, to Tunis to meet with Ward and try to convince him to stop his criminal activities. When Ward would not listen, Pepwell persuaded one of the pirate's followers, a German sailor named Kerson, to murder Ward. In return Kerson would be granted asylum in England. The plot failed. Ward offered big cash payments to Pepwell's crew, and many of them deserted their captain to join Ward as pirates. Kerson, meanwhile, was captured by a Venetian ship and hanged.

In the summer of 1609, Portugal sent a fleet of twelve huge battleships to Tunis to try to destroy Ward. In a stealthy night mission, the Portuguese succeeded in burning most of Ward's fleet, which lay at anchor. Although this was a devastating loss, Ward recovered quickly. Within about six months he had obtained new ships and was once again in business in the shipping lanes of the eastern Mediterranean.

A Tragic Hero

Although the Barbary pirates were widely feared, their exploits also inspired awe. Europeans were particularly fascinated by the idea of women being captured by corsairs and sold into slavery. This theme inspired the plot of *The Corsair*, a long narrative poem by English poet George Gordon, better known as Lord Byron (1788–1824). The hero of the poem, Conrad, is a pirate captain based on an island in the Mediterranean Sea, near Greece. Conrad rescues a slave woman belonging to the Ottoman ruler of this region. English readers were thrilled with the exotic aspects of this story. When the poem was first published in London in 1814, it sold out all ten thousand copies of its first print run in just one day. Within a month, it had sold twenty-five thousand copies.

Byron made Conrad an idealistic hero who turned to piracy because his society rejected him. But actual corsairs were very different. They were motivated primarily by a desire for money. And they were far more likely to kidnap and sell women than to rescue them from captivity. Even so, Byron's poem created an image of the corsairs that remained popular for many years and that inspired other works of art. Among them are *Il corsaro*, an opera by Giuseppe Verdi

Lord Byron, author of The Corsair. © WORLD HISTORY ARCHIVE/ALAMY.

(1813–1901); *Le Corsaire*, a ballet popularized by Russian choreographer Marius Petipa (1818–1910); and *The Corsair*, a painting by Eugene Delacroix (1798–1863).

Later life

Ward's last-known pirate action occurred in 1617, when he attacked and burned the *Foscarina*, a Venetian merchant vessel. He was reportedly seen at sea the following year, but it is not known what happened to him after that. According to many reports, he retired in Tunis around 1622 and died there of plague the following year. He reportedly had an Italian wife in Tunis, as well as a wife in England whom he continued to support.

Ward's adventures captured the imagination of people living in seventeenth-century England. Tales of his exploits were reported in the news and were the subject of ballads and other entertainments. A ballad known as "The Famous Sea-Fight between Captain Ward and the Rain-bow," the lyrics of which are available on the *Contemplations from the Marianas Trench* Web site, describes the pirate as "the biggest robber that ever you did hear." The balled recounts a battle between Ward and an English ship sent to fight him. Winning this battle, Ward boasts, "Tell your king for me, If he reigns king all on the land Ward will reign king on the sea."

Historians debate Ward's importance in the history of piracy. Some think that his activities, while spectacular, did not have much lasting effect. Others point out that his activities helped to expand Barbary piracy. Raids by the corsairs became so frequent that England responded by building naval bases in Gibraltar, at the Atlantic entrance to the Mediterranean, and at the island of Minorca. These were significant steps in the expansion of the British Empire.

For More Information

BOOKS

Earle, Peter. *The Pirate Wars.* New York: Macmillan, 2006, p. 29.

Malam, John. *The Barbaraossa Brothers and the Pirates of the Mediterranean.* Laguna Hills, CA: QEB, 2008.

PERIODICALS

Hotson, Leslie. "Pirates in Parchment." *Atlantic Monthly* (August 1927). Available online at www.theatlantic.com/past/docs/issues/27aug/hotson.htm (accessed on January 3, 2011).

Tinniswood, Adrian. "Captain Jennings Causes Chaos." *History Today* (May 2010): 48 (6).

WEB SITES

" 'The Corsair', Lord Byron's Best Seller." *National Public Radio.* www.npr.org/templates/story/story.php?storyId=4487368 (accessed on January 3, 2011).

"Ward the Pirate." *Contemplations from the Marianas Trench.* www.contemplator.com/sea/ward.html (accessed on January 3, 2011).

Where to Learn More

Books

Burgess, Douglas R., Jr. *The Pirates' Pact: The Secret Alliances Between History's Most Notorious Buccaneers and Colonial America.* New York: McGraw-Hill, 2009.

Carpenter, John Reeve. *Pirates: Scourge of the Seas.* New York: Sterling, 2006.

Cawthorne, Nigel. *Pirates of the 21st Century: How Modern-day Buccaneers Are Terrorising the World's Oceans.* London: John Blake, 2010.

Clifford, Barry. *Expedition Whydah: The Story of the World's First Excavation of a Pirate Ship.* New York: Cliff Street Books, 1999.

Cordingly, David. *Under the Black Flag: The Romance and the Reality of Life Among the Pirates.* New York: Random House, 2006.

————, ed. *Pirates: Terror on the High Seas from the Caribbean to the South China Sea.* North Dighton, MA: World Publications Group, 2006.

Crowley, Roger. *Empires of the Sea: The Siege of Malta, the Battle of Lepanto, and the Contest for the Center of the World.* New York: Random House, 2008.

Druett, Joan. *She Captains: Heroines and Hellions of the Sea.* New York: Simon and Schuster, 2001.

Forester, C.S. *The Barbary Pirates.* New York: Sterling Point, 2008.

Heller-Roazen, Daniel. *The Enemy of All: Piracy and the Law of Nations.* New York: Zone Books, 2009.

Johnson, Captain Charles. *A General History of the Robberies and Murders of the Most Notorious Pirates.* Guilford, CT: The Lyons Press, 1998, 2002.

Konstam, Angus. *The History of Pirates.* Guilford, CT: The Lyons Press, 2002.

————. *Piracy: The Complete History.* Oxford, England: Osprey, 2008.

Lane, Kris E. *Pillaging the Empire: Piracy in the Americas, 1500–1750.* Armonk, NY: Sharpe, 1998.

Lewis, Jon E., ed. *The Mammoth Book of Pirates: Over 25 True Tales of Devilry and Daring by the Most Infamous Pirates of All Time.* Philadelphia, PA: Running Press, 2006.

Little, Benerson. *The Sea Rover's Practice: Pirate Tactics and Techniques, 1630–1730.* Dulles, VA: Potomac Books, 2007.

Lloyd, Christopher. *English Corsairs on the Barbary Coast.* London: William Collins Sons, 1981.

Matthews, John. *Pirates.* New York: Atheneum, 2006.

Murray, Dian H. *Pirates of the South China Coast, 1790–1810.* California: Stanford University Press, 1987.

Ormerod, Henry A. *Piracy in the Ancient World.* Baltimore: Johns Hopkins University Press, 1996.

Pennell, C.R., ed. *Bandits at Sea.* New York: New York University Press, 2001.

Perry, Dan. *Blackbeard: The Real Pirate of the Caribbean.* New York: Basic Books, 2006.

Rediker, Marcus. *Between the Devil and the Deep Blue Sea: Merchant Seamen, Pirates and the Anglo-American Maritime World, 1700–1750.* Cambridge, UK: Cambridge University Press, 1987.

———. *Villains of All Nations: Atlantic Pirates in the Golden Age.* Boston, MA: Beacon Press, 2004.

Sanders, Richard. *If a Pirate I Must Be… The True Story of "Black Bart," King of the Caribbean Pirates.* New York: Skyhorse Publishing, 2009.

Sharp, Anne Wallace. *Daring Pirate Women.* Minneapolis, MN: Lerner, 2002.

Travers, Tim. *Pirates: A History.* Stroud, Gloucestershire, UK: Tempus, 2007.

Wilson, Peter Lamborn. *Pirate Utopias: Moorish Corsairs and European Renegades.* 2nd ed. Rye Brook, NY: Autonomedia, 2003.

Woodard, Colin. *The Republic of Pirates: Being the True and Surprising Story of the Caribbean Pirates and the Man Who Brought Them Down.* New York: Harcourt, 2007.

Wren, Laura Lee. *Pirates and Privateers of the High Seas.* Berkeley Heights, NJ: Enslow, 2003.

Yolen, Jane. *Sea Queens: Women Pirates Around the World.* Watertown, MA: Charlesbridge, 2008.

Zacks, Richard. *The Pirate Coast: Thomas Jefferson, the First Marines, and the Secret Mission of 1805.* New York: Hyperion, 2005.

Periodicals

Antony, Robert. "Piracy in Early Modern China," *IIAS Newsletter,* 36 (March 2005). Also available online at http://www.iias.nl/nl/36/IIAS_NL36_07.pdf (accessed on January 3, 2011).

Baldauf, Scott. "Who Are Somalia's Pirates?" *Christian Science Monitor* (November 20, 2008). Also available online at http://www.csmonitor.com/World/Africa/2008/1120/p25s22-woaf.html (accessed on January 3, 2011).

De Souza, Philip. "Ancient Rome and the Pirates." *History Today* 51, no. 7 (2001).

Gettleman, Jeffrey. "Somalia's Pirates Flourish in a Lawless Nation" *New York Times* (October 31, 2008). Available online at www.nytimes.com/2008/10/31/world/africa/31pirates.html (accessed on January 3, 2011).

Gwin, Peter. "Dangerous Straits." *National Geographic* (October 2007). Also available online at http://ngm.nationalgeographic.com/2007/10/malacca-strait-pirates/pirates-text.html (accessed on January 3, 2011).

Johnson, Keith. "Who's a Pirate? U.S. Court Sees Duel over Definition." *Wall Street Journal* (August 14, 2010). Available online at http://online.wsj.com/article/SB20001424052748703988304575413470900570834.html (accessed on January 3, 2011).

Murray, Dian H. "Pirates of the South China Coast 1790–1810," *Journal of the Economic and Social History of the Orient* 33, no. 2 (1990): 234–6.

Rediker, Marcus. "When Women Pirates Sailed the Seas." *The Wilson Quarterly* 17, no. 4 (Autumn 1993): 102–10.

Tabarrok, Alexander. "The Rise, Fall, and Rise Again of Privateers," *Independent Review* 11, no. 4 (Spring 2007): 565–77.

Web Sites

Adow, Mohammed. "The Pirate Kings of Puntland." *Al Jazeera.net* (June 17, 2009). http://english.aljazeera.net/news/africa/2009/06/2009614125245860630.html (accessed on January 3, 2011).

Davis, Robert. "British Slaves on the Barbary Coast." *BBC British History in Depth.* http://www.bbc.co.uk/history/british/empire_seapower/white_slaves_01.shtml (accessed on January 3, 2011).

Krystek, Lee. "The Golden Age of Piracy." *The Unmuseum.* www.unmuseum.org/pirate.htm (accessed on January 3, 2011).

"Pirates." *National Maritime Museum.* http://www.nmm.ac.uk/explore/sea-and-ships/facts/ships-and-seafarers/pirates (accessed on January 3, 2011).

"Pirates of the Whydah." *National Geographic.* http://www.nationalgeographic.com/whydah/main.html (accessed on January 3, 2011).

Rothwell, Donald R. "Maritime Piracy and International Law." *Crimes of War Project* (February 24, 2009). http://www.crimesofwar.org/onnews/news-piracy.html (accessed on January 3, 2011).

Index

Bold type indicates major entries. Illustrations are marked by (ill.).

S